W9-DCH-100

Protestantism in America

The Columbia Contemporary American Religion Series

The Columbia Contemporary American Religion Series

The spiritual landscape of contemporary America is as varied and complex as that of any country in the world. The books in this new series, written by leading scholars for students and general readers alike, fall into two categories: Some titles are portraits of the country's major religious groups. They describe and explain particular religious practices and rituals, beliefs, and major challenges facing a given community today. Others explore current themes and topics in American religion that cut across denominational lines. The texts are supplemented with carefully selected photographs and artwork, and annotated bibliographies.

—

Roman Catholicism in America
CHESTER GILLIS

Islam in America
JANE I. SMITH

Buddhism in America
RICHARD HUGHES SEAGER

PROTESTANTISM

in America

Randall Balmer and Lauren F. Winner

COLUMBIA UNIVERSITY PRESS

NEW YORK

COLUMBIA UNIVERSITY PRESS

Publishers Since 1893

New York, Chichester, West Sussex

Copyright © 2002 Columbia University Press

All rights reserved

Library of Congress Cataloging-in-Publication Data

Balmer, Randall Herbert.

Protestantism in America / Randall Balmer and Lauren F. Winner.

p. cm. — (Columbia contemporary American religion series)

Includes bibliographical references and index.

ISBN 978-0-231-11130-0 (cloth : alk. paper)—ISBN 978-0-231-11131-7 (pbk. : alk. paper)

1. Protestant churches—United States. 2. United States—Church history.

3. Protestantism—United States. I. Winner, Lauren F. II. Title. III. Series.

BR515 .R36 2002

280'.4'0973—dc21

2002023859

Columbia University Press books are printed on
permanent and durable acid-free paper.

Printed in the United States of America

For John Wilson

(editor, *Books and Culture*)

and for John F. Wilson

(professor of religion, Princeton University)

CONTENTS

At one time—and not so long ago—Protestantism served as the organizing principle for any survey of religious life in America. Not without reason. Ever since the early days of European colonization of North America in the seventeenth century, America has been both overwhelmingly diverse and overwhelmingly Protestant, and these characteristics gave religious historians plenty to work with. Charting the permutations of American Protestantism could easily consume an entire career, as reflected in the work of such worthies as Robert Baird, Winthrop S. Hudson, Edwin S. Gaustad, Sidney E. Ahlstrom, Robert T. Handy, and Martin E. Marty, among others.[1] All of these historians produced important surveys of religious life in America, and all of them located Protestantism at its center.

Shortly after the publication of Ahlstrom's magisterial *A Religious History of the American People* in 1972, however, the "Protestant consensus" began to unravel, both in reality and in the historiography. Americans had, after all, elected a Roman Catholic to the presidency in 1960. More significantly, changes in the immigration laws in 1965 together with the rise of the counterculture in the late 1960s conspired to alter the American religious landscape. Muslim mosques, Hindu temples, Buddhist shrines, and Sikh gurdwārās appeared in places as diverse as Queens, New York, and Toledo, Ohio. Hare Krishna proselytizers patrolled airports and street corners, seeking converts. Followers of Maharishi Mahesh Yogi conducted lectures about Transcendental Meditation on college and university campuses. Native American religious practices enjoyed a resurgence following the occupation of Wounded Knee, South Dakota, in 1973. Middle-class Americans (and their children) dabbled in Eastern and New Age spirituality. In short, the Protestant center was no longer holding.

Students of religion in America eventually caught on to this phenomenon. The past several decades have seen a remarkable surge of scholarly studies that shed light on the religious life of Americans outside the ambit of Protestantism. Even the historiography of Protestantism itself has been Balkanized or (to use a favorite jargon term of academics) "problematized." For much of the twentieth century, historians viewed Protestantism in America as "liberal" or "mainline" Protestantism writ large, excluding the most populous and most vibrant strain of American Protestantism, evangelicalism. That began to change in 1980, with the publication of *Fundamentalism and American Culture* by George M. Marsden, whose work provided an intellectual legitimacy to an important but long-neglected (and much reviled) movement within evangelicalism.[2]

Others followed Marsden's lead, exploring various dimensions of evangelicalism in America—fundamentalism, pentecostalism, African American traditions, and the holiness movement. This work, together with the studies of non-Christian religions, has rendered a more complex portrait of American religious life, but it has also rendered it impossible any longer to rely on Protestantism as the sole organizing principle for understanding religious life in America.

The Columbia Contemporary American Religion Series is a reflection of this new historiographical complexity. Each book in the series treats a different religious tradition, and none pretends to offer a survey of all of American religious life. When James Warren of Columbia University Press first approached us about writing one of the volumes, he suggested evangelicalism, which we agreed to do. A while later, when he asked for suggestions about a volume on mainline Protestantism, a larger discussion ensued, at the conclusion of which it seemed sensible to combine the two projects into a single book, thereby restoring some balance and perspective to Protestantism in America.

This is what we have sought to do. Following an account of a Protestant Easter Sunday service, the first part of the book provides an introduction to Protestantism, a brief history, and a taxonomy of the varieties of Protestantism in America. Part Two comprises a series of three ethnographic accounts of Protestant worship services. The final section looks more closely at three issues that currently divide American Protestants—feminism, homosexuality, and social justice. This section also provides a glimpse into the everyday lives of Protestants in America—their beliefs, their anxieties, the way they try to configure their lives around their convictions. The first of the worship services takes place in the Williston Federated Church of Williston, Vermont, which is affiliated with both the United Church of Christ (a distant descendant of New England Puritanism) and the United Methodist Church. This congregation, housed in an archetypal white clapboard New England meetinghouse, illustrates several themes of so-called mainline Protestantism, including a generally liberal theology, a concern with social justice, and a strong interest in ecumenism (cooperation and unity among various Protestant denominations).

The second worship service is that of the redoubtable Abyssinian Baptist Church of New York City. Organized in 1808 and relocated to 138th Street during the Harlem Renaissance, Abyssinian boasts a proud history of social activism, racial uplift, and stentorian preaching. The famous (or infamous) Adam Clayton Powell Jr. used its pulpit as a springboard for election to Congress, and the current minister, Calvin O. Butts, is an articulate political spokesman for the African American community and the subject of frequent speculation as a candidate for mayor of New York City. A visit to Abyssinian Baptist Church illustrates the breadth and the depth of Protestant sentiment within the black community. Abyssinian also demonstrates how, for African Americans, theology and worship can never be divorced from social awareness (as happens frequently within white Protestantism). Laboring under the scourge of slavery and lacking other avenues for the expression of leadership, African Americans historically looked to the church for direction on matters both sacred and secular. Martin Luther King Jr. was, of course, the best example of this phenomenon during the twentieth century, but hundreds of black Protestant ministers in America intercede for their flocks before both God and Caesar.

The New Life Family Fellowship in Santa Fe, New Mexico, illustrates the most durable strain of Protestantism in America: evangelicalism. Consigned to the margins of American religion after the infamous Scopes trial of 1925, evangelicalism in all of its various forms—fundamentalism, pentecostalism, neo-evangelicalism, the holiness movement—came roaring back with a vengeance in the second half of the twentieth century. The church in Santa Fe, a venue not often associated with the "Bible belt," shows how tenacious evangelicalism is in American culture and how it envelops the lives of its followers by means of both programs and piety.

The chapters on feminism, homosexuality, and social justice require some context and explanation. Among the myriad religions in the United States, only Protestantism has approached anything closely resembling hegemony. Its status as by far the most significant expression of religion in America has allowed Protestants to shape the culture in ways that other traditions have not. Put another way, freed from the struggle for mere survival in America's religious marketplace, Protestantism has had a much more tentacular reach in the United States than has any other religion. Protestant sensibilities shaped healthcare and welfare in the nineteenth century, for example, and Protestants have had a profound effect on everything from labor relations and gender roles to political discourse.

Any assessment of contemporary Protestantism, then, must include an account of how Protestants have both influenced—and in turn have been influenced by—popular culture. The publication of Betty Friedan's *The Feminine Mystique* in 1963, for instance, set in motion cultural debates that have still not been resolved, and American Protestants span the ideological spectrum on issues of gender and sexuality. The movement for gay and lesbian rights has triggered debates and confrontations throughout American society and its institutions; Protestantism has by no means been immune to these discussions. The chapters on feminism and homosexuality offer insight into the variety of Protestant attitudes on these topics.

Finally, Protestants in America have had a vexed relationship with social justice. While Martin Luther believed that the function of the state was to restrain evil, John Calvin believed that the Christian should reform society according to the norms of godliness, and the Anabaptists taught that the true follower of Jesus should shun government altogether. American history has seen examples of all of these Protestant attitudes toward the social order. Some Protestants called for the abolition of slavery as early as the eighteenth century, while others defended the institution. In the twentieth century, theologically liberal Protestants generally adopted politically liberal positions, while many theological conservatives gravitated toward the other end of the political spectrum. Still, as the chapter on social justice demonstrates, Protestant attitudes toward social justice vary so widely as to make generalizations risky.

We could have focused on other challenges facing American Protestants. (Indeed, as the book went to press, we were pleased to see that Mark Noll had chosen to focus the second section of his impressive *American Evangelical Christianity: An Introduction* on "flashpoints," and we were amused to see that he had chosen three different issues—Roman Catholicism, science, and politics.[3])

Technology, for example, might merit its own chapter. Protestants are wrestling with their response to scientific advances in human cloning and stem cell research. Protestants have also struggled to come to terms with the new pluralism that has reshaped the American religious landscape since changes to the immigration laws of 1965. The issue is not so much the loss of cultural hegemony—America is still in many ways a Protestant nation—but rather the faithful struggle of Protestant believers to be good neighbors to people of other faiths. As Diana Eck, a Methodist and a professor of religion at Harvard University, has noted, it is one thing for Southern Baptists to wring their hands about the millions of lost souls in polytheistic India; it is quite another for them to walk across the street and break bread with their Hindu neighbors. Finally, at the turn of the twenty-first century, there are indications that the tectonic plates of Protestant theology are shifting. Evangelicals like Kevin Vanhoozer articulate a postmodern theology. John Milbank, impresario of the Radical Orthodoxy movement, argues that theology must be the grounds of society following the end of modernity. And with pentecostalism having eclipsed liberation theology as the "theology of the people" in Latin America, liberal Protestant theologians will have to reconsider their allegiance to the various forms of liberation theology—womanist theology, black theology, Latino theology, even ecospirituality (which seeks to liberate kelp beds)—that has been the mainstay of Protestant liberalism since Reinhold Niebuhr.

Our focus on feminism, sexual orientation, and social justice, we concede, is somewhat subjective, informed not only by our scholarly angle of vision, but also by our own religious lives in American Protestant churches. The books we have read and the people we have interviewed persuade us that these are three of the most crucial issues facing the church today, and our experiences, Sunday after Sunday, as members of fractious and fissiparous churches have confirmed that.

Taken together, the chapters of Part Three provide, if not a portrait, at least a collage of contemporary Protestantism in all its variety and complexity. The final section includes biographical sketches of notable Protestant leaders, a chronology, and a glossary.

Protestantism in America

Easter Sunday

The sound of a trumpet signals that this is not an ordinary Sunday. The chancel choir, bedecked in red robes with white stoles, sings "Alleluia" from the balcony, and members of the congregation crane their necks to take in the spectacle. At the front of the sanctuary, a jungle of Easter lilies, so densely packed that they appear intertwined, frames the pulpit on the left and the lectern on the right. At the conclusion of the "Alleluia" a disembodied voice from the rear, authoritative but friendly, instructs the congregation to stand.

"People of God—Friday was not the end of God's story!" the same voice declaims. "Our God is a God of the living! Jesus Christ has risen to save you! He has risen to give you life! People of God—look! The tomb is empty! He has risen!"

The congregation, reading from the bulletin, responds, "The tomb is empty! Alleluia!"

The voice again: "Alleluia! Christ is risen!"

"He is risen, indeed! Alleluia!"

The pipe organ strikes the opening chords of the processional hymn, "Jesus Christ Is Risen Today, Alleluia," and the choir, redeployed to the narthex, now advances down the center aisle to their place behind the lectern on the right side of the center altar. The pastor, dressed in a white cassock and white stole, brings up the rear of the procession. As he reaches the front he pirouettes and offers the invocation. "In the name of the Father and of the Son and of the Holy Spirit," he intones, and the congregation responds, "Amen."

"Middling" Protestantism

Bethlehem Lutheran Church in Ridgewood, New Jersey, may not be a typical Protestant church, but that is only because there is no such thing. Protestantism in America encompasses everything theologically from evangelicals and fundamentalists, on the one hand, to Episcopalians and the United Church of Christ, on the other; their worship styles range from the relative simplicity of Baptists and Congregationalists to the ceremonialism of Lutherans and Episcopalians. While the worship of the latter tends toward the formal and liturgical, the former generally eschew ritual; their clergy wear business suits or even sport shirts, not vestments. Some evangelicals even refuse to recite the Lord's Prayer because it smacks of liturgy.

Bethlehem Lutheran falls somewhere in the middle. Its worship service offers a blend of liturgy and extemporaneous preaching, a characteristic usually associated with evangelicalism, and yet the clergy wear vestments. The service regularly invokes the Holy Trinity—"Father, Son, and Holy Spirit"—but very few parishioners genuflect, as they might in an Episcopal church. To underscore further the "middling" character of this congregation on the spectrum of American Protestantism, Bethlehem Lutheran is part of the Lutheran Church–Missouri Synod, a denomination known for its blend of liturgy and conservative theology. The Missouri Synod, which published its devotional guides in German as well as English until 2000, sees itself as following most closely in the tradition of Martin Luther, the progenitor of Protestantism.

"Jesus has carried our sins to His own death," the pastor declares following the congregation's confession of sins. "His sacrifice is complete and full. He has won the victory!"

Luther himself would certainly endorse such language. One of the hallmarks of Protestantism in the sixteenth century was the centrality of Christ in the theological drama of redemption. In opposition to the Roman Catholic Church, Luther emphasized the New Testament notion that we are saved by grace, through faith. The Christian no longer needed the mediation of the church. All believers have direct access to God through Jesus, who, in Christian theology, died for the sins of humanity on Good Friday. More important, however, Jesus rose from the dead "on the third day," which provides the occasion for the celebrations of Easter Sunday.

"Alleluia! Christ is risen!" the pastor announces once again, and the congregation responds: "He is risen, indeed! Alleluia!"

The reading from the Old Testament, or the Hebrew Bible, follows another congregational hymn, "Jesus Lives! The Victory's Won." A layman, dressed in a beige double-breasted suit, steps to the lectern and announces the passage, Isaiah 25:6–9. He reads it, concluding with the words, "The Word of the Lord."

The pastor, a tall man with graying hair and a winsome smile, leads the congregation in another responsive reading, and the layman returns to the lectern to read the epistle, 1 Corinthians 15:19–28, Paul's declaration that without the resurrection there is no hope. The pastor slips into the back row of the choir to help out with the anthem, a piece from *The Creation* by Franz Joseph Haydn, and then re-emerges to read the Gospel, the resurrection narrative from Mark 16:1–8.

Luther would surely approve of all the readings from the Bible. One of the hallmarks of Protestantism is *sola scriptura*, a reliance on the Bible alone as the source of authority. Whereas the Roman Catholic church insists on twin bases of authority—Scripture and tradition—Luther believed that church leaders and church councils were fallible and that only the Bible remained as the true guide for the believer. To that end, Luther advocated the availability of the Scriptures in vernacular translation so that everyone could read and interpret the Bible for himself or herself. Luther himself undertook the translation of the New Testament into German from the Greek, and the spread of Protestantism throughout Europe, England, and Scandinavia gave rise both to vernacular translations and to a dramatic increase in literacy, as individuals sought access to the Bible through their own eyes and not as filtered through the teachings and theology of the Roman Catholic Church. The plethora of Bible readings at Bethlehem Lutheran, then, represents an assertion of Protestant distinctiveness over against what Protestants have generally considered the overbearing authority and pretensions of Roman Catholicism.

Centrality of the Sermon

The pastor concludes the Gospel reading and segues into his sermon. The Reverend Andrew D. Nelson doesn't step behind the pulpit for his homily; he stands in front of his congregation and uses a wireless microphone, clipped to his stole, for amplification. "I always looked forward to my birthday," Nelson begins, adding after a pause, "at one time." He recalled receiving Fort Apache as a gift one year and a Schwinn ten-speed bicycle another. He remembered with particular fondness the birthday that signaled he could drive a car. Sometime in his early twenties, however, he stopped looking forward to birthdays and now, pushing fifty, he recognizes the inevitability of aging. "We can't avoid death," Nelson declares, thereby providing a nice segue into the resurrection account.

Nelson's preaching style is congenial, informal, and folksy—even on this Easter Sunday. He takes pains to appear accessible to his congregation, preaching extemporaneously with only a Bible and a couple of notes clutched in his hand. Sometimes he asks for a response from the congregation, and on a recent Sunday he offered a kind of dramatization: the life of a church pew, recalling the generations that had used it over the years. The relaxed style represents an attempt to break with the stodginess of other Protestant ministers, those who hide behind pulpits and read from prepared texts. In that way, Nelson's preaching style more closely resembles the approach of those in the evangelical wing of Protestantism, which saw enormous growth over the last half of the twentieth century.

Nelson rehearses Mary Magdalene's surprise at the absence of the body when she visits the tomb on Easter morning. In her distress, according to the account in the Gospel of Mark, she encounters an apparent stranger, who asks why she is crying. "What a question to ask in a cemetery!" Nelson exclaims. The congregation responds with a murmur, but that is not the only noise in the sanctuary. Children walk (sometimes run) up and down the side aisle, and babies cry. This congregation includes young parents, a demographic group much in demand among religious organizations, especially Protestants. Evangelicals have generally had more success in luring this group back into the churches, in part because of the range of youth programs they offer, but more traditional or mainline Protestant churches have been trying to market themselves more aggressively. Nelson's casual homiletical style is part of that approach.

Andrew Nelson is something of a returnee himself. He grew up in northern New Jersey, attended Norwich University, where he earned a B.S. in biology, went off to the army, and then to Rutgers for a master's degree in environmental sciences. His first career path was civil engineering and environmental sciences, but a personal crisis prompted him to shift direction. After working with a high school youth program, he enrolled at Concordia Seminary, the Lutheran Church–Missouri Synod's school in St. Louis, where he earned the Master of Divinity degree at age thirty-four. He also met fellow student Gretchen there, and they married in 1982.

Nelson is winding up his Easter sermon with a rush of enthusiasm.

"Surprise! I've seen the Lord," he says, paraphrasing Mary from the passage in the Gospel. "He's alive!" Nelson goes on to ask rhetorically, not to mention autobiographically: "Whose life could be the same after you've met the living Lord?"

"On Good Friday the Son of God went to the cross and died for you," the pastor continues. "Today he rose from the dead." Then one final appeal: "Call upon the name of the Lord and you'll be saved."

Evangelical Versus Liberal

Nelson's sermon underscores the evangelical nature of his congregation and its underlying conservative theology. The notion of a personal conversion—being "saved" or "born again"—once was unremarkable among Protestants, but the liberal wing of Protestantism has gravitated away from such notions. Evangelicals might talk about Jesus as their "personal Lord and Savior," but liberals generally eschew such language in favor of social concerns: civil rights, peace and justice, inclusive language, and acceptance of homosexuals, among other issues. Whereas evangelicals emphasize evangelism, bringing others into the fold, liberals talk about "bearing witness" against evil in the world.

The divide between the two ends of the spectrum sometimes makes it appear that evangelical Protestants have more in common with, say, conservative Catholics than they do with liberal Protestants, who in turn are more akin to Unitarians or Reform Jews. The ecclesiastical topography in Ridgewood, New Jersey, provides an example. Bethlehem Lutheran is located approximately two blocks from Christ Church, one of two Episcopal parishes in town. Christ Church flies a flag celebrating racial and sexual diversity next to the United States flag and the flag of the Episcopal church; several months ago the parish devoted a Sunday service to the affirmation of gays and lesbians, who were openly affectionate with one another during the processional. Nelson, on the other hand, preached a pro-life sermon on "Life Sunday" at Bethlehem Lutheran, and a recent initiative within the congregation encourages members to place a large sign on their front lawns, white letters on a red background: "John 3:16," a reference to the New Testament verse that provides the cornerstone of evangelical theology: "For God so loved the world that he gave his only Son, that whosoever believeth in Him shall not perish but have everlasting life."

Nelson's pro-life affirmations, however, should not be confused with the Religious Right. He is friendly and engaging, not mean-spirited or even overtly political. In the tradition of Luther himself, Nelson sees his role as both pastoral and pedagogical. He devotes a great deal of energy to teaching the scriptures to his congregation, and his sermons are decidedly more biblical than topical. "I want every sermon to reflect the love of Jesus Christ and his desire for every person to come to him for salvation," Nelson says. "I want every person to walk out of church—no matter how burdened they are when they come in—knowing that they can come to Christ for salvation."

Protestant Sacramentalism

The offering follows the sermon, with a gentle reminder in the bulletin that "God loves a cheerful giver," quoting from 2 Corinthians 9:7. The service then moves into the Holy Eucharist or the Lord's Supper, when Christians observe the sacramental feast that Jesus instituted during his Last Supper with his disciples. "The Lord be with you," Nelson intones, and the congregation responds, "And with your spirit." He continues: "The Lord continues to come to us boldly and lovingly through His true body and blood—in, with, and under the bread and wine in this meal."

The theology surrounding the Lord's Supper has been contested among Protestants since the sixteenth century. Whereas the Roman Catholic Church holds to the doctrine of transubstantiation—the bread and wine of Holy Communion *actually become* the body and blood of Christ in the course of the mass, even though they retain the outward forms of bread and wine—Luther could not abide such teaching. He talked about the real presence of Jesus in the Eucharist (hence the language "in, with, and under"), but some of the more radical Protestants, following the lead of Zurich reformer Ulrich Zwingli, adopted a "memorialist" theology of the Lord's Supper: Its purpose was merely to remind us of the life and death of Jesus. Those Protestants—most Baptists, for example—take a "lower" view of Holy Communion, observing it perhaps once a month or even less frequently. High-church Protestants, on the other hand, such as Episcopalians and Lutherans, celebrate the Lord's Supper or Holy Eucharist more frequently—once a week, typically—because they believe that the sacraments impart grace to the believer.

At Bethlehem Lutheran the congregation partakes of Holy Communion every other week. After the words of institution, Nelson summons the congregation to the altar where, in groups of a dozen or so, they kneel at the altar rail and hold out their hands. A layman drops a communion wafer into each set of hands, and another offers a tray of thimble-sized cups—most filled with red wine, but the cups in the center, as noted in the bulletin, are filled with "non-alcoholic white wine." The pastor then dismisses each set of communicants with a blessing, and they return to their pews to make room for the next group.

The ritual surrounding Holy Communion here at Bethlehem Lutheran also represents a middle way for American Protestantism. Those who adopted the memorialist theology of the Lord's Supper—we *remember* the life and death of Christ—also tended to have been influenced by the temperance movement. These Protestants have foresworn the use of wine in Holy Communion in favor of grape juice. At about the same time (and for reasons of hygiene) they shunned the communion chalice, which had been customary throughout most of church history. These churches, then, served the "wine" (grape juice) of Holy Communion in individual cups. Many of these same churches (although not Bethlehem Lutheran) routinely distribute the elements of Holy Communion to the congregation seated in their pews—by means of church elders passing around trays of wafers and thimble-sized cups—rather than have congregants come to the altar, which some Protestants regard as too high church, or Catholic.

Bethlehem Lutheran, however, treads the middle ground—using small containers of wine and requiring able-bodied parishioners to come forward to the altar (Nelson comes down to serve those in wheelchairs after the remainder of the congregation has communicated). Another indication of the relatively "high" view of the sacraments at Bethlehem Lutheran is the place that Holy Communion occupies in the service. In more low-church Protestant denominations, such as Baptist or Congregational, everything in the service leads up to the sermon, which is generally delivered from a central pulpit. Among Lutherans and Episcopalians, however, the climax of the worship service is the Holy Eucharist, which comes after the sermon and just before the closing hymn and recessional.

Everyone Welcome

Not everyone in the congregation receives Communion, but most do. After filing up the center aisle to the altar and kneeling at the altar rail, after receiving the bread and the wine and a blessing, members of the congregation return to their seats by the side aisles. The choir sings a couple of hymns, and some members of the congregation join in. Some kneel in prayer, and others take in the surroundings.

Bethlehem Lutheran Church was founded in the early years of the twentieth century, and the present sanctuary was constructed in 1958 (an educational wing, with Sunday school classrooms and a gymnasium, was added in 1968). The main building, constructed of brick and stone, is vaguely gothic in architecture. The etched stained-glass windows, popular in the 1950s, show scenes from the New Testament with the accompanying text below.

The observance of Holy Communion on Easter Sunday takes a bit longer than on most other Sundays. Almost every Protestant church in America must accommodate larger crowds at Christmas and Easter than on ordinary Sundays. (Mount Olivet Lutheran Church in Minneapolis schedules eight services on Christmas Eve.) Here at Bethlehem Lutheran in Ridgewood the congregation offers three services on Easter instead of the usual one service. Whereas some Protestant clergy once scolded those who showed up only once or twice a year, they now tend to be more accommodating, seeing the holidays as their opportunity to make their best pitch for congregants. Nelson avoids browbeating the Christmas and Easter crowds, and he takes pains to be especially friendly as congregants file past to greet him at the conclusion of the service.

On this Easter Sunday, the parishioners of Bethlehem Lutheran Church greet one another in the narthex and just outside the front door. On their way to the parking lot, they pass the well-manicured front lawn with a church sign built of stone, matching the main building, and a scattering of red signs with white lettering, placed there especially for Easter: "John 3:16."

Part One

BACKGROUND

CHAPTER ONE

Protestantism in America

The term "Protestant" derives from Martin Luther's sixteenth-century assault on the corruptions of the Roman Catholic Church. Luther, an Augustinian friar, could not escape a sense of his own unworthiness before God, despite his frequent confession of sins and his partaking of the sacraments. He sought solace in even more confessions and even more assiduous attendance to the church's sacramental life, but he could not escape a sense of his own insouciance before a holy and demanding God. An exasperated confessor finally suggested that Luther study the New Testament, especially Paul's epistles to the Romans and the Galatians. There, Luther found the truth that liberated him from what he came to revile as the "works righteousness" of medieval Catholicism. We are saved by grace through faith, Luther concluded after his study of the New Testament. There is *nothing* we can do to earn our salvation; it is the gift of God, an insight that freed him from responsibility for making himself worthy before a righteous God.[1]

Luther's "rediscovery of the Gospel" had far-reaching implications. When he tacked his *Ninety-five Theses* to the cathedral door at Wittenberg on All Hallow's Eve, 1517, Luther still considered himself a loyal son of the Roman Catholic Church. He professed confidence that once the pope learned of the abuses committed in the name of the faith—Luther was especially exercised by the sale of indulgences or freedom from the penalty of sin—the pope would step in and mandate the appropriate reforms to restore the church to biblical faith. The Vatican, however, responded petulantly. Pope Leo X threatened Luther with excommunication, Luther remained defiant, and the pope finally issued his decree of excommunication in 1520. Luther then set about a "re-formation" of the church, a comprehensive program known collectively as the Protestant Reformation.

Specifically, Luther emphasized the "priesthood of believers," that each individual has access to God directly through Jesus. No longer did the believer need to rely on the agency of the church or its priests, and in the newly formed Protestant church the clergy served as spiritual guides and especially as preachers, whose task it was to provide at least the rudiments of theological instruction. Luther also taught *sola scriptura*, that the Bible alone, the inspired Word of God, was the source of authority for the believer. This contrasted with the Roman Catholic notion of twin fonts of authority: Scripture and tradition. Luther's reliance on Scripture and the believers' priesthood led to the conviction that the Bible should be available in the vernacular. Luther himself contributed by translating the New Testament into German during his exile in Wartburg Castle (1520–21), and Protestants across northern Europe and England followed suit with other translations into the vernacular for the benefit and edification of the faithful.

The Bible, however, admits of many interpretations. Much to the chagrin of Luther himself, others infected with the Protestant spirit offered their own prescriptions for reform and standards for godliness. Luther tried to rein in some of the more unruly spirits—criticizing the "enthusiasts" of his day, for example, for behaving as though they had swallowed the Holy Ghost "feathers and all"—but he had unleashed a zeal for reform that could not be extinguished, and one of the characteristics of Protestantism to this day is its divisiveness. In Luther's day some groups went in the direction of Anabaptism (insisting that baptism was for adult believers only, not infants), and others prosecuted reforms according to their own interpretations of the Bible. In Geneva, for instance, John Calvin sought to restructure society according to biblical norms, and he set about writing a systematic theology for Protestantism, *The Institutes of the Christian Religion*, which went through several editions in his lifetime and remains influential among many American Protestants. Calvin articulated a variant of Protestant theology known as the "Reformed tradition," with its emphasis on the doctrine of election (Jesus died to redeem only the elect, who are saved regardless of merit) and the regeneration of society.

Protestantism in Colonial America

By the end of the sixteenth century, Protestantism had already divided into several groups. Lutherans, the followers of Martin Luther, dominated Germany and Scandinavia. Anabaptists, who were persecuted both by Catholics and by other Protestants, fled to eastern Europe, Russia, and eventually North America. The Reformed tradition, which became a significant force in such cities as Geneva, Strasbourg, and Frankfurt-am-Main, eventually spread to England after the Marian Exiles (Protestant refugees from England during the reign of Mary Tudor, "Bloody Mary") returned to England in 1558. The Reformed tradition sought to "purify" both church and state in England from the vestiges of Roman Catholicism. This last branch of Protestantism provided a significant bridge to North America.

The presence of Protestants in the New World, however, began with the settlement at Jamestown in 1607, with its population of Anglicans (members of the Church of England). A group of Protestant dissenters, the Pilgrims, arrived from England in 1620 by way of Leiden, in the Netherlands. In the spring of 1628 Jonas Michaëlius, a minister in the Dutch Reformed Church, held a Protestant service in New Amsterdam, offering Holy Communion to "fully fifty communicants." By the late 1620s a group of Puritans in England had despaired of ever reforming the Church of England, so they sought and obtained a charter for the Massachusetts Bay Company and set sail for the New World in 1630. Aboard the *Arbella*, John Winthrop summarized their mission: "We shall be as a city upon a hill," he declared to his fellow Puritans. Massachusetts would set the standard and provide a beacon to the rest of the world (England especially), showing how church and state should be configured in a godly commonwealth.

Other Protestants sought religious refuge in the New World: Anglicans in Virginia; Huguenots (French Protestants) in the Middle Colonies; Swedish Lutherans along the Delaware River; Scottish Presbyterians in New Jersey; Quakers and numerous Anabaptist groups in Pennsylvania; Moravians in Georgia, the Carolinas, and Pennsylvania; and German Lutherans in Georgia, New York, and Pennsylvania; among many others. By the middle of the eighteenth century the Atlantic seaboard provided a virtual laboratory for Protestant groups, who had migrated from the Old World to the New World, impatient with the entrenched Catholic institutions—churches, governments, universities—that had thwarted Protestant reforms across the Atlantic. North America offered a chance to start anew, a *tabula rasa*, free from the restraints of the Old World.

Throughout American history, Protestants have taken full advantage of that freedom. Protestantism has splintered further in the context of religious disestablishment, giving rise to countless varieties of Lutherans, Presbyterians, Methodists, Anabaptists, and Baptists, not to mention independent congregations that also fall beneath the rubric of Protestantism.

Classifying American Protestants in the Nineteenth Century

Imposing any tidy taxonomy on such an internally diverse movement necessarily distorts the varieties of Protestantism in America. One dichotomy might be liturgical and nonliturgical. In this scheme, such Protestant groups as Lutherans and Episcopalians (part of the worldwide Anglican Communion) would be classified as liturgical, while Methodists, Baptists, Presbyterians, and various Anabaptists (Mennonites, Amish, Hutterites, et al.) would demonstrate a lesser reliance on liturgy and the sacraments in their worship. Another dichotomy might be theological, with a division between Calvinists and Arminians. Here the distinction centers on soteriology, the doctrine of salvation. Those in the Reformed tradition (the theological descendants of John Calvin) hold to the view of election: Salvation comes only to the elect, who are chosen according to the mysterious councils of God rather than with regard to good works or individual merit. Arminianism, on the other hand, became popular among American Protestants after the American Revolution; it insisted that the individual could initiate the salvation process by the exercise of his or her own volition. Salvation, in this *democratic* soteriology, was available to everyone; one had merely to decide or choose to be saved, rather than wait on God to initiate the process.

No dichotomy is perfect—many Presbyterian congregations, for instance, are quite liturgical, and many avowed Calvinists are in fact rather Arminian in their approach to soteriology. Perhaps the most useful distinction in American Protestantism is that between evangelical and nonevangelical or, to use the argot of the eighteenth century, between New Lights and Old Lights. As early as the 1720s, controversies arose among American Protestants over the importance of conversion or "new birth." Jonathan Edwards and other evangelicals, drawing on John 3 in the New Testament, where Jesus tells Nicodemus that he must be "born again" to enter the kingdom of heaven, insisted on the centrality of conversion in the religious life. Their opponents, led in the eighteenth century by Boston minister Charles Chauncy, proposed more rationalistic alternatives to this warm-hearted conversion experience. By the nineteenth century many of the followers of Chauncy had drifted toward various forms of theological liberalism, ranging from a nonrevivalistic Protestantism and Universalism (based on the doctrine of universal salvation) to Unitarianism and Transcendentalism, while evangelicals conducted a massive series of revivals and sought to reform society and usher in the kingdom of God. The fight against slavery held these two strands of Protestantism together—in the North, at least—but the fissures between evangelical and nonevangelical Protestantism again emerged later in the nineteenth century. In response to intellectual assaults against the Bible and the overwhelming social problems caused by industrialization, urbanization, and the arrival of non-Protestant immigrants, evangelical Protestants withdrew from society and from various projects of social reform. More liberal, nonevangelical Protestants opted for the Social Gospel, with its emphasis on the regeneration of society and its de-emphasis on individual conversion.

By the 1920s the line of demarcation was even more firmly drawn between evangelical Protestants, on the one hand, who took pride in their theological and social conservatism and in their fidelity to Scripture; and on the other hand, nonevangelical Protestant liberals, who became known as "mainline Protestants" for the remainder of the twentieth century.

Definitions: *Evangelical* and *Liberal*

The term "evangelical" refers generally to the New Testament and, more specifically, to Martin Luther's "rediscovery of the gospel" in the sixteenth century. The evolution of evangelicalism in America, its emergence as one of the most influential religious and social movements in American history, has produced some specialized characteristics that set it apart from the mainstream of American Protestantism. The visits of George Whitefield, an Anglican itinerant preacher, to the American colonies in the 1730s and 1740s triggered a widespread evangelical revival known as the Great Awakening. Whitefield built upon and knit together disparate revivals in the colonies— the pietistic awakenings among the Dutch in the Raritan Valley of New Jersey, the revival in Jonathan Edwards's congregation in Northampton, Massachusetts, and the sacramental seasons among the Scots-Irish Presbyterians in the Middle Colonies. Despite the persistence of some ethnic and theo-

Fig. 1.1. Charles Chauncy (1705–87), pastor of the First Congregational Church in Boston, was one of the first theological liberals in America. He criticized such revival preachers as George Whitefield and Jonathan Edwards, and he believed that a benevolent deity would ultimately grant everyone salvation.

logical differences, all manifestations of the Great Awakening emphasized the necessity of some kind of conversion followed by a piety that was warm-hearted and experiential—or, in the argot of the day, "experimental"—over against the coldly rationalistic religion characteristic of the upper classes and the ecclesiastical establishment. Although it is perilous to generalize about such a broad and internally diverse movement, evangelicalism in America has largely retained those characteristics—the centrality of conversion, the quest for an affective piety (perhaps best exemplified by John Wesley's Aldersgate experience in 1738, when he found his heart "strangely warmed"), and a suspicion of wealth, worldliness, and ecclesiastical pretension.

Eighteenth-century evangelicals, known as New Lights, helped to shape American culture in the Revolutionary era and beyond. Evangelicals generally lined up with the Patriots during the Revolution, and such evangelical leaders as Isaac Backus joined Enlightenment deists such as Thomas Jefferson in an unlikely alliance to press for religious disestablishment. The Second Great Awakening stoked the revival fires once again in three different theaters of the new nation: New England, western New York, and the Cumberland Valley.[2] Each theater made its own distinctive contribution to antebellum evangelicalism. The revival fervor in New England gave rise to benevolent and reform societies such as the temperance movement, the female seminary movement, prison reform, and abolitionism. Lyman Beecher, for example, invested considerable energy in his campaign to outlaw dueling after Aaron Burr killed Alexander Hamilton in a duel in Weehawken, New Jersey, in 1804.

of a conversion or "born-again" experience as the criterion for entering the kingdom of heaven. Evangelicals take this from the third chapter of Saint John in the New Testament, where Nicodemus approaches Jesus by night and asks what he must do to inherit the kingdom of heaven. Jesus replied, as recorded in John 3:3, "I tell you the truth, unless a man is born again, he cannot see the kingdom of God."[5]

Although the precise theology surrounding it may vary, the conversion experience for most evangelicals occurs instantaneously, and it is often (though not always) attended by emotion. It is a datable moment, when the individual turns from darkness to light, from sin to salvation, from unrighteousness to righteousness. It marks the beginning of a new life in which the believer, despite occasional reversals (known as "backsliding"), strives to live a godly life, engaging in such spiritual disciplines as church attendance, prayer, Bible reading and study, and acts of kindness toward others.

The moment of conversion generally culminates in the repetition of something that has come to be known as the "sinner's prayer." While no one has prescribed any one formula, the prayer usually includes some acknowledgment that the individual is a sinner, the intention to turn from sinfulness, and then a willingness to embrace Jesus as savior. From that moment on, as long as the prayer is offered in sincerity, the individual is "born again."

The second general characteristic of evangelicals is that they take the Bible seriously—many of them to the point of interpreting it literally. This biblicism derives from the conviction that the Bible is the "Word of God," God's special revelation to humanity. The centrality of the Bible is also a legacy from Martin Luther's notion of *sola scriptura*, the idea that the Scriptures alone provide the basis for authority. Luther used the Bible as a corrective to what he saw as the corruptions of medieval Roman Catholicism, and he asserted that the Bible alone—not Scripture and tradition— was the appropriate guide for the believer.

More often than not evangelicals have approached the Bible literally, from Genesis and the account of creation at the beginning of the Hebrew Bible to the book of Revelation at the end of the New Testament. (The former has led to attempts on the part of politically conservative evangelicals to push for the teaching of "scientific creationism" in the schools, and the latter has led to a fixation with the "end times," which, many evangelicals believe, are upon us.) Evangelical theologians in the nineteenth century fastened onto Scottish Common Sense Realism, a mode of biblical interpretation which insisted that the simplest, most obvious reading of the Bible was the correct one. Common Sense Realism then reinforced the notion that individuals could be their own interpreters of Scripture.

Luther's notion of *sola scriptura* combined with the doctrine of the priesthood of believers—the conviction that everyone was responsible directly to God, without the intermediary of the priest or the church—led to a splintering of Protestantism as various individuals read the Bible for themselves and came up with variant interpretations. Without the ballast of history and tradition, evangelicals (who are overwhelmingly Protestant) sailed in many different directions, giving rise to a great deal of internal diversity within the movement. Nowhere is this tendency more apparent than in North America. Denominationally, evangelicals can be found in all of the mainline Protestant denominations—the United Methodist Church, the United Church of Christ, the Evangelical Lutheran Church of America, the Presbyterian Church, and the Episcopal Church, among others—even though those bodies are generally associated with more liberal theology. Since 1967, a strong, vibrant presence of evangelicals has also emerged within the Roman Catholic Church.

Most evangelicals, however, are affiliated with evangelical denominations—from a variety of Baptist groups to the Assemblies of God to the Evangelical Free Church—or with independent, nondenominational congregations that might be identified simply as Community Bible Church or, depending on the locality, Winnetka Bible Church or Princeton Bible Church.

Characteristics of a Liberal Protestant

Whereas many Protestant evangelicals demonstrate a profound otherworldliness, Protestant liberals generally exhibit a greater comfort with *this* world. In its extreme forms, liberal Protestantism falls into H. Richard Niebuhr's "Christ of Culture" category, whereas evangelicals gravitate toward his "Christ against Culture" scheme, with its suspicion of the larger culture.[6] One example of the liberal accommodation to culture was a book entitled *The Secular City*, written by Harvey Cox of Harvard Divinity School. Published in 1965, *The Secular City* argued that Christianity and secular culture were approaching the point where the two would intersect like circles on a Venn diagram; there would no longer be a distinction between the two categories.[7] Although Cox repented of that view twenty years later (in a book entitled *Religion in the Secular City*), the earlier statement remains a classic articulation of the liberal view that Christianity is not at war with the culture; indeed, it has "baptized" the culture.[8]

A second characteristic of liberal Protestants is that they tend to have a somewhat less exalted view of the Bible than evangelical Protestants. Whereas evangelicals want to approach the Bible literally—many insisting, for example, on seven literal days of creation—liberals are more likely to see the biblical writings as time-bound and open to allegorical interpretations. Liberals take the New Testament proscriptions against long hair for men or against women as teachers, for instance, as reflections of the sensibilities of first-century culture, while evangelicals have more difficulty maneuvering around such statements. Historically as well, liberal Protestants evinced a great deal less distress over nineteenth-century assaults on biblical authority—in particular, Darwinism and the German discipline of higher criticism, which cast doubts on the authorship of several biblical books.

In the eyes of many evangelicals, liberal Protestants' comfort with the larger culture and attenuated liberal views of biblical authority have led to such compromises of the faith that liberal Protestantism bears scant resemblance to true Christianity. Liberals, on the other hand, accuse evangelicals of being slavishly literal in their interpretations of the Bible, so much so that their moralistic stances on such issues as women's leadership and homosexuality eclipse what liberals see as the larger messages of the Bible: compassion and forgiveness.

Protestant Sacramentalism

While the Roman Catholic Church had seven sacraments at the time of the Protestant Reformation and many more during the Middle Ages, Luther and the Protestants reduced that number to two: baptism and the Lord's Supper. Luther's own theology of those two sacraments did not stray very far from that of the Roman Catholic Church, although he rejected the doctrine of transubstantiation, the conviction that the bread and wine of Holy Communion actually become the body and blood of Christ.

Among Protestants in America, the rite of baptism has sparked considerable debate and controversy. While the Roman Catholic Church believes that the sacrament of baptism, usually done in infancy, removes the taint of original sin, most Protestants offer different interpretations. Some, following Luther and John Calvin, see infant baptism as the rite of initiation into the community of faith. A larger number of evangelicals, however, follow the Baptist tradition, which insists upon adult (or believer's) baptism. In this theology, inherited from Conrad Grebel and Roger Williams, among many others, baptism—by immersion, not sprinkling—follows conversion; it is a public testimony on the part of the believer to his or her salvation and therefore cannot be done in infancy. While those evangelicals who believe in infant baptism defend it as the New Testament counterpart to circumcision, Baptists point out that no clear instance of a child being baptized exists in the New Testament. Even the baptism of Jesus, as recorded in the Gospels, took place when Jesus was an adult.

The Lord's Supper, also known as Holy Communion or, in more high-church circles, Holy Eucharist, refers to a commemoration of the Last Supper Jesus shared with his disciples before his crucifixion. Liberal Protestants view Holy Communion as essential to the building of community, but because evangelicals have generally shied away from sacramentalism (in part because of its association with Roman Catholicism), many hold to a "memorialist" view of the Lord's Supper. In this interpretation, the bread and the wine of Holy Communion merely *remind* us of the death of Christ; they do not necessarily impart grace to the believer, as in the Roman Catholic doctrine of transubstantiation.

The memorialist view has led, in turn, to a diminution of observance among evangelicals. Whereas faithful Catholics or Episcopalians receive Holy Communion at least once a week, most evangelical churches offer the Lord's Supper once a month at most, perhaps as seldom as once a quarter or a couple of times a year. The temperance movement in nineteenth-century America also wrought changes in evangelical practice. Unfermented wine—grape juice—was substituted for wine, and the common cup was jettisoned for hygienic reasons in favor of small, individual-sized containers.

Protestant Demographics

Several factors make quantification of Protestants difficult. First, it is nearly impossible to find evangelicals by denomination. While many denominations are identifiably evangelical—the Assemblies of God, the General Association of Regular Baptists, or the Church of God in Christ, among many others—many evangelicals remain part of mainline Protestant denominations, so they would not show up in statistical analysis by denominations. Another complication revolves around the way that membership is reckoned. For many Protestant churches membership is almost a birthright, bestowed on the children of the faithful through baptism or confirmation, whereas most evangelical churches have more exacting standards for membership, which might require a candidate to stand in front of the elders or the entire congregation and give a detailed account of her conversion and spiritual pilgrimage. This divergence in standards for membership has given rise to the odd situation wherein a local mainline Protestant congregation might have 2,000 members on the rolls and 200 who show up for Sunday worship, while an evangelical church might have the opposite: 2,000 in attendance and only 200 members. This strange divergence contributed to the widespread impression throughout most of the twentieth century that liberal or mainline Protestants were more significant numerically than they actually were.

Having said that, however, pollsters have become more sophisticated in recent years in calculating the number of evangelicals. A 1998 Gallup poll, for instance, placed the number at 39 percent of the population of the United States, using the three criteria of personal conversion, belief in the Bible as the Word of God, and a desire "to lead nonbelievers to the point of conversion."[9] The poll found that, among the African American population, the percentage rose to 58 percent, and 21 percent of Roman Catholics fit the definition of evangelical, up from 12 percent in 1988.[10] Gallup also identified large numbers of evangelicals in every region of the country, from a low of 26 percent in the East to 54 percent in the South.[11]

Lyman A. Kellstedt and John C. Green lay out four criteria for locating evangelicals: belief that salvation comes only through faith in Jesus, conversion experience, belief in the importance of missions and evangelism, and "belief in the truth or inerrancy of Scripture."[12] Only 14 percent of Americans, they found, met all four tests, but 31 percent affirmed the importance of being born again, 37 percent said it was essential to witness to the faith, 44 percent said the Bible was true, and 46 percent insisted that Jesus was the only way to salvation.[13] Kellstedt and Green also sought to get at the question in a slightly different way, dividing the population into five groups: white evangelical Protestants, Roman Catholics, black Protestants, white mainline Protestants, and others. Using this tool, they found that white evangelical Protestants made up the largest percentage at 26 percent, followed by Roman Catholics at 23 percent and mainline Protestants at 17 percent.[14]

A survey conducted by Christian Smith, Michael Emerson, Sally Gallagher, and Paul Kennedy asked Americans to classify themselves according to different religious identities. Mainline Protestants numbered 27 percent of the population, and the category "theologically liberal Christian" claimed 20 percent. Nineteen percent said they were fundamentalists, and 21 percent were evangelicals.[15]

The Angus Reid Group of Canada conducted a poll in 1996 which compared religious affiliations in the United States and Canada. The poll found that while 55 percent of the population in the United States "believe the Bible is God's word, to be taken literally word for word," only 28 percent of Canadians agreed. As for reading the Bible, 21 percent of Canadians said they did so at least weekly, while the number rose to 43 percent in the United States. As for the number of evangelicals overall, the survey identified 15 percent of the Canadian population as "non-black evangelical Protestant," whereas the percentage in the United States was more than double: 33 percent.

The Aberration of "Mainline Protestantism"

The ascendance of liberal or mainline Protestantism in the middle decades of the twentieth century was transitory and, to some extent, illusory. Evangelicalism has been the most influential social and religious movement in American history, but the repercussions from the fundamentalist-modernist controversy during the 1910s and 1920s temporarily changed the dynamics of American Protestantism in the twentieth century. The abridged version of the story is that the modernists or the liberals won, at least in the short term. Half a century later, though, evangelicals vigorously reasserted themselves in politics, religion, and culture.

In 1923 J. Gresham Machen, then a professor at Princeton Theological Seminary, published a book entitled *Christianity and Liberalism*, which drew a distinction between the two—Christianity and liberalism—and called on liberals within his own Presbyterian denomination to do the honorable thing, to acknowledge their theological deviance and withdraw from the denomination. The Presbyterian modernists, of course, refused Machen's challenge, so it was Machen and the conservatives who were forced to leave and form their own congregations, schools, colleges, seminaries, mission societies, and denominations. That move proved costly, and it provided the liberals (those who would eventually become known as the "Protestant mainline") with a tactical, if temporary, advantage. They held on to their ecclesiastical institutions, along with the endowments that sustained them, while the evangelicals had to start over and build from scratch, thereby skewing the relative strength of the two strains of American Protestantism.

Without any question, evangelicals, including fundamentalists, pentecostals, and the holiness people, represented the growth sector of American Protestantism at the turn of the twenty-first century, increasing in numbers, visibility, and cultural influence. Those generally associated with mainline Protestantism, on the other hand—Lutherans, Methodists, Episcopalians, Congregationalists, Presbyterians, and some Baptists—have faltered since the mid-1960s by almost any index: membership, church attendance, or giving. Mainline Protestants, now called "Old-Line Protestants" by some observers, invested heavily in the ecumenical movement and in such political causes as civil rights, opposition to the war in Vietnam, and the pursuit of equal rights for women. For their part, evangelicals, after a half-century hiatus, reclaimed their place in American public discourse in the mid-to-late 1970s, although, tragically, the political agenda that leaders of the Religious Right espouse betrays the noble legacy of evangelical activism in the nineteenth century.

In short, the religious landscape of the United States has shifted dramatically since the editors of the *Christian Century* exulted in 1951 that "America should be grateful for the spiritual tide which flows unceasingly into our national life through its institutions of religion." The "institutions of religion," of course, were mainline Protestant denominations, for the editors of the *Christian Century*, a magazine long associated with liberal Protestantism, rarely deigned to speak of evangelical Protestants, and when they did so their tone was one of barely concealed contempt.

The Roots of Division

The Emancipation Proclamation and the conclusion of the Civil War fractured the unity of American Protestants. In the decades after the war two rather distinct factions emerged: conservative or evangelical versus liberal or nonevangelical. In a sense the first salvo had arrived from Great Britain on the eve of the Civil War. Charles Darwin's *The Origin of Species* hit American bookstores on November 24, 1859, and all 1,250 copies sold that same day. Darwin's theory of evolution struck at the core of Protestant beliefs about the authority and reliability of the Scriptures because, taken to its logical conclusions, Darwinism undermined the credibility of literal readings of the Genesis account of creation. A second threat also arrived from across the Atlantic. The German discipline of higher criticism cast further doubt on the reliability of the Bible by calling into question the authorship of several books in the Bible. The higher critics insisted that the book of Isaiah, for instance, was written by two or three different authors; they also provided textual evidence that the Torah or the Pentateuch (the first five books of the Hebrew Bible) came from several sources and not from the single hand of Moses himself—who in any case presumably would have had trouble recording his own death at the conclusion of Deuteronomy. Conservative Protestants saw ominous signs that the intellectual climate was turning hostile to the Bible and against orthodox Christianity; some academics were calling into question such doctrines as the virgin birth of Jesus, the inspiration of the Scriptures, and the authenticity of miracles.

Conservative Protestants also became uneasy about the direction the culture was taking, expressing alarm over the social changes occasioned by rapid urbanization, industrialization, and the arrival of non-Protestant immigrants. Taken together, these developments undermined evangelicals' confidence in their ability to construct the kingdom of God on earth.

Liberal Protestants, however, took another tack. As evangelicals retreated into an otherworldly posture, emphasizing the importance of individual conversions over social amelioration, liberals rose to the social challenges of the late nineteenth century. Led by such ministers and theorists as Walter Rauschenbusch, Washington Gladden, and Richard T. Ely and by the example of Jane Addams, founder of Hull settlement house in Chicago, liberal Protestants embraced what became known as the Social Gospel, which insisted that God was capable of redeeming sinful social institutions as well as sinful individuals. The Social Gospelers, as they became known, plunged into the herculean, Progressive-era task of cleaning up the tenements, ending machine-type political corruption, ministering to the poor, and abolishing child labor and the seven-day workweek.

Evangelicals, meanwhile, became increasingly alienated from the larger culture. They viewed with suspicion everything from the Bolshevik Revolution to the bobbed hairstyles fashionable among women in the 1920s. Conservatives were especially alarmed by the incursion of liberal or "modernist" ideas into Protestant denominations. They sought to defeat the liberals, but they repeatedly fell short. Machen, the professor at Princeton Seminary, for instance, was forced out of Princeton in 1929, whereupon he started his own seminary, Westminster Theological Seminary, in Philadelphia and eventually his own conservative denomination, the Orthodox Presbyterian Church. Similar scenarios unfolded in other denominations, with the evangelicals, by and large, bolting from institutions that they regarded as fatally tainted with heresy.

The "Mainline Mirage"

While mainline Protestants were exulting over their victories in the fundamentalist-modernist controversy, having finally banished those pesky conservatives, the evangelicals were busy building the foundations for their return to cultural ascendance in the mid-1970s. What is remarkable about this period of evangelical activity is not merely that evangelicals managed to organize a vast network of congregations and denominations and to construct Bible institutes and seminaries—what is remarkable is the way they went about it. They accomplished this formidable task by relying on their time-honored appeal to the masses, by speaking the idiom of the people. Throughout American history evangelicals have displayed an almost unerring knack for tapping into popular sentiments, and during these years of rebuilding they reached out to the public in innovative, often ingenious ways—from Aimee Semple McPherson's radio broadcasts and theatrical sermons at Angelus Temple in Los Angeles to Billy Graham's stadium crusades to Charles E. Fuller's *Old Fashioned Revival Hour*. While mainline Protestants basked in their pyrrhic victory in the fundamentalist-modernist controversy, the forces they thought they had vanquished were merely regrouping to fight another day, having mustered their troops at the grass roots.

Protestant liberalism itself faced some challenges in these years. The world emerged from the First World War, in the words of F. Scott Fitzgerald, "to find all gods dead, all wars fought, all faiths in man shaken."[16] In the judgment of some theologians, the suffering and the atrocities associated with the "Great War" had sounded the death knell for liberalism, with its rosy assessment of human nature and its assertion of the "immanence" of God. A group of theologians, who became known as Neo-Orthodox, reasserted the transcendence of God and took a more sober appraisal of human nature. In so doing, they staked out a middle ground between the liberals and moderates on the one hand and the conservatives and evangelicals on the other. But occupying the middle ground too often entailed getting caught in a crossfire; evangelicals criticized what they regarded as

Neo-Orthodoxy's inadequate appreciation for the authority of the Bible, while liberals objected to Neo-Orthodoxy's dim view of human nature.

For the most part, however, liberal Protestants enjoyed their ascendance during the middle decades of the twentieth century, at the same time that evangelicals were struggling to build their institutions. "Mainline Protestantism," as it came to be called, aspired to represent the middle-class aspirations of the American way of life. In a grand gesture of corporate efficiency and Cold War solidarity they organized themselves into the National Council of Churches during a November 1949 snowstorm in Cleveland. Ignoring the warnings of the Protestant magazine *Christian Century* and other Protestants who feared that the National Council of Churches would lose touch with its Protestant constituents, the new organization chose the upper west side of Manhattan for its new headquarters, a towering International-style building known officially as the Interchurch Center but almost universally as the "God Box." President Dwight D. Eisenhower laid the cornerstone for the new building on October 12, 1958, thereby symbolizing the convergence of mainline Protestantism and the American way of life.

Although the logic behind denominational cooperation and avoiding the duplication of efforts was unassailable, mainline Protestants also plunged into the currents of ecumenism, the impulse toward Christian unity. Taking their cue from John 17, where Jesus expresses the hope that his followers "may all be one," the ecumenical movement sought, in effect, to reverse the fractiousness of the Protestant Reformation, seeking theological unity among all Protestants—at least among mainline Protestants. Several initiatives were launched, many of which led to intercommunion. Theologically, however, the ecumenical movement proved disastrous as mainline Protestants ratcheted their distinctive doctrines down to the lowest common denominator of agreement, generally expressed in trinitarian terms: peace, justice, and inclusiveness.

Though few would quibble with those noble ideals, many of the people in the pews became restive. The so-called decline of mainline Protestantism began to show up in various indices (membership, giving, attendance) as early as 1965. The reasons are complex—and hotly disputed—but several factors must be taken into account. The first is demographic and geographic. As white America fled to the suburbs after World War II, many mainline congregations had difficulty keeping up with their congregants. Many of these redoubtable churches were downtown congregations, with expensive buildings and an elaborate infrastructure that could not be easily transplanted to the suburbs. First, finding a buyer who could give fair value for the property was nearly impossible, and a flight to the suburbs would represent a betrayal of both the Social Gospel legacy of Protestant liberalism and the ecumenical cant of peace, justice, and inclusiveness. Failure to relocate, however, had other adverse effects. As congregants moved to the suburbs they organized other churches, and many of the churches waiting for them were evangelical congregations.[17]

Another factor leading to the mainline decline was the insularity of denominational leaders. Once the executives settled into their offices overlooking Riverside Drive in Manhattan they started to lose touch with the people in the pews, many of whom considered denominational officials too liberal, both theologically and politically. These congregants voted with their feet, many of them finding their way to evangelical churches. Belatedly (almost comically), mainline denominations recognized the folly of their New York City location and sought to reconnect with the grass roots by moving their offices to the heartland—the Presbyterians to Louisville, Kentucky; the United Church of Christ to Cleveland; the Evangelical Lutheran Church to Chicago.

A third difficulty facing the Protestant mainline was blurred identity, a direct consequence of the ecumenical movement. By the 1980s it had become virtually impossible to distinguish between a Methodist and a Presbyterian or a Lutheran and an Episcopalian. Indeed, little set them apart from one another, aside from their history, which they seemed all too eager to elide in favor of a kind of pan-Protestantism. That impulse was understandable during the Cold War, when Protestants had taken it upon themselves to present a united front against the perils of communism. By the late 1980s, though, as the Soviet empire teetered and finally collapsed, Americans sought more definition and particularity, whether in ethnicity or theology. Evangelicals offered theological definition and unambiguous morality in an uncertain age. Many Protestants found that attractive.

The Evangelical Resurgence

In 1949, Billy Graham, a dynamic young preacher, agonized over a friend's challenge to attend seminary. Charles Templeton, an evangelist for a new organization called Youth for Christ, possessed an intellectual restlessness that finally got the better of him, and, in a famous meeting at the Taft Hotel in New York City, Templeton challenged Graham to enroll with him at Princeton Theological Seminary. Graham considered the offer at some length but finally, during a retreat in the San Bernardino Mountains of southern California, decided to reject the offer and simply "preach the Gospel." Graham left the retreat for Los Angeles, where he conducted a revival (which he called a "crusade") beneath a huge tent, dubbed the "Canvas Cathedral." Graham's preaching made him a celebrity in the land of celebrities, and his anticommunist rhetoric caught the attention of newspaper magnate William Randolph Hearst, who instructed his papers to "puff Graham."

Graham and his "team" translated his popularity into something of an empire, with a magazine, a radio program, television specials, and even a motion picture company. More important for evangelicals, however, Graham represented a kind of advance guard, moving beyond their evangelical subculture and circulating in the wider world. Evangelicals took a vicarious satisfaction in Graham's very public friendships with a succession of U.S. presidents, from Dwight Eisenhower to Bill Clinton. For evangel-

Fig. 1.5. Throughout a career that lasted more than half a century, Billy Graham invited millions to come to Jesus with his simple, homespun preaching. Bettmann/Corbis.

icals themselves, a half century of institution building had begun to pay off by the 1970s. They had laid the foundation for their return to the public arena, with a flourishing subculture of colleges and seminaries, missions and publications, and they had made their presence felt in the media, not only radio but television.

The catalyst for their re-entry into the public arena was the presidential campaign of a Southern Baptist Sunday school teacher, Jimmy Carter. The former governor of Georgia spoke openly about being a born-again Christian and promised that he "would never knowingly lie to the American people." To an electorate wearied of Watergate and Richard Nixon's endless prevarications, the pledge resonated; for evangelicals, Carter represented one of their own, someone who was unafraid to articulate his faith. By no means did all evangelicals cast their votes for Carter (many, in fact, remained unregistered), but the Democratic candidate lured many—southerners especially—out of their apolitical torpor and back into the political arena.

One of the ironies of American political life in the 1970s and 1980s was that many evangelicals turned against Carter in favor of Ronald Reagan in the 1980 election, which featured three candidates for president—Carter, Reagan, and independent candidate John B. Anderson—who all claimed to be born-again Christians. The Religious Right, a loose coalition of politically conservative evangelicals that had emerged during the Carter presidency, helped to ensure the election and re-election of Reagan in 1980 and 1984, respectively.

In other ways as well, evangelicals grew more and more comfortable with the world outside of their subculture. For example, while evangelicals had once harbored deep suspicions about the perils of affluence, many adopted a kind of "spiritualized Reaganism" with their embrace of the so-called prosperity theology in the 1980s, insisting that God was eager to shower material blandishments on the faithful. Evangelicals had reestablished their presence in politics, in media, in higher education, and (to a somewhat lesser degree) in the arts. The so-called megachurches (generally defined as congregations of 1,000 or more) sprouted up across North America, spreading their evangelical message to their communities and beyond. While evangelicals remained deeply rooted within their own subculture, sometime during the 1980s evangelicalism ceased being a counterculture. Evangelicals had reasserted themselves as the major force in American Protantism.

American Protestantism at the Turn of the Twenty-first Century

By the turn of the twenty-first century mainline Protestantism was languishing. When Robert Edgar, former U.S. Congressman and former president of Claremont School of Theology, assumed leadership of the National Council of Churches at the turn of the millennium, he inherited an organization deeply divided and dispirited and more than $4 million in debt. Several mainline Protestant seminaries were equally divided along ideological lines and even more grievously in debt, forced to siphon off their endowments to meet operating expenses. Not all mainline Protestant institutions were in such dire straits, of course, but the momentum of American Protestantism clearly had shifted away from liberalism and back to evangelicalism.

The mainline ascendance during the middle decades of the twentieth century, then, was transitory, but it may have been illusory as well due to the failure of social scientists to assess accurately the numerical strength of evangelical and mainline Protestantism. The challenge in many mainline congregations lies in getting your name *off* of the membership rolls, while evangelical standards for church membership are much more exacting. Add to this the fact that many evangelicals are affiliated with independent congregations, who do not divulge membership figures to denominational entities, let alone social scientists, and you have a rather skewed picture of the relative importance of evangelical and mainline Protestants in the twentieth century.

Assessing the real picture is no easy matter. Without any question liberal or mainline Protestantism retained considerable resources at the turn of the twenty-first century, especially institutional assets: universities, seminaries, church endowments, pension funds, and the like. The folly of evangelicals in thinking they could match those resources was underscored when Jerry Falwell announced that his Liberty University would be the next Harvard. Evangelicals, however, building on the foundation of their own subculture, which they had painstakingly constructed during the middle decades of the twentieth century, had made impressive institutional advances. More important, they had retained the loyalty of their constituents, in part because of a clearly articulated theology but also because of an insistence on communicating with the grass roots. As mainline Protestants would learn belatedly, no money and no endowment could buy that.

CHAPTER TWO

A Brief History of Protestantism in America

Protestantism in America claims a number of historical antecedents, from German-speaking Reformers to English religious dissidents. Most Protestants, moreover, would want to trace their religious roots back even further, to biblical times. Many Protestants, especially evangelicals, claim they are the remnant of the true church, the church unfettered by doctrinal minutiae and fractious factionalism, a back-to-the-biblical-basics church, whose members draw not from the manners and teachings of Ulrich Zwingli or Thomas Hooker, but Scripture itself, and little else. Another milepost, of course, is Martin Luther and the Protestant Reformation. Protestant belief, for both evangelical and mainline Protestants, is grounded in Luther's insistence on individual authority—what he called the "priesthood of believers." Even though they read the Scripture through the lens of a variety of interpretive eyeglasses, American Protestants claim Luther's *sola scriptura*—his insistence that each person read Scripture for herself or himself, aided by the Holy Spirit, rather than have the interpretation of a handful of church officials imposed from above.

Luther scarcely would have recognized the phenomenon he wrought. Protestants in America have taken the sentiments Luther advocated to their logical conclusion, but were Luther around today, he might not have very much in common with his religious descendants, and he would doubtless be distressed by the endless splintering that has characterized Protestantism in America.

The Legacy of Puritanism

Evangelicalism, the more aggressive strain in American Protestantism, traces its roots to the twin influences of Puritanism and Pietism, religious movements that dominated the Middle Colonies and New England from the early seventeenth century for the next hundred years. If you mention "Puritans," most Americans conjure cookie-cutter stereotypes from fourth grade Thanksgiving skits—righteous (or self-righteous), black-clad, sexually repressed cardboard clichés, ever worried, as historian Perry Miller once put it, that somebody, somewhere might be having fun. But Puritans were in fact a diverse and contentious lot—and American evangelicals three centuries later continue to draw on both the normative Puritan ideal as well as the vociferous minority that strayed from it. Puritans' rigorous moral standards, their emphasis on Scripture, and their demand for a conversion experience continue as hallmarks of American evangelicals today.

Orthodox Puritans were devout—some would say dour—Calvinists. They believed that all humanity was sinful ever since Adam and Eve bit into the fruit of the forbidden Tree of Knowledge of Good and Evil. Even primers for children emphasized the sinful nature of humanity—in teaching the alphabet, Puritan schoolbooks linked each letter to a biblical lesson, and "A" usually stood for "In Adam's fall, we sinned all." A portion of humanity, the elect, was predestined for salvation, and that salvation could not come through doing good works but only through God's grace. The elect could never be sure that they were saved, and consequently, Puritan poetry tells us, even those most confident Christians spent their lives tormented over the status of their souls. Nonetheless, Puritan divines developed an elaborate "morphology of conversion"—believers could analyze their own lives and determine whether it was likely that they were among the elect. The linchpin was the conversion experience. The Puritan who believed he was saved would testify to his community about why he thought he was saved. Church elders then determined, based on his conversion narrative, whether he was sincere and whether he had in fact undergone a conversion. If so, the believer was assumed to be a member of the elect, the saved on earth, and was admitted as a communicating member of the church.[1]

Indeed, church membership was not only a statement about one's heavenly lot, it also determined the shape of one's earthly life as well. In the theocracy of colonial New England, the franchise was determined not by property ownership, but by church membership; only church members—male church members—could vote.

If American evangelicalism was influenced by Puritanism's reliance on scripture and emphasis on conversion, it was no less shaped by Puritan dissenters, of whom there were not a few in New England. Anne Hutchinson and Roger Williams were the most famous dissenters, but lesser-known Puritans throughout colonial New England protested against what they saw as deadened spiritual hypocrisy, far from the "city on a hill" that John Winthrop had envisioned in his famous sermon aboard the *Arbella*. Among the many Puritan dissenters were Separatists, Radical Spiritists, Anabaptists, and Millenarians; American Protestants find antecedents in each of their belief systems. The Separatists—better known as Pilgrims—were the first settlers of Plymouth Colony and Salem, where Roger Williams first preached. Separatists shared with Puritans their criticisms of the Church of England; they differed, however, on one crucial point: Puritans wanted to remain part of the Anglican Church and purify it (hence the moniker) from within, while Separatists believed that in order to be the true church of God they needed to sever ties completely with corrupt, "popish" Anglicanism. Their message of primitive piety and separation from worldly corruption has resonated with Protestants, especially evangelicals, throughout American history, especially during the mid-twentieth century.

Evangelicals in the wake of the Great Awakening and later would also be profoundly influenced by the Radical Spiritists, a diverse group of Puritan dissenters led by Samuel Gorton, Randall Holden, and others. These believers preached utter dependence on the Holy Spirit and eschewed orthodox teaching on conversion. Conversion, Gorton and others argued, could only be determined by the individual—church elders who tried to evaluate parishioners' conversion narratives were wasting their time, since conversion and salvation defied logic. One hallmark of conversion, according to the Spiritists, was the certainty that the believer himself experienced, something no church elder could assess. As Peter Sterry, an intimate of Oliver Cromwell, put it, for Spiritists, "Spiritual truth discovered by demonstration of reason" made no more sense than "the mistresse in her Cookmaid's clothes."

This emphasis on individual authority extended beyond the realm of conversion. Spiritists, most famously Anne Hutchinson, questioned the authority of ministers generally. They particularly criticized the emphasis the clergy placed on education, because in their understanding, book learning did not give a person any special insight into matters of the Spirit. Gorton

PUBLIC WORSHIP AT PLYMOUTH BY THE PILGRIMS.

Fig. 2.1. After the Pilgrims crossed the Atlantic in 1620, they established places of worship free from governmental interference. The Puritans began arriving a decade later. New York Public Library.

bemoaned the clergy who belittled the "immediate inspiration and revelation of the Spirit" instead of believing that "all must be hewed out by study and so kept in schools of humane learning, Libraries, and in men who have most means and time to exercise themselves in such things."

Finally, the Anabaptists and Millenarians left a legacy to American Protestantism. Anabaptists, who from the 1640s on emphasized the necessity of an adult's, or "believer's," baptism, are the ancestors of today's Baptists. Roger Williams, usually recognized as the father of the Baptist tradition in America, was rebaptized as an adult in 1639, although some evidence suggests there was a movement afoot for adult baptism even before then.[2] Although the debate over the timing of baptism may seem prosaic today, it animated heated debate among Protestants in the seventeenth, eighteenth, and nineteenth centuries. Baptists argued that there was no scriptural evidence for the baptism of children; Jesus and John, after all, were both adults when they were baptized. Furthermore, the Baptists argued, a child cannot make an informed commitment to Christianity, as an adult can. The Puritans, on the other hand, saw baptism as a rite of inclusion into the com-

Fig. 2.2. Anne Hutchinson (1591–1643) tested the limits of Puritan tolerance in the 1630s. She was banished from Massachusetts in 1638. Bettmann/Corbis.

munity of faith, the New Testament counterpart to the Old Testament rite of circumcision.

Millenarians emphasized, as have some American evangelicals ever since, the immediacy of Christ's reign on Earth. While Quakers believed that the colonists were already living in the Kingdom of God, other colonial millenarians urged New Englanders to take steps to hasten the return of

Christ to Earth. Thomas Venner embodied the most radical strain of seventeenth-century millennarianism. A member of the church of Salem who spoke urgently about the need to bring about God's kingdom on Earth, Venner returned to England in 1655 in the wake of the Puritan Revolution, which he took as a clear sign that the kingdom was at hand. In 1656, he led a radical conventicle in Swan Alley, Coleman Street, in London, where he and his followers stockpiled arms in anticipation of the coming Armageddon.

Not all millennarians were so ardent in their expression of faith, but they did share with Venner a reading of Scripture that used the prophecies in Daniel and the book of Revelation to interpret the events of the day. The migration to America itself played no less an important cosmic role than the English Revolution, for many Puritan colonists believed that the immigration was the age of glory that Scripture said would precede the last judgment, and some radical Protestants speculated about the exact date of Christ's return.

If contemporary Protestants seldom look to the English Revolution and the settling of Massachusetts Bay Colony as important moments in God's eschatological calendar, they do share the millennarians' penchant for singling out specific human events—the fall of the Berlin Wall, for example, or the Gulf War—as fulfillments of biblical prophecies. And predicting the precise day that Jesus would return to earth has been a favorite theological parlor game for evangelicals ever since.

The Legacy of Pietism

Puritans were not the only European settlers to bequeath a religious tradition to later American Protestants. Evangelicalism emerged from two strands of early American religion, and Pietist traditions played no less a role in shaping American evangelicalism than did Puritan practices. Historians often point to the Great Awakening, a series of religious revivals in the 1730s and 1740s, as the moment when evangelicalism took hold in America. Indeed, there is some truth in this claim: The American South was populated by lukewarm Anglicans and African slaves trying to hold on to their indigenous religious practices through the early eighteenth century, and the South did not become anything resembling today's Bible Belt until the preachers of the Great Awakening converted thousands of planters, yeomen, and slaves in the 1730s and 1740s, and, even more significantly, during the Second Great Awakening at the turn of the nineteenth century. But pointing to the Great Awakening as a starting point can be misleading, for really the religious fervor that marked these decades of revival no more began with the preaching of George Whitefield than it ended by the 1750s. Some scholars have seen the Awakening as Puritanism's last-ditch effort to survive into the eighteenth century, but it is more accurately conceived of as one incarnation of a durable Pietistic tradition that was alive and influential in the colonies long before the 1730s.[3]

Sermons from the Awakening emphasized two themes that were staples of Pietistic preaching and teaching as far back as the late seventeenth century: the necessity of spiritual rebirth and demands for upright living. At the same time that Congregationalist divines were commenting on the wondrous revivals sweeping the Connecticut Valley, Guiliam Bertholf led a Pietistic revival in northern New Jersey, and Swedish Lutherans in the Delaware Valley were divided over the meaning of Lars Tollstadius's Pietistic preaching. Pietism influenced even the most conventional Great Awakening preachers. Gilbert Tennent, one of the day's leading revivalists, imbibed Pietistic teachings and fervor from the Pietist master preacher Theodorus Jacobus Frelinghuysen, a Dutch Reformed minister with whom Tennent preached in the Raritan Valley of New Jersey.[4]

Not only did Tennent learn from Frelinghuysen, and vice versa, Pietism also served to link non-English-speaking colonists with the English. Puritans like Williams Perkins and Williams Ames wrote tracts that were translated into Dutch and read by Pietist leaders—and those English Puritans read writings by myriad Dutch Pietist leaders, from Willem Teelinck to Gysbertus Voetius. In itself, Pietism was just as transatlantic a movement as Puritanism, with Pietist leaders maintaining close ties to religious leaders in the Old World well into the eighteenth century.

Pietism largely disappeared from America around the middle of the eighteenth century—that is, it disappeared as a distinctive, identifiable movement, for it was melded with Puritanism to form the American evangelical tradition. Evangelicalism owes its fervor and much of its doctrine to these Pietistic roots. Today's evangelical Bible studies evince the influence of the Bible studies conducted in the Scandinavian *Bede Hus* (prayer house), today's prayer meetings mimic the eighteenth-century pietist conventicles, and evangelical sermons echo the Pietistic warnings about leading a life that is outwardly religious but bereft of inner spiritual fervor. Perhaps more than anything, though, evangelicalism and Pietism share the sometimes futile aim of preventing the religious life from growing ossified.

The Age of Awakenings

Historians have debated the phenomenon that we now call the Great Awakening. Several things are misleading about the term, not least its implication that there was one, unified, dramatic religious event—which was certainly not the case.[5] Rather, the religious awakenings of this period were erratic, disparate events interrupted by the American Revolution. Whatever we call it, the wave of revivals was ignited by the preaching of George Whitefield in Georgia and New England in the 1740s and 1750s. Whitefield first arrived in Georgia in 1738 on a brief fund-raising stint for an orphanage. The next year, he returned to the colonies, and in 1740 he preached revivals all over New England; reports from the time portray Whitefield preaching to crowds of 8,000 people every day for month-long stretches.

Like many evangelical leaders after Whitefield, he was a charismatic, compelling presence, and some commentators even claim that his curiously crossed eyes were engaging, not distracting. Whitefield had been drawn to a career on the stage as a young man, but he gave that up when he became a Christian. His dramatic flair continued to captivate audiences in his new calling, however, especially in a culture that, at that time, had no theatrical tradition.[6] Contemporaries claimed that Whitefield could bring tears to your eyes simply by uttering the word "Mesopotamia." Benjamin Franklin had this to say about Whitefield's oratorical finesse and persuasive powers:

> I happened soon after to attend one of [Whitefield's] Sermons, in the Course of which I perceived he intended to finish with a Collection, and I silently resolved he should get nothing from me. I had in my Pocket a Handful of Copper Money, three or four silver Dollars, and five Pistoles in Gold. As he proceeded, I began to soften, and concluded to give the Coppers. Another stroke of his Oratory made me asham'd of that, and determin'd me to give the Silver; and he finish'd so admirably, that I empty'd my Pocket wholly into the Collector's Dish, Gold and all.[7]

Phillis Wheatley, the noted early American black poet, took Whitefield as the subject of her first published poem: Whitefield, she wrote, preached "Take him, ye Africans, he longs for you, / Impartial Saviour is his title due."

Whitefield alone did not preach the colonies into a religious frenzy. Jonathan Edwards, pastor of a congregation in Northampton, Massachusetts, had led what he later described as a surprising work of God—a revival in the Connecticut River Valley. A strict Calvinist who believed, in the tradition of his Puritan forebears, that all people were sinful and only some were called out for salvation by the grace of God, Edwards emphasized how a completely depraved humanity depended on God. His Northampton congregation responded with an outbreak of piety and revival that overwhelmed the community.

The revivals in America were not an isolated occurrence; they were part of a larger transatlantic religious revival. Whitefield himself was influential in leading not only the revival in the American colonies, but also the Evangelical Awakening in England and the Welsh revival, called the *Cabuslang werk*. Eighteenth-century evangelicals themselves understood that these three religious revivals were not isolated events but were part of the same work of the Holy Spirit. As John Wesley, the English founder of Methodism, noted, the American revival was "Evidently one work with what we have here." Evangelical leaders in the mother country were linked through correspondence and newspapers to the revivals in the mainland colonies. From Halle, the center of German Pietism, revival leader A. E. Francke wrote letters to some five thousand correspondents, and he subscribed to newspapers from all over the Atlantic world. In 1734 and 1735, Francke and many British Isle evangelicals read Edwards's account of God's surprising Connecticut Valley work in newspapers published in London, Boston, and Glasgow. Likewise, many evangelicals in America kept abreast of Scottish revivalism by reading *Glasgow Weekly History* and various revival magazines from Edinburgh.

Henry Davidson of Galashiels, Scotland, described himself as an "omne-gatherum" of pamphlets from throughout the Atlantic world. In a web of Atlantic evangelicalism, Davidson corresponded with a minister at Braintree, in Essex, England, and with an evangelical merchant in Edinburgh who himself had contacts at Whitefield's London tabernacle, through which he received frequent updates about revivals in the American colonies.

New Lights Versus Old Lights

Not all Americans took kindly to the evangelical revivalism sweeping the colonies. Rifts in local churches and towns developed between the supporters of the revivals, called New Lights because of their enthusiasm for revival, and those who opposed the religious enthusiasm and fervor of the revivals, the Old Lights. One of the most dramatic expressions of the divisive nature of the revivals can be found on the village green in New Haven, Connecticut, where the New Light meetinghouse sits alongside the Old Light meetinghouse. The Old Lights were simultaneously liberal and conservative. Culturally, they were conservative insofar as they detested the enthusiasm and fervor of the revivals; they distrusted the ways the preaching was shaking up American culture. Theologically, the Old Lights were much more liberal than their revivalist counterparts. In fact, Charles Chauncy, the most vituperative and vitriolic of all Edwards's critics, went on to found the Unitarian Church, but his cultural conservatism came through in his nickname: "Old Brick."

Although the South could not boast as many prominent native son preachers as New England, there too the revivals had a profound impact. Although the South now bears the distinction of being the nation's Bible Belt, its religious commitments before the Great Awakening were quite tenuous. The seeds of the devout evangelical fervor that has come to mark the South were planted during the Awakenings. In particular, the Baptists had a tremendous impact on the mid-eighteenth-century South. In the 1750s Shubal Stearns and Daniel Marshall evangelized the Carolinas, and in 1755 they established the first Baptist church in the South, in Sandy Creek, North Carolina. Samuel Davies was another preacher, a Presbyterian, who led southern revivals, notably among slaves. As early as 1758 northern preachers helped black slaves on William Byrd III's Virginia plantation establish a formal fellowship for worship.

The most important Christian center for African Americans in pre-Revolutionary America was Savannah. Like the evangelists on the British Isles, the religious leaders of Savannah's black community demonstrate the transatlantic nature of the revivals during this period. David George was a slave who ran away from Virginia and worked as a servant to the Natchez Indians before being sold to a plantation on the Savannah River. There, he was converted to the Baptist faith by a slave named Cyrus. When low-country Georgia fell to British rule in 1778, George's Patriot owner abandoned the plantation, and George moved his congregation to Savannah, where he remained for the next three years. When, at the end of the war, the British army left Georgia, George followed the British to Nova Scotia, where he established another black Baptist church. In 1793, he emigrated to Africa, founding the first West African Baptist church.

George Leile was another Georgian slave who was significant in shaping Afro-Southern—and Atlantic—Christianity. He was the slave of a Loyalist

Baptist deacon who freed Leile before the British occupation. After his manumission, Leile moved to Savannah and, like George, left Georgia when the British troops left. Leile went to Jamaica, establishing a church in Kingston. When Liele left Savannah, many African Americans in the area concluded that organized, black Christianity was over in Savannah, but just before he departed, Leile baptized Andrew Bryan, a slave on Brampton Plantation. Bryan gathered fellow slaves in regular worship, which was scheduled early in the morning and late at night so that it did not conflict with work schedules. In 1788, Bryan was ordained as a Baptist preacher; he baptized forty-five slaves the next day, and Savannah's first Baptist church was organized. Initially called the Ethiopian Church of Jesus Christ at Savannah, the congregation was known by the 1820s as the First African Baptist Church.

Only a few months after the church was established, a group of white Savannahians on a grand jury stated that it was a "grevance" that African Americans were "being permitted to assemble in large bodies under the pretence of religion." William Bryan was singled out as having violated the law. Bryan's owner, whose father had been a strong supporter of Whitefield, intervened and allowed Bryan the use of his barn for worship services; local animosity died down, though not before Bryan was publicly whipped. At Bryan's death in 1812, the church had 1,498 members, 28 percent of the Savannah River Association, of which First African Baptist was a member. One of the most important black religious institutions in the South, First African has been called by one historian the "mother church of black religious institutions."

Even those white southern Christians who did not object to sharing the gospel with African Americans did not hold their black coreligionists in the highest esteem. Charles Colcock Jones, a Georgia planter who advocated evangelizing the slaves, complained about their "stupid looks, their indifferent staring, their profound sleeps." But, as in so many cases, the white observers misconstrued the meanings of their slaves' actions. Jones concluded that black churchgoers were too daft or uneducated to understand highfalutin sermons or too heathenish to care about their salvation. But these same African Americans who dozed in white churches were devoted and passionate in the black "invisible churches" that populated southern plantations.

These black churches provided more than spiritual succor for enduring the hardships of slavery; they were the only institutions in slave society where African Americans had any measure of autonomy. The churches helped care for the infirm, facilitated the development of families, and created a rich tradition of black music.

Protestantism and the American Revolution

Many scholars have argued that the religious awakenings of the 1740s were intimately connected to the American Revolution: The revivals established patterns of communication among the colonists and helped to erode ethnic barriers so that the colonists had more of a common identity as Americans. If the revivals influenced the Revolution, the Revolution would influence subsequent revivals as well. The Revolution led to religious disestablishment, the proscription against a state church, and it inculcated in the republic the value of religious freedom rather than merely religious toleration. Prior to the Revolution, many of the thirteen colonies boasted a state-established church, but state after state followed the example of disestablishment set by the Middle Colonies, with the last colony, Massachusetts, disestablishing the Congregational Church in 1833.

Long before separation of church and state was codified in the Constitution and the churches disestablished, evangelicals had pushed for the separation of church and state. The Baptists going back all the way to Roger Williams were most ardent in pursuing this goal. When in 1764 a Baptist college—later to become Brown University—was founded, the charter determined to uphold "Absolute and uninterrupted Liberty of Conscience" and proclaimed that the school would admit students of any religious denomination. Isaac Backus, the leader of New England Baptists, raised the issue of formal separation of church and state with Massachusetts and Connecticut during the Revolution (although these two states would be the last to disestablish their state churches).

Although religious disestablishment is often credited to Thomas Jefferson's Deistic leanings—and Jefferson did pen the elegant Virginia Statute for Religious Freedom, based upon an earlier statement by James Madison—it was in fact evangelicals who forged the separation of church and state. The Baptists in Virginia wielded significant political muscle after the Revolution both because of their burgeoning numbers and because they had ardently supported the revolutionary effort. Irate that they were legally required to support the Anglican Church, Baptists collected thousands of signatures and petitioned the Assembly for disestablishment. The Assembly

Fig. 2.3. The Great Awakening prompted the formation of several schools—today's Princeton, Rutgers, Brown, and Dartmouth—in order to provide for an educated, revival-minded clergy. Rhode Island College, founded by the Baptists in 1764, eventually became Brown University. John Hay Library Archives for Brown University.

took action: They disestablished the Anglican Church but required all citizens to pay taxes to support some church of their own choosing. The religious dissenters found this *via media* unsatisfactory, and they continued the fight that culminated in the Virginia Statute for Religious Freedom— the basis for the First Amendment in the Bill of Rights. In this statute, religion is separated from the state not because religion might impinge on government but the other way around—because state interference would be bad for religion.

The postrevolutionary trend toward disestablishment only furthered the spread of Protestantism, but other factors contributed to religious revival as well. Regionalism was particularly important in shaping evangelicalism's spread in America. The form of revivalism in the North was influenced by the relatively dense population that was increasingly concentrated in urban areas. The South, on the other hand, was less densely populated and had few urban centers. Southern revivalism occurred in homes, small meetinghouses, and open fields. Denominations were dispersed differently throughout the country. Baptists and Methodists predominated in the South, as they do today. Presbyterianism tended to follow the migration and settlement patterns of the Scots-Irish, taking hold, for example, in the Piedmont area and great valley of Virginia. Baptists tended to settle in coastal areas, tackling first the Tidewater when they evangelized Virginia and Savannah when they set out to convert Georgia. Methodism established itself very early in the South, where Methodists tended to be attracted first to small urban centers from which they would then send out circuit-riding preachers.

Protestantism and Democracy

As the eighteenth century progressed, migration carried evangelical Protestantism across the mountains into Alabama, Mississippi, Kentucky, Ohio, Indiana, and Illinois. The spread of evangelicalism produced both denominational rivalry in the competitive American religious marketplace—another Protestant legacy still with us today—and interdenominational cooperative programs. Protestantism, moreover, with its emphasis on the priesthood of believers—each of us is equal before God—had an undeniable appeal to Americans newly intoxicated with democratic ideals in the early national period.[8] At times, the Protestant egalitarianism extended even to women and to African Americans, a radical notion at the time.

Particularly after 1800 both the egalitarian and the ecumenical character of Protestantism became pronounced, with camp meetings and other revivals presided over by preachers of different denominations. A meeting where "5 or 6 Methodist preachers" together with "5 Calvinists . . . some Presbyterians—some Baptists" debated matters of faith and urged conversion long into the night, as described by Methodist minister Jacob Young, was not atypical. The element that most distinguished southern revivalism from its northern cousin was the large presence of African American slaves. The promise of spiritual equality drew not only thousands of African Americans to evangelical churches but appealed to white women as well. Indeed, at its inception southern evangelicalism was dominated—at least numerically—by African Americans and white women. Through the early nineteenth century the specter of black and white ministers sharing the same pulpit was not uncommon. Nor was it rare to hear a white Christian comment enthusiastically about a black coreligionist's powerful prayers and exhortations. A white Methodist in Mississippi, for example, recalled that at one camp meeting, when a black slave called Pompey prayed and exhorted, "The earth seemed to tremble under the weight of that power . . . the whole audience seemed to sway to and fro . . . cries for mercy, groans of agony and shouts of praise were so numerous and loud that, strong and loud as his voice was, one could scarcely hear him."

The spiritual equality between black and white—and the limitations of that spiritual equality—can be seen in how white and black evangelicals addressed one another; "brother" and "sister" were the evangelical appellations of choice. Often black church members were referred to in just this way, Brother John or Sister Rebecca. Just as often, they were referred to as Black Brother and Black Sister, qualifiers that marked black Christians as still set apart from their white brothers and sisters in Christ.

Black women played a role as spiritual leaders in many African societies, and this role carried over into southern culture: In many accounts of revival, it is a black woman who was the catalyst for the conversion experiences of many. Thomas Rankin, a Methodist clergyman, reported presiding over one love-feast, a congregational celebration of the Last Supper, during which he looked up into the gallery where the black worshipers were seated and pointed out one particular black woman. Rankin does not tell us what she was doing, but he does tell us she brought the house down, inspiring in other congregants verbal and physical manifestations of conversion as they became, in Rankin's parlance, overcome by the Spirit.

Evangelicalism offered women an opportunity for self-expression and leadership. Although not usually serving as preachers (licensed clergy who could expound on a biblical text), women, black and white, exhorted, bringing people to an emotional pitch and preparing them for conversion. As historian Evelyn Brooks Higginbotham has noted, scholars of American religion have given so much attention to the role of the preacher that we have tended to overlook the role of the exhorter, who often played a crucial role in preparing people to experience dramatic spiritual rebirth.

The relative freedom of white women and African Americans eroded over time, however, as a glance at church seating arrangements reveals. As white men became disturbed by the predominance of women and African American men in the churches, they began to separate women from men and blacks from whites. Black worshipers were often relegated to the gallery (where they, too, would sit in sex-segregated sections) or, in some churches, to pews painted black. At least one Virginia church initiated a campaign to build a wall down the middle of the church—on one side black worshipers would sit, whites on the other. (The campaign was successful, although two prominent black worshipers left in protest before it was completed.)

Unlike the segregation of black and white worshipers, the physical segregation of men from women did not last in southern churches. As Christine

Leigh Heyrman has argued, the division of men from women was considered an affront to the authority of the southern family. White men saw their control of their wives being challenged, and they believed evangelical preachers were encouraging women to put church before family, to listen to the church's authority rather than their husbands' authority. In the end, to win the support of white men, evangelical churches capitulated on this point and restored the old family seating.[9]

Segregation in seating led to other rebellions. In 1787 Richard Allen, a freed slave, led a contingent of other African Americans away from the segregated galleries of the Saint George Methodist Episcopal Church in Philadelphia and eventually formed the Bethel African Methodist Episcopal Church.[10] The persistence of the formal segregation of African Americans also drove many black southerners out of biracial churches and left them to establish their own autonomous churches, one of the most important accomplishments in African American history. Traditional interpretations have argued that evangelicalism was imposed by the planter class on slaves as a mechanism for social control, but many planters, in fact, vigorously opposed the evangelization of slaves because they rightly feared the consequences of Christian—especially Protestant—claims about spiritual equality. African Americans appropriated evangelical Protestantism, and, within their own Christian communities, the leadership skills of black men and women were allowed to flourish.

In some regions, the establishment of black Protestant churches predated the establishment of white churches. The first black church in Savannah, for example, was built before the construction of the first white Baptist church in 1803. The same pattern prevailed in Fayetteville, North Carolina; Wilmington, North Carolina; and other towns across the South. These black churches were fundamental to the formation of culture and identity among African Americans, providing the Protestant assurance of a God who viewed all beings—women and men, black and white, slave and free, lay and clerical—as equal.

Although the first wave of evangelization saw a decline in traditional African practices, the introduction of Christianity to the South, on the whole, had positive effects on black slaves, providing avenues for the expression of leadership within the African American community. How women were affected by evangelization is less clear. Many scholars have argued that churches in the North developed as centers of female philanthropy. Because the actual work of northern revivals took place in churches, where women could gather, opportunities arose for the development of a collective identity among women that was a direct antecedent of the

Fig. 2.4. Richard Allen (1760–1831), a freed slave, led a contingent of blacks away from Philadelphia's Saint George Methodist Episcopal Church in 1787 to form Bethel Church, which later became the flagship of the African Methodist Episcopal (AME) Church. Billy Graham Center Museum.

women's rights movement. In the South, certainly, things proceeded differently. Because revivalism was more diffuse, often based in the home, there was no comparable opportunity for the development of female collectivity.

Even in the North, however, the story may not be as upbeat as it seems at first blush. Women in the post-Revolutionary era were increasingly marginalized in northern evangelical churches. Sin itself was feminized, with sexual offenses in particular being identified with women. Furthermore, even those voluntary reform organizations that came out of the evangelical churches ultimately served to undercut women's authority. These organizations were by and large led by men but run on a day-to-day basis by women—and they aimed to reform women, not men, especially in the arena of sexuality. The Magdalen Society, for example, founded in 1800, attempted to reform prostitutes by reintegrating young women into society through marriage and respectable jobs—and to restore, the leaders of the society made quite clear, male authority.

In the end, evangelicalism failed to bring equality to African Americans or white women. Evangelicals in the South who, under northern and English leadership, initially offered trenchant criticisms of slavery silenced their critiques as evangelical leadership was consolidated into southern hands. Even sectarian groups who initially offered African Americans something that resembled equality had retreated from this position. Consider the Moravians of North Carolina. When the Moravians, ardent Pietists from central Europe, first arrived in North Carolina, they attracted black members and opposed slavery. But as the eighteenth century wore on, the Moravians themselves began buying slaves, and they started treating Afro-Moravians as subordinates. Black and white Moravians once lived together, ate together, and were buried together. But by the 1820s Moravian graveyards tell a different story: Afro-Moravians were buried separately, kept apart in death as they had come to be in life.

Protestantism and the Sectional Crisis

Protestantism did not appeal only to black southerners and elite white women. As Randy Sparks has written, evangelicalism began in the eighteenth-century South as a revolutionary movement of the plain folk, "who consciously set themselves in opposition to the dominant culture of the gentry."[11] Yeomen found that evangelicalism challenged, however obliquely, the authority of the slave-owning gentry. Their very body language, that evocative and dramatic hallmark of evangelical revival, where new Christians rolled on the ground or jumped up and down infused by the Spirit, challenged elite notions of proper carriage, proper posture, proper gestures. Southern elites looked on in horror at what they deemed barbaric and animalistic physical behavior. In this atmosphere, the mingling of rich and poor, black and white, men and women, seemed especially threatening, for surely in the emotionally and spiritually charged physical expressions of the dancing exercise, the laughing exercise, and the jumping exercise, a challenge to traditional patterns of authority could not lag far behind.

Antebellum coastal North Carolina illustrates the anxiety that evangelical revival inspired in white planters. In the 1830s Methodist revivals flourished along the North Carolina coast, and elite white women were drawn to the meetings. Their unchurched husbands panicked because their wives were worshiping next to—and mingling with—slaves, free African Americans, and the "lower sorts" of white southerners. The planters decided that if they could convince their wives to trade the raucous Methodist revivalism for the comparatively staid Episcopal Church, the dangerous intermingling and all the potential alliances it implied would cease. In some cases, husbands went so far as to reopen Episcopal churches that had been dormant since the Revolution. Their experiment met with mixed results—their wives no longer had the opportunity to mix with unfit company, but they did not lapse into rote Episcopal ritual as was hoped. Rather, the women infused the Episcopal churches with evangelical fervor, demanding the same conversion experiences and devotion to Scripture that had been preached by Methodist itinerants.

Not only does this Episcopal revival illustrate the challenge that elite southern men perceived evangelicalism as posing, but it also belies the myth that evangelicalism was confined to the ranks of Baptists, Methodists, and Presbyterians. Just as regionalism was critical to the spread and development of evangelical Protestantism during the First Great Awakening, so too regionalism must play a part in any understanding of evangelicalism during the antebellum years, because slavery split American Protestants, as it split the rest of the nation, into two distinct societies. Although the Protestant churches did not formally separate into regionally distinct denominations until the 1840s—the Methodists split in 1844, Baptists in 1845, and Presbyterians in 1861, although any Presbyterian could have seen what was coming in 1838, when the church established two general assemblies, one that accepted slavery and one opposed to it—the mores at the root of those splits predated the Civil War by decades.[12]

No better illustration of the Devil's fondness for citing Scripture can be found than the rhetoric of antebellum Protestants. Northern Protestants drew on Scripture to buttress all manner of reform movements, from temperance to abolition. White southern preachers based their defenses of slavery on the same Bible, and their black coreligionists used Scripture to frame their claims for freedom and to criticize their masters' pretensions to Christianity. By the 1830s, especially after Nat Turner's slave rebellion in Southampton County, Virginia, it was no longer acceptable in white southern evangelical circles to criticize the institution of slavery. In the early decades of the century, slaveholders had been content to characterize slavery as a "necessary evil." Many, most famously Thomas Jefferson, evaluated the future of tobacco in the South and suggested that slavery would eventually die out. But those soothsayers failed to account for cotton; with the ascension of that crop, slavery would not fade away, but grow more entrenched. In the 1840s, slave owners no longer thought of slavery as a necessary evil, but as a good.

The cornerstone of white southerners' defense of slavery was the Bible—and one could argue that given Protestants' historical penchant for reading Scripture literally, the pro-slavery theologians' arguments were better than those of their northern coreligionists. Slavery, theologians from R. L. Dabney to James Henley Thornwell said, is allowed in both the Old and New Testaments. Paul specifically urges those in bondage to remain in bondage, and, in Philemon and elsewhere, he emphasizes servants' duty to obey their masters. Another favorite text was the story of Ham, a son of Noah. In Genesis, Ham is punished and his descendants cursed; according to pro-slavery theologians, those descendants were Africans, whose enslavement fulfilled the biblical curse.

The influence of pro-slavery ideologues spread far beyond the pulpits. In contrast to the more egalitarian leanings of earlier southern evangelicals, the antebellum ministers' emphasis on hierarchy and order appealed to white men and women across the region. Men understood that the ministers' teachings about the hierarchy of master and slave bolstered their position as head of the household, while plantation mistresses understood that their wealth depended on slavery, and if slavery required a hierarchical society where white women were subject to the wills of their husbands, then so be it. As the message of spiritual equality had earlier attracted African Americans to Christianity, the message of temporal inequality brought heads of southern households to church. Planters and lawyers, politicians and educators took up the message of the pro-slavery divines. In the Mississippi state legislature, as the nation headed toward war, a resolution declaring slavery "a blessing . . . the legitimate condition of the African race, as authorized . . . by the law of God" was introduced.

It is hardly surprising that black Christians had a markedly different reading of Scripture. Focusing more on Moses than Philemon, black Christians interpreted God's promises to deliver the Israelites from the Egypt of slavery to the Promised Land of freedom as directly applicable to their own bondage. They cherished Paul's assertion that in Christ "there is neither bond nor free because you all are one in Christ Jesus."[13] Black Christians concluded that physical and legal equality followed spiritual equality, and they preached that the white Southerners holding them in bondage might profess to be Christians, but really they were sinners. As Charles Moses, a black preacher and former slave, bluntly put it: "My Master was mean an' cruel an' I hates him, hates him. That God Almighty has condemned him to eternal fiah', of that I is certain." In 1864, one runaway slave wrote to his former mistress to say, "I want you to understand that mary is my Child and she is a God given rite of my own and you may hold on to hear as long as you can but I want you to remembor this one thing that the longor you keep my Child from me the longor you will have to burn in hell and the qwicer youll get their." Indeed, not only was the content of the slaves' claims inspired by the Bible, but the form too—though they might not be able to spell, they could write eloquently and poetically, echoing the cadences of the book they knew the best, the King James Version of the Bible.

Northern evangelicals embraced abolition. From Harriet Beecher Stowe (daughter, sister, and wife of three notable ministers) to Julia Ward Howe, who describes being called out of bed by God in the middle of the night to pen *The Battle Hymn of the Republic*, evangelicals crusaded against the evil that was slavery. Arthur Tappan, the first president of the American Antislavery Society; Joshua Levitt, editor of *The Evangelist* and *The Emancipator*; Edward Norris Kirk; Nathan S. S. Beman; and Jacob Knapp all were Protestants who led the fight against slavery.

Postmillennialism and Arminianism

Northern Protestants' zeal to make the world more godly was reflected not merely in their actions, but also in their theology. At least since Jonathan Edwards in the middle of the eighteenth century, the majority of American evangelicals had subscribed to the doctrine of postmillennialism, the conviction that Christ would return after the millennium, the 1,000 years of peace and righteousness predicted in the book of Revelation. This theology was essentially optimistic, because it held that the millennium, a time of joy and happiness, would occur before Christ's return, and in fact could be happening even now. It was the duty of evangelicals, therefore, to reform the world according to the norms of godliness in order to usher in the millennium and prepare for the return of Christ. If Christians led ethical lives and reformed society, they could hasten the arrival of the millennium. By midcentury, some evangelicals boldly claimed that, if only Christians would carry on in their zealous good works, the millennium could be initiated in as little as three years.

American evangelicals' commitment to postmillennialism had been shored up during the Second Great Awakening, a series of revivals led most notably by Charles Grandison Finney that swept America in the antebellum period. But the Second Great Awakening did not just confirm a postmillennial impulse; it also wrought a major theological revolution that dethroned Calvinism as the regnant Protestant theology. Until the early nineteenth century Calvinist doctrine held sway among American Protestants. Brought to America by English Puritans but first articulated by Geneva theologian John Calvin, Calvinism held that salvation was entirely in the hands of God. Some people, the "elect," were predestined by God for salvation, and others were consigned to damnation. There was nothing an individual could do to change his or her fate. Good works could not earn salvation; they were merely a byproduct of the believer's redemption.

In the early republic, however, many American theologians were beginning to challenge these Calvinistic tenets. Nathaniel William Taylor of Yale, for example, asserted that a loving God would offer salvation to all who sought it earnestly, not merely to a predestined few. This Arminian idea (named for Dutch theologian Jacobus Arminius) that an individual could choose salvation is, in a nutshell, the core of the theology that came to dominate American Protestant thinking from the mid-nineteenth century to the present.

Revivals, in fact, made little sense without Arminian theology: What good would an evangelist's exhortations do if no one in the audience could *choose* to accept the call to Christ? Rather than merely wait for God to call upon the elect, revivalists beginning early in the nineteenth century wheedled and cajoled their auditors to take matters into their own hands and choose their own salvation. That evangelical revivals remain, essentially, Arminian gatherings is reflected in Billy Graham's entreaties to "make a decision for Christ."

Such language, which lies at the heart of contemporary American evangelicalism, would have made little sense to Americans before the early nineteenth century. Charles Finney prefigured Graham's revival tactics. People could, to borrow the title of one of Finney's sermons, "change their own hearts," abandoning their sinful ways and choosing a life of Christian salvation. Finney believed that if he ran a revival correctly he would harvest converts. Indeed, he often compared a revival meeting to the planting of a crop: If he did everything just so, his toil would produce fruits and vegetables.

Finney's revivals were planned to the smallest detail. He trained local clergy and laity to counsel new converts at the end of revival meetings (another nineteenth-century innovation found in Graham revivals today). He advertised his meetings in newspapers and distributed leaflets door to door. In fact, it was not until the Second Great Awakening that the term "revival" was used to describe the organized, efficient, ritualized service conducted by evangelicals designed to bring about new conversions and reinvigorate faith. Although they initially criticized Finney's methods as too pragmatic, other Protestants began to adopt his practices when they saw just how many converts Finney could win in a single night of preaching.

Protestants and Social Reform

Finney's message did not merely pertain to salvation in the afterlife; it also taught people how to live in this life, and he emphasized the importance of good works. This move away from salvation by grace to a works-oriented theology was yet another way in which Finney and his contemporaries broke with the old Calvinism. Northern Protestants were inspired not just to work for abolition, but to reform all corners of society; they worked on behalf of children and the mentally ill, they offered education to women, they were devoted in their service to the poor, and they led America's fight for temperance. Around the time of the Revolution, New England boasted only about fifty charitable organizations. By 1820, there were between 1,500 and 2,000 Bible societies, orphanages, and other centers of organized charity, the vast majority of them founded and operated by Protestants.

Although theologically liberal Protestants participated zealously in reform, the largest impetus for this frenzy of charity came from evangelical fervor. As a writer for the New York *Observer* noted in 1855, "Infidelity makes great outcry about its philanthropy, but religion does the work." Nineteenth-century evangelicals forged a close link between faith and good works. In the rapidly urbanizing North, evangelicals were beset by problems they blamed on immigration, alcohol, Catholicism, and general indifference to the Bible and the church; the only cure was Protestant piety.

Baptist Henry Clay Fish asked in 1857: "What can save our cities but a powerful revival of religion? What one thing does this whole country call so loudly for as the descent of the Holy Ghost upon the churches?" In 1868 Finney declared that "the loss of interest in benevolent enterprises" was no less a sign of backsliding than adultery or drunkenness.

Examples of Protestants' commitment to reform abound—witness the career of Phoebe Palmer, a leader of the Methodist holiness movement. Beginning in the 1840s, she worked as a tract distributor in the slums of New York and participated in a prison ministry at the Tombs. She served for eleven years as the corresponding secretary of the New York Female Assistance Society for the Relief and Religious Instruction of the Sick Poor, and in 1850 she established the Five Points Mission, which opened a chapel, schoolrooms, baths, and twenty furnished apartments for the use of New York's poor.

Throughout their reforming efforts, Palmer and other northern evangelicals emphasized stewardship, the notion that people are earthly stewards caring for that which rightly belongs to God; time, money, and other material possessions are to be used in a godly way, not for selfish ends. Palmer, for example, believed that there was nothing inherently wrong with being wealthy, but she cautioned that money and possessions are "social responsibilities, for which an account of stewardship must be rendered." Gilbert Haven, a prominent Methodist abolitionist, warned that he found congregants were more willing to sit through a sermon that condemned slavery than a sermon that condemned usury. "Some rich brother, who waxed fat on these ill-gotten gains," he observed, "will denounce you as an intermeddler, while his conduct uncensured, and himself undisciplined, keeps scores from the church."

The desire to perfect the world dovetailed with another theological platform that Finney was crucial in inaugurating: perfectionism. This was not a new notion, but one culled from Wesleyan Methodism. Perfectionism taught that one could receive a "second blessing" of the Holy Spirit, a second conversion of sorts, which rendered the individual incapable of sinning. As Charles Trumbull would articulate his doctrine in its twentieth-century incarnation, "the very desire for sin is taken from you; you do not want to do anything that you know to be sin."

At the same moment that Finney's revivals were bringing this Wesleyan doctrine to Christians outside of Methodist circles, Palmer and others were reviving perfectionism within Methodist circles. Perfectionism came to be known as Victorious Life theology because at its core was the teaching that through Christ one could be victorious over sin, not just in the hereafter but in this life as well. Although Victorious Life theology persisted well into the twentieth century—a Victorious Life conference was held as late as 1916—this theology was especially appropriate for the late nineteenth century. These years were flush times for American Protestants, who then held tremendous cultural sway in the nation. Indeed, it did seem that one could live the good life, a "victorious life," on Earth even as one remained committed to the religious guidelines that could assure one's salvation in the afterlife.

Victorious Life theology, however, was not a homegrown product. Not only did it originate in English Wesleyanism, but it received another hearing during the revivals that began in 1875 in the Lake District town of Keswick (hence, Victorious Life theology also answers to the less colorful moniker "the Keswick movement"). In 1891, a popular English speaker in the Keswick tradition, F. B. Meyer, came to the United States to speak at Dwight L. Moody's annual summer conference in Northfield, Massachusetts. Throughout the 1890s, American and English advocates of perfectionism shuttled back and forth between the two countries, exchanging ideas and doctrine. Like so much of American Protestantism, then, perfectionism was not unique to the United States but part of a larger transatlantic movement.

The Keswick emphasis on the Victorious Life endures in American Protestantism, even into the twenty-first century. Evangelicals, in particular, emphasize the importance of spiritual discipline—daily Bible reading, prayer, attendance at worship services—as a means of attaining "victory" over sin and leading godly lives.

Amid the theological transformations convulsing nineteenth-century American Protestantism—postmillennialism, Arminianism, Keswick teachings—there were other changes afoot that were even more important—namely, the emancipation of African American slaves and the failure of Reconstruction. Northern evangelicals, white and black, had contributed in no small measure to the abolitionist movement, but there were other American Protestants even more directly involved in Emancipation—the slaves themselves.

The failure of white evangelicals to follow through on the promises of spiritual equality in the early nineteenth century led some black southerners to follow Richard Allen's lead in Philadelphia and establish their own separate churches. By and large, though, biracial worship proved the rule until Reconstruction, when the freedmen, stung by the persistence of racism and segregation, left the biracial churches and established their own independent black congregations. These churches were one of many expressions of black independence after Emancipation, but as one historian has written, "Among the most lasting and important achievements of the period, the churches were the first and by far the largest institutions under black control."

The Emergence of Liberal Protestantism

The conclusion of the nineteenth century witnessed another new trend— the development of liberal Protestantism as a distinct movement within American Protestantism. Although there had been liberal dissenters from the evangelical norm throughout American history, a rich, liberal theological tradition did not come into its own until the turn of the twentieth century, when the Social Gospel of Walter Rauschenbusch and Washington Gladden caught on. The Social Gospel echoed the optimism of the antebellum reformers, but it sought to bring the good news and good works of the Gospel to people without necessarily bringing a traditional Gospel message about the unique saving power of Christ along with it. The Social Gospelers, as they were known, insisted not only on the redemption of sinful individuals but on the redemption of sinful social structures as well. Such a theology dovetailed with the agenda of Progressives in the political arena, and so the Social Gospelers worked toward the enactment of child labor laws, the end of the seven-day work week, the cleanup of slums and tenements, the right of workers to organize, and the eradication of corrupt political machines.

The engagement of liberal Protestants in social reform coincided with an opposite trend among conservative, or evangelical, Protestants. Rather than seeing the cities as a challenge to their postmillennial optimism about the formation of a godly society—and rising to that challenge, as the liberals did—evangelicals saw urban ills and corruptions as a repudiation of postmillennialism. In response, they fastened on to a new scheme of biblical interpretation, premillennialism, the notion that Jesus would return at any moment to rescue the true Christians and to unleash judgment against the unfaithful. Evangelicals then largely abandoned the task of social amelioration in favor of individual regeneration, leaving the arena of social reform to Protestant liberals.

In addition to changing the direction of Protestant social activism, the emergence of liberalism as a distinct strain in American Protestantism also called old theological verities into question: Was the Bible perfect and infallible? Did the historic creeds of the church capture an eternal truth? Was Jesus to be understood as God made man, the only path to salvation, or as one insightful teacher among many, whose words were recorded in a book with great wisdom but no necessary binding authority? Was ethics, rather than salvation, the main end of religion? Were the feelings and experiences of religion more important than the philosophy of religion?

As this more liberal Protestant thinking became increasingly dominant, evangelicals felt that this newly popular liberal Protestantism was little better than heresy, and they sought to shore up the ramparts of orthodoxy. Evangelicals, for instance, argued against Charles Darwin's evolutionary theory, which undermined literal understandings of the Bible when pressed to its logical conclusions. They also sought to counter the effects of higher criticism, a method of biblical criticism emanating from Germany that called into question the integrity of the biblical texts, by essentially sidestepping the issue. In an article entitled "Inspiration" in the 1881 issue of the *Presbyterian Review*, A. A. Hodge and B. B. Warfield argued that the Bible was fully inspired and utterly without error—"inerrant"—in the *original* autographs (which are no longer extant); any apparent mistake or discrepancy in our current texts had crept in through the agency of copyists. Although this argument was not new in the annals of church history, it allowed conservative Protestants to hold on to the traditional doctrine of biblical inspiration by adding the codicil of "inerrancy" in the originals and thereby protect the integrity of Scripture from the meddling of liberals.[14]

Such strategies were not always successful. Among northern Presbyterians, for example, attitudes toward the Bible proved crucial. When Charles A. Briggs was named to the Edward Robinson Chair of Biblical Theology at Union Theological Seminary in New York City, conservatives within the denomination brought him up on charges of heresy because of his affection for higher criticism and because of what they saw as his compromises on biblical inspiration. Briggs was acquitted twice by the presbytery of New York, but on the third try the conviction stuck. In the meantime, however, both Briggs and Union Seminary had made moves to sever their ties with the denomination: Briggs became an Episcopal priest, and Union became independent. Within a couple of decades, however, northern Presbyterians had eased away from conservative doctrines, thereby precipitating a split between liberals and evangelicals in the 1920s.

Twentieth-Century Evangelicalism

American evangelicalism in the twentieth century moved through four different phases, which can be divided (albeit with some contrivance) into periods of twenty-five years apiece. For the first quarter of the century, evangelicals became increasingly marginalized in the broader culture. As the rest of America discovered the appeal of liberal Christianity or a more secular outlook on life, evangelicals were derided as backwards yahoos who, like so many Luddites, swam against the tide of progress and modernization. Faced with the twin evils of Darwin's theory of evolution and German higher criticism of the Bible, evangelicals saw the world marching in a direction they did not wish to follow.

In the second decade of the twentieth century, two Los Angeles evangelicals named Milton and Lyman Stewart put up $250,000 to publish a series of booklets that would propagate the basics of the faith to teachers, preachers, theological students, and YMCA secretaries throughout the English-speaking world. The booklets were called *The Fundamentals* because they outlined the fundamental teachings of the faith—the inerrancy of Scripture, the virgin birth of Jesus, the authenticity of miracles, the imminent return of Jesus—and they gave the movement called fundamentalism its name. Each volume contained several articles written by conservative Protestant theologians from North America and Great Britain, providing "orthodox" counterarguments to Protestant liberals on issues ranging from evolution to the divinity of Jesus.

But even the new fundamentalism could not derail the march of liberal Protestantism. Evangelicals were losing their toehold in the wider culture. Their symbolic loss came in 1925, in a hot, stuffy courtroom in a small town in eastern Tennessee. On the face of it, evangelicals won the Scopes trial—John T. Scopes, a rather inarticulate substitute biology teacher, was found guilty of teaching the theory of evolution. But evangelicals lost the more important battle, the larger cultural battle. Through the combined efforts of Clarence Darrow, lawyer for the defendant, and H. L. Mencken, the acerbic reporter for the Baltimore *Sun*, evangelicals were mocked and ridiculed. Even as the supposedly victorious verdict was delivered, evangelicals knew they had lost. William Jennings Bryan, famed orator and presidential candidate who had argued the state's case, had been reduced to incoherence when he allowed himself to be cross-examined under oath by Darrow about the truth of the Bible. Bryan died just two days after the trial ended.[15]

In the wake of the Scopes trial, evangelicals moved into the second phase of their twentieth-century history—they went underground. As the world mocked evangelicals, evangelicals in turn condemned the world. They felt besieged. They retreated and retrenched, building an elaborate subculture of institutions where their faith could remain intact, free from assault by the larger hostile world. Evangelicals created their own colleges and seminaries, summer camps, presses and bookstores, and grammar schools. The fortress mentality of this period is reflected in the very architecture of evangelical buildings, buildings that loomed large and massive, garrisons against attack. So too, evangelical theology turned against the world, condemning "worldliness" in all of its insipid forms, from affluence and gambling to motion pictures and the use of cosmetics.

During this second quarter of the twentieth century evangelicals honed their dualism, the us-versus-them theology that came to characterize evangelical rhetoric for the remainder of the twentieth century. In 1940 fundamentalist preacher John Rice declared, "One can be a modernist and a pastor. But one cannot be a modernist and a real evangelist. For that reason there is an antipathy between modernists and evangelists, a fight to the very death." Here, Rice referred to two types of liberalism or modernism— theological modernism, which strayed from a literal approach to the Bible, and modernism in society generally. One cultural development that Rice and his fellow travelers especially abhorred was the expanding role of women. Rice inveighed against three trends he could not abide in his popular book whose title summarized his antipathy: *Bobbed Hair, Bossy Wives, and Women Preachers.* Charles R. Scoville condemned the "French-heeled, kangaroo-shaped, fresco-faced, frizzle-headed flapper." The changes in women's status, of course, were linked with liberal theology: A literal reading of Scripture suggested that women were to submit to their husbands as to the church. Sporting lipstick and short skirts were sure signs of worldliness, and cigarette smoking was beyond the pale; one woman was dismissed simply as a "cigarette smoker and a theological liberal," as though the two were inseparable.

The generation of evangelicals from 1950 to 1975 both maintained and challenged the antiworld stance characteristic of Rice and his fellow fundamentalists. While continuing to support their own schools and camps— and, by this time, their own movie studios and radio stations—evangelicals began a tentative rapprochement with the world, an overture epitomized by Billy Graham's 1950 revival "crusade" in Portland, Oregon. There, Graham decided to initiate a radio program and to incorporate his operations under the rubric of the Billy Graham Evangelistic Association. Graham did more to draw evangelicalism back into the public arena than anyone else, and he was roundly criticized for it. Those evangelicals with more fundamentalist leanings attacked Graham for making ecumenical overtures to Catholics and for aligning himself with more liberal Christian ministers in cities where he preached. These fundamentalists held fast to the notion that evangelicals should remain separate from the world, and Graham, with his unabashed appeal to the masses, was challenging that assumption.

The split between hard-line fundamentalists and more ecumenical evangelicals persisted into the twenty-first century. Many fundamentalists, for instance, regarded Graham himself as hopelessly liberal. Although the theological differences between the two groups are less glaring than the theological differences between evangelicals and mainline Protestants, each camp has its own magazine (*Christianity Today* for the evangelicals, *World* for the fundamentalists) and their own colleges (Wheaton for the evangelicals, Bob Jones University for the fundamentalists, to cite just two examples).

Despite Graham's extraordinary visibility in American society, the years after 1950 were the heyday of liberal, or mainline, Protestantism. Paul Tillich and Reinhold Niebuhr dominated the American theological scene and were public intellectuals, gracing the cover of major news magazines and appearing as commentators in the news media. Mainline churches were ascendant—in America, at midcentury, it was in vogue to be a churchgoer but not to be too devout, lest you be seen as a religious fanatic. Scripture was a guide for mainline Protestants, but not an inerrant one, and Jesus was a teacher, but not necessarily God made flesh. When Will Herberg wrote in 1955 that "the past quarter of a century has witnessed what is probably the most impressive renewal of Protestant religious thinking since the days of Jonathan Edwards," he was thinking of a renewal of what became known as mainline Protestantism.[16] "Religious movements that dimly recall the old evangelical crusade are to be found," he conceded, but only "among some of the 'fringe' sects." On the whole, mainline Protestantism at midcentury had "settle[d] down to a stable, respectable, 'domesticated' existence."[17]

Within a generation that would be different—mainline Protestantism would be on the wane, and evangelicals would be back in the spotlight. Twenty-one years after Herberg dismissed evangelicalism as peripheral, a born-again Christian was elected president of the United States. Jimmy Carter was no closet evangelical, either; he was forthright in his campaign about the importance of his evangelical commitments. In his 1980 campaign for re-election, one of Carter's television ads featured an open Bible, described in a voiceover as the place he turned when he needed guidance.

The election of Carter in 1976 ushered in the final quarter of the twentieth century, and, once again, the disposition of evangelicals toward the larger culture changed. The rise of politically conservative evangelicals— on the surface, at least—recalled the activism of nineteenth-century evangelicals. The movement known loosely as the Religious Right, which galvanized, ironically, to oppose Carter in the 1980 presidential election, represents a latter-day attempt to reform society. Although these activists maintained that they were premillennialists, thereby adhering to the pessimistic theology of their turn-of-the-century forebears, they were in fact acting like postmillennialists, out to remodel the world according to what they had determined were the norms of godliness.

The overall agenda of the Religious Right, however, especially its opposition to feminism, belied the legacy of evangelical activism in the nineteenth century, which unfailingly had taken up the cause of the marginalized in society, especially women and minorities. As politically conservative evangelicals achieved at least a measure of success in the political arena, moreover, their suspicions of "worldliness" began to fade. Especially during the 1980s, many evangelicals who had once heard sermons about the difficulty of a rich man entering the kingdom of heaven became comfortable with the trappings of affluence. Evangelicals also enjoyed "worldly" success in popular music, with the advent of the phenomenon of contemporary Christian music, and in the academy, where a significant number of evangelicals held tenured positions at prestigious universities.

American Protestantism at the Turn of the Twenty-first Century

Protestantism at the turn of the twenty-first century embodies many of the themes of American history. Evangelicalism has thrived because of its relentless populism and its ability to adapt its message to the latest means of communication. Indeed, contrary to H. L. Mencken's caricature of evangelicals as backwards country bumpkins, evangelicals have, from the earliest days of American history, been great technological innovators, beginning with open-air preaching and the eighteenth-century print revolution through Aimee Semple McPherson's adoption of radio waves and Billy Graham's use of television to spread the Gospel.

Protestant liberals who, with their confidence in the essential goodness of humanity, want to see progress in history, took justifiable pride in their advocacy of equality and civil rights for minorities, women, and homosexuals. Liberals also pushed for unity, seeking to erode theological and institutional differences among mainline Protestant denominations. In America, however, under the disestablishment protection of the First Amendment, the splintering tendencies of Protestantism have always predominated. They have been played out more extensively in America than anywhere else on earth, with numberless divisions according to denomination, race, region, ethnicity, gender, and theology.

CHAPTER THREE

The Varieties of Protestantism in America

Martin Luther's notion of *sola scriptura*, the idea that the Bible alone served as the source of authority for the believer, gave Protestants the warrant to interpret the Scriptures for themselves. The Bible, in turn, because of its complexity and even its apparent contradictions, allowed for a multitude of interpretations and led to a splintering of Protestantism, as each interpreter made his (and sometimes her) own claims for having truly understood the mind of God.

Nowhere has this Protestant fissiparousness manifested itself more completely than in America. The New World offered Protestants (and others) a chance to start anew, to sculpt their religious lives from scratch, without having first to destroy the entrenched religious institutions—churches, hierarchies, universities—of Europe, still overwhelmingly in thrall to the Roman Catholic Church. In the United States, the First Amendment guarantee of free exercise of religion, coupled with the proscription against a state church, established a free marketplace of religion, where religious entrepreneurs (to extend the metaphor) could compete with one another for popular approbation. Protestants especially, having overthrown the ballast of history, tradition, and creeds during the Protestant Reformation, took advantage of the opportunities to create, recreate, and sometimes even create again Protestant churches, denominations, and institutions. In short, Protestantism in America is endlessly creative—or, in less flattering terms, endlessly schismatic—which renders any attempt to comprehend its diversity exceedingly difficult.

A Taxonomy of Liberal Protestantism

The beginnings of Protestant liberalism in America can probably be traced
to the formation of the Brattle Street Church in Boston in 1699. In Massachusetts at the end of the sixteenth century, liberalism was defined as a
protest against the regnant Puritan theology of the day, especially the Puritan adherence to Calvinism. Liberals objected to the perceived determinism of Calvinist theology (the notion that only the elect would be delivered
from damnation) and asserted that redemption was available to everyone.

The demarcation separating liberal from evangelical became wider during a colonies'-wide revival known to historians as the Great Awakening,
which took place in the 1730s and 1740s. In the course of the revival, two
extraordinary intellects—Jonathan Edwards, Congregational minister in
Northampton, Massachusetts, and Charles Chauncy of Boston's Brattle
Street Church—conducted a pamphlet war on the nature of revivals and
conversions. Whereas Edwards, representing the evangelical emphasis on
conversion, insisted that God worked in mysterious ways, visiting revival
upon the elect, Chauncy argued that one's journey toward redemption
might be gradual or evolutionary, rather than instantaneous. Chauncy made
the case for a more rational understanding of God and theology, while
Edwards (himself perhaps the most formidable intellect ever to inhabit
America) defended the importance of what he called the "religious affections" in the life of the believer.[1]

As the differences between evangelical and liberal developed in the
eighteenth and nineteenth centuries, liberals called into question the Protestant doctrine of depravity or original sin—that all humanity has inherited
Adam's sin. They also attacked the notion of hell, arguing that a gracious
and benevolent God would never consign one of his children to damnation,
and they gravitated toward universalism or universal salvation, the doctrine
that everyone will be saved, in this world or the next. Finally, beginning
in the mid-nineteenth century, Protestant liberals questioned the "inspiration" of the Bible, suggesting that the Bible was a collection of human
writings—not the timeless truths of the inerrant "word of God"—that
must be adapted to modern circumstances and reinterpreted by contemporary believers.

These theological issues—original sin, eternal damnation, biblical inspiration—remain points of difference between evangelical and liberal
Protestants. Implicit in liberal Protestantism is the notion of progress, the

idea that we are coming to a fuller understanding of the mind of God, that we are inching closer to realizing the kingdom of God on earth.

In institutional terms, liberal—or, in the twentieth century, mainline— Protestants are those generally associated with the major Protestant denominations: the United Methodist Church, the United Church of Christ, the Episcopal Church, the Presbyterian Church (U.S.A.), the Christian Church (Disciples of Christ), the American Baptist Church, and (according to some criteria) the Evangelical Lutheran Church in America. Such categorization is not fail-safe, however, because many evangelicals maintain their presence in these denominations, seeing themselves as defenders of orthodoxy in the midst of a drift toward liberalism.

In keeping with their theological outlook and their essential optimism about human goodness, liberal Protestants tended much more than evangelical Protestants to take liberal or progressive stances toward the social issues of the day, especially in the twentieth century. Despite evangelical Protestantism's feminism in the nineteenth and early twentieth centuries, liberal Protestants generally led the way on women's ordination during the latter half of the twentieth century. Liberal Protestants were active in the civil rights movement and in opposition to the war in Vietnam. They have also been more accommodating to gays and lesbians than evangelicals, who have, by and large, censured homosexuality.

A Taxonomy of Evangelical Protestantism

Although other criteria can factor into identifications of evangelical Protestants, a twofold definition—the centrality of conversion and a belief that the Bible is God's Word and therefore lies at the core of the Christian life—provides the most reliable guide to identifying evangelicals. Polling data are elusive (and somewhat unreliable) on this subject, but the data suggest that anywhere from 25 to 46 percent of the population in the United States would fit the definition of evangelical. Such numbers, however, are somewhat deceptive because of the diversity within the movement. One way to think of "evangelicalism" is as an umbrella term, and beneath that umbrella are many variations. Or, to shift the image somewhat, evangelicalism is like a vast corporation, say, General Motors; within General Motors are several divisions: Oldsmobile, Cadillac, Buick, Chevrolet, Pontiac, Saturn, and GMC Trucks. All of those divisions are part of General Motors, but (to some extent, at least) they maintain their own identities.

So too, with evangelicalism. Someone who is an evangelical is also a particular sort of evangelical—a pentecostal or a fundamentalist or a neo-evangelical or part of the holiness movement or even some combination—and each strain has its own characteristics.

Holiness Movement

The holiness movement emerged from John Wesley's emphasis on Christian perfection, the doctrine that the believer could attain "perfect love" in this life after the born-again experience. Wesley's notion of perfect love freed the believer from the disposition to sin, although he allowed for failings rooted in "infirmity" and "ignorance."

Holiness teachings achieved their best hearing in Methodist circles, but as Methodism expanded, became more respectable, and acquired middle-class trappings in the nineteenth century, holiness doctrines faded into the background. Though rooted in the Methodist Episcopal Church, the holiness movement was interdenominational and sought to revitalize the piety in Methodism and other denominations. Holiness—also called "sanctification" or "second blessing" (after the first, conversion)—was promoted in the antebellum period by Sarah Lankford and Phoebe Palmer in their

Fig. 3.1. The Ocean Grove Camp Meeting Association was formed in 1867 by those who sought to reinvigorate the piety of Protestant denominations, principally Methodism, in the nineteenth century. Historical Society of Ocean Grove/Courtesy of Wayne T. Bell, from the book *Images of America: Ocean Grove*.

Tuesday Meetings for the Promotion of Holiness, by Timothy Merritt in his *Guide to Holiness* magazine, and by Charles Finney and Asa Mahan at Oberlin College. After the Civil War it thrived in independent camp meeting associations, such as those at Ocean Grove, New Jersey, and Oak Bluffs, Massachusetts.

By the final decade of the nineteenth century holiness evangelists numbered more than 300. The Methodist hierarchy grew uneasy about the holiness influence, especially the apparent lack of denominational loyalty of holiness people. As they came under increased pressure, some submitted to the Methodist hierarchy, while others joined emerging holiness denominations, such as the Church of God (Anderson, Indiana), the Church of the Nazarene, the Pentecostal Holiness Church, or the Fire-Baptized Holiness Church, among others. These groups generally emphasize the importance of probity and ask their adherents to shun worldliness in all its insipid forms. The holiness movement also survives in regular camp meetings throughout North America.

Fundamentalism

The term "fundamentalism" derives from a series of pamphlets that appeared between 1910 and 1915 called *The Fundamentals; or, Testimony to the Truth*. The publishing project was financed by Lyman and Milton Stewart of Union Oil Company of California, who set up a fund of $250,000 dollars to publish the booklets and to distribute them to Protestant leaders throughout the English-speaking world. *The Fundamentals* contained conservative statements on doctrinal issues and were meant to counteract the perceived drift toward liberal theology or "modernism" within Protestantism. Those who subscribed to these doctrines became known as "fundamentalists," and "fundamentalism" came to refer to the entire movement.[2]

Fundamentalism has also been described as a militant antimodernism, but that characterization must be qualified. Fundamentalists are not opposed to modernism in the sense of being suspicious of innovation or technology; indeed, fundamentalists (and evangelicals generally) have often been in the forefront in the uses of technology, especially communications technology. Fundamentalists have an aversion to modernity only when it is invested with a moral valence, when it represents a departure from orthodoxy or "traditional values," however they might be defined.

Finally, fundamentalism is characterized by militancy, at least as it has developed in the United States; Jerry Falwell, for instance, has insisted that

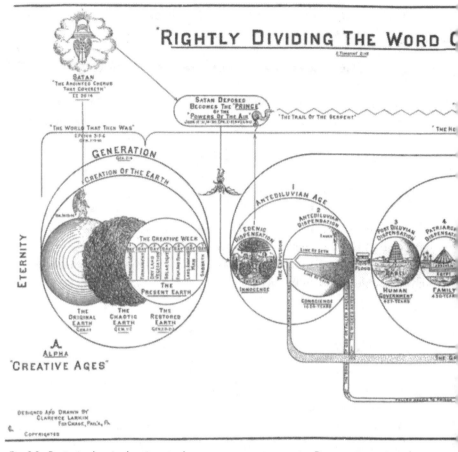

Fig. 3.2. Beginning late in the nineteenth century many conservative Protestants gravitated toward a new mode of biblical interpretation called "dispensationalism," which divided all of history into ages or dispensations. This 1918 chart, drawn by Clarence Larkin, was an attempt to illustrate apocalyptic themes in the Bible and warn sinners of their impending doom. © 1918. All Rights Reserved. From *Dispensational Truth or God's Plan and Purpose in the Ages* by Clarence Larkin.

he is a *fundamentalist*, not an *evangelical*. This militancy—on matters of doctrine, ecclesiology, dress, personal behavior, or politics—has prompted some historians to remark that the difference between an evangelical and a fundamentalist is that a fundamentalist is an evangelical who is mad about something.

Fundamentalism is also the strain of evangelicalism most identified with a doctrine known as "dispensational premillennialism." Dispensationalism was a scheme of biblical interpretation that became popular among evan-

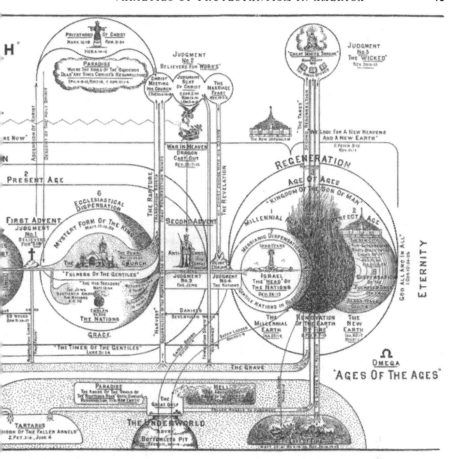

gelicals in the late nineteenth and early twentieth centuries. John Nelson Darby, an early leader of the Plymouth Brethren in Great Britain, postulated that all of human history could be divided into different ages or dispensations and that God had dealt differently with humanity in each of these dispensations. Dispensationalists further insisted that we are now poised at the end of the final dispensation and that Jesus will return at any moment.

The scheme was especially attractive to evangelicals in America because it offered an explanation for why the postmillennial kingdom so confidently predicted earlier in the nineteenth century had failed to materialize. Instead, dispensational premillennialism insisted that the world was growing more and more sinful, and that the imminent return of Jesus offered the only escape from the scourge of the cities, overrun, in the opinion of evangelicals, by non-Protestant immigrants.

Dispensationalism also offered evangelicals a rubric for understanding Israel and the Jews. Yes, the promises made to Israel in the Hebrew Bible (which evangelicals refer to as the Old Testament) were valid, but the Jews' rejection of Jesus as messiah prompted a postponement of the messianic kingdom and the creation of a new heir out of the Gentiles, the church.

Darby's ideas caught on with evangelicals in North America and were popularized by means of prophetic conferences, Bible institutes, and especially the *Scofield Reference Bible*, compiled by Cyrus Ingerson Scofield and published by Oxford University Press in 1909. Scofield insisted upon seven dispensations (although other dispensationalists have come up with other figures), and his scheme became especially popular among fundamentalists. Dallas Theological Seminary remains the intellectual center of dispensationalism, and it was perpetuated in the twentieth century by such Dallas theologians as Lewis Sperry Chafer, John F. Walvoord, Charles C. Ryrie, and J. Dwight Pentecost.

Examples of fundamentalist churches abound, ranging from Falwell's Thomas Road Baptist Church in Lynchburg, Virginia, to Moody Memorial Church on the north side of Chicago (which has been very much at the center of fundamentalism ever since the 1910s), to Calvary Chapel of Costa Mesa, California, which lay at the center of the Jesus Movement in the early 1970s. In any of these churches a visitor will take a seat in a rather large auditorium, which is configured in a way that suggests that the sermon is the central feature of the worship service: The pulpit, rather than the altar, stands at the center of the stage or platform. The service itself most likely will open with congregational singing, followed by a reading or readings from the Bible, announcements, and the offering. Every element of the worship service leads up to the sermon.

The sermon itself in a fundamentalist church will typically last twenty to thirty minutes, perhaps longer. It might touch on a number of themes, including the importance of conversion (perhaps described as "giving your life to Jesus"), the necessity of hewing to various behavioral standards (avoiding drugs, alcohol, and tobacco—except in the South—and dressing modestly, an injunction addressed especially to women), or premillennialism. The fundamentalist preacher—almost invariably a man—will seek to ground his sermon in the Bible, often quoting from memory and using proof texts. The general tone of the sermon and the fundamentalist congregation itself is one of militancy and suspicion of what fundamentalists regard as a corrupt and corrupting world.

Pentecostalism

In some respects pentecostalism is the opposite of fundamentalism, at least beneath the umbrella of evangelicalism. Whereas fundamentalist theology tends to be highly ratiocinated, pentecostals emphasize the importance of the affections. Pentecostal worship can be very enthusiastic, with individuals speaking in tongues or even dancing in ecstasy under the influence of the Holy Spirit.[3]

Pentecostalism, which emerged out of nineteenth-century holiness impulses, coalesced as a movement in the early years of the twentieth century. On the first day of the new century, January 1, 1901, a student at Bethel Bible College in Topeka, Kansas, Agnes Ozman, began speaking in tongues, an indecipherable spiritual language. This experience, also known as "glossolalia," was explicitly linked to the first Pentecost, recorded in Acts 2, when the early Christians were filled with the Holy Spirit. The movement, with its teachings about the baptism of the Holy Spirit, spread to Texas and then to Los Angeles, where it burst into broader consciousness during the Azusa Street Revival.

The roots of pentecostalism, however, reached back into the nineteenth century and the holiness movement, which sought to promote personal holiness (and John Wesley's doctrine of Christian perfection) within Methodism and other American denominations. By the end of the century, however, holiness advocates were feeling increasingly marginalized, and many left Methodism to form their own denominations. The pentecostal movement, with its distinctive emphasis on the second blessing or baptism of the Holy Spirit, as evidenced by glossolalia, spread quickly after the Azusa Street Revival. Pentecostalism took various denominational forms, including the Pentecostal Holiness Church, the Church of God in Christ, the Church of God (Cleveland, Tennessee), and the Assemblies of God, which was organized in 1914 and is the largest pentecostal denomination in North America.

Pentecostal worship today is characterized by ecstasy and the familiar posture of upraised arms, a gesture of openness to the Holy Spirit. Pentecostals generally believe in the many gifts of the Holy Spirit, including divine healing, in addition to speaking in tongues. Those denominations associated with pentecostalism would include the aforementioned Assemblies of God and the Church of God in Christ, among many others. Some of the more visible of the televangelists of the 1980s, including Jim Bakker and Jimmy Swaggart, were pentecostals.

Charismatics

Although the terms "charismatic" and "pentecostal" have been used inter-changeably in recent years, a distinction remains. Both believe in the gifts of the Holy Spirit, especially divine healing and speaking in tongues, but while a pentecostal is affiliated with a pentecostal denomination, a charismatic is part of a church or denomination that, as a whole, looks askance at the exercise of pentecostal gifts.

Whereas classical pentecostalism traces its origins to Agnes Ozman's speaking in tongues on the first day of the twentieth century, the charismatic movement brought pentecostal fervor into mainline denominations beginning in the 1960s. The groundwork for such an incursion, however, was laid in the previous decade by such pentecostal ecumenists as David Du Plessis, Oral Roberts, and Demos Shakarian, a California layman and founder of the Full Gospel Businessman's Fellowship International.

The charismatic movement, also known as the "charismatic renewal" or "neo-pentecostalism," erupted in 1960 among mainline Protestants with the news that Dennis J. Bennett, rector of Saint Mark's Episcopal Church in Van Nuys, California, had received the baptism of the Holy Spirit and had spoken in tongues. About one hundred parishioners followed suit, to the dismay of other parishioners, members of the vestry, and the Episcopal bishop of Los Angeles. Although Bennett left Van Nuys for Seattle, Washington, he remained with the Episcopal Church, taking over a struggling parish, Saint Luke's, and transforming it into an outpost of the charismatic movement. Bennett's decision to remain an Episcopalian illustrates the distinction between pentecostals and charismatics, even though both believe in the baptism of the Holy Spirit. Whereas "pentecostal" refers to someone affiliated with one of the pentecostal denominations, such as the Assemblies of God or the Church of God in Christ, a "charismatic" remains identified with a tradition that, on the whole, looks askance at pentecostal enthusiasm.

The movement spread to other mainline Protestant denominations in the 1960s: the American Lutheran Church, the Lutheran Church in America (united in 1988 under the name Evangelical Lutheran Church in America), the United Presbyterian Church (U.S.A.), the American Baptist Church, and the United Methodist Church. Charismatic influences also took root in such unlikely settings as the Mennonites, the Churches of Christ, and the United Church of Christ. The Lutheran Church–Missouri Synod, however, vigorously resisted charismatic incursions, as did the Southern Baptist Convention, although Pat Robertson—a self-identified charismatic—retained his ordination as a Southern Baptist until his campaign for the presidency in 1988.

Charismatic impulses made their way into the Roman Catholic Church beginning in February 1967, when a group of students from Duquesne University in Pittsburgh attended a spiritual retreat and received the baptism of the Holy Spirit. The Duquesne Weekend, as it came to be known, led to other gatherings of Roman Catholics looking for spiritual renewal, notably in South Bend, Indiana, and Ann Arbor, Michigan. Both venues became majors centers of the Catholic Charismatic Renewal.

The charismatic movement also finds expression in independent congregations and in a number of larger churches that have begun to form their own network of affiliated congregations similar to denominations. Notable examples include Calvary Chapel in Santa Ana, California; Cathedral of Praise in South Bend, Indiana; Victory Christian Center in Tulsa, Oklahoma; Rock Church in Virginia Beach, Virginia; and Vineyard Christian Fellowship in Anaheim, California.

The New Evangelicalism

Apart from the final word on its sign, "Willow Creek Community Church," nothing about the buildings and grounds of Willow Creek suggests a religious institution—with the exception, perhaps, of the traffic congestion on Sunday morning. Several lanes of traffic turn simultaneously into the driveway, which is more than a mile long. The four lanes of automobiles meander past a duck pond with the obligatory corporate fountain. A squadron of traffic controllers funnel the cars—station wagons, sedans, sport utility vehicles—into one parking lot or another, obeying orders relayed by radio from the master traffic controller perched atop the roof of the sprawling steel and glass building. Willow Creek has provided airport-style numbering—Pink 53 or Orange 22—on the stanchions of the light poles in the parking lots so that congregants can locate their automobiles upon leaving the building.

Willow Creek Community Church represents the broad mainstream of American evangelicalism, sometimes called "neo-evangelicalism" or the "new evangelicalism." The new evangelicalism, which emerged in the middle of the twentieth century, is characterized by the ability to speak the idiom of the surrounding culture. It is unabashedly populist, and it is merely one recent example of the evangelical genius for reaching the masses. In the case of Willow Creek, the church was founded in the mid-1970s by Bill Hybels, a student at Trinity College in nearby Deerfield, Illinois. Hybels wanted to know why suburbanites stayed away from church, so he came up with a door-to-door market research survey and, on the basis of his findings, proceeded to design a church that would overcome their objections. The survey showed, for example, that churchgoers did not like being dunned for money, so Willow Creek makes it clear that visitors should consider themselves guests and need not feel obligated to contribute when the offering plate passes by.

The survey also suggested that suburbanites were put off by religious symbols—crosses, icons, and the like—and so the architecture and the appointments at Willow Creek are utterly without religiously symbolic reference. The place looks, in fact, like a suburban corporate office park, with its steel and glass facade, the meticulous landscaping, and the massive parking lot. This, too, is not coincidental. Willow Creek Community Church, located in the northwest suburbs of Chicago, attracts many people associated in one way or another with the corporate world, so the architecture quite deliberately has a corporate feel, something that suburbanites would find familiar. A recent addition to the Willow Creek physical plant was a food court, similar to those found in suburban shopping malls. Between Sunday school and the morning worship service, for example, or after a meeting of junior high school parents on Tuesday morning, con-

Fig. 3.3. Willow Creek Community Church, founded in 1975, has become a prototype for megachurches. It offers a variety of programs, recreational opportunities, and even a food court. Approximately 17,000 attend the weekend services at its property in South Barrington, Illinois. Courtesy of Willow Creek Community Church.

gregants can stop by the cinnamon bun concession or grab a slice of pizza and talk with friends or prepare for the next meeting.

Somewhere in the neighborhood of 17,000 suburbanites come to worship at Willow Creek every weekend (two services Saturday evening and two Sunday morning). As they file into the main auditorium and find a place in the theater-style seats, they settle in for a service that would seem rather exotic to those accustomed to a Methodist worship service or a Roman Catholic mass. The congregants gather to the sounds of musicians, usually some ensemble of guitars, drums, and keyboard, and then the service opens with a congregational hymn. The program varies from there, but the service includes a dramatic presentation, the reading of Scripture, an offering (with newcomers instructed not to contribute; they should think of themselves as guests), and a sermon from Hybels or one of his many associates.

With its unabashed catering to the tastes of its congregants, Willow Creek Community Church stands as the preeminent example of the new evangelicalism, which is characterized by the ability to speak the idiom of the surrounding culture. New evangelicalism, also known as "neo-evangelicalism," began as a movement among conservative Protestants in the 1940s and 1950s to go beyond the contentious fundamentalism of the 1920s and 1930s and adopt a more irenic posture toward the world in general and other Protestants in particular.[4] Harold John Ockenga, pastor of Park Street Church in Boston, and president of the newly formed Fuller Theological Seminary, probably coined the term in 1948. He characterized neo-evangelicalism as "progressive fundamentalism with a social message." Ockenga and a cohort of others, including Carl F. H. Henry, Edward J. Carnell, Vernon Grounds, and others, hoped to counteract the anti-intellectualism associated with fundamentalism, and the new evangelicals sought to build an evangelical coalition with the help of such institutions as the National Association of Evangelicals, *Christianity Today*, the Evangelical Theological Society, and Fuller Seminary.

Neo-evangelicals retained a conservative theology, especially on the issue of biblical inerrancy, but they cautiously entertained the discipline of biblical criticism. Dispensational theology was called into question, thereby arousing the suspicion and ire of many fundamentalists. Billy Graham's cooperation with liberal clergy during his 1957 crusade at Madison Square Garden in New York City was interpreted by many fundamentalists as a sellout to "modernism." The new movement prospered, however, because of its willingness to adapt to changing cultural forms, although the insis-

tence on a kind of litmus test over the doctrine of inerrancy in the 1970s
sapped some of the energy from neo-evangelicalism at the same time that
the televangelists, most of them either fundamentalists or pentecostals, were
gathering momentum.

This taxonomy of evangelicalism in America by no means exhausts the
categories. The Southern Baptist Convention, the largest Protestant denomination in America, belongs under the general rubric of evangelicalism,
but it does not fit comfortably into any one of the strains described above.
A small but growing movement of evangelicals is gravitating toward Eastern Orthodoxy, much to the consternation of the church hierarchy. Many
African American churches would fit the general definitions of evangelicalism, and they might well be included in the taxonomy, but the sorry
history of racism and segregation in American history has meant that there
has been precious little interaction between black and white fellow believers.

Taken together, however, evangelicals in America make for a formidable
movement. Evangelicalism set the social and political agenda for much of
the nineteenth century, and the machinations of politically conservative
evangelicals, often lumped into the general category of the Religious Right,
reshaped the political landscape of the last quarter of the twentieth century.
The larger, incalculable impact of evangelicalism, however, has been its
effect on ordinary believers—ordering their beliefs, their piety, their social
relationships, and their attitudes toward the broader culture.

Evangelicals and the End of Time

America's evangelicals, because of their literalistic reading of the Bible,
especially the book of Revelation, have long been fixated on the end of
time. This fixation sets them apart from liberal Protestants, who generally
pay the book of Revelation little heed. Like Augustine and Martin Luther
and any number of Christian theologians, evangelicals hold to a linear view
of history, one that sees the present world collapsing in some form of
apocalyptic judgment.

No less a figure than Jonathan Edwards believed that the Millennium,
one thousand years of righteous rule described in Revelation 20, was at
hand. In the early 1840s a farmer and biblical interpreter from Low Hampton, New York, calculated that Jesus would return sometime in 1843 or
1844. William Miller publicized his predictions, and by the time the deadline
arrived, October 22, 1844, more than 50,000 people had expressed sympathy
with his teachings. So frenzied was some of the rhetoric about the imminent

VARIETIES OF PROTESTANTISM IN AMERICA   83

Second Coming that Horace Greeley felt obliged to publish a special edition of the *New-York Tribune* to refute Miller's teachings.

Other religious groups in American history have fashioned their beliefs around the conviction that human history will soon come to an end. Joseph Smith taught (and Mormons still believe) that the center stake of Zion, the heavenly city, will be in Jackson County, Missouri. Charles Taze Russell and a handful of his followers gathered on the Sixth Street Bridge in Pittsburgh on Good Friday 1878 to await their translation into heaven; Russell's present-day followers, the Jehovah's Witnesses, still carry the message of apocalyptic judgment throughout the world.

Evocations about the end of time, however, also permeate numberless evangelical sermons, motion pictures, and books. Billy Graham, for instance, often talks about the return of Jesus, and he has written several books about the apocalypse predicted in the Bible. With the approach of the year 2000 and the turn of the millennium, moreover, speculation about the apocalypse reached a fever pitch, not only in religious circles but in the broader culture as well.

Evangelicals and the Apocalypse

Most of the rhetoric about the end times, then, comes out of this dominant strain of American Protestantism, evangelicalism. Evangelicals read the words of Revelation not as comfort to the early Christians during their time of persecution, an assurance that God would eventually avenge their sufferings (as liberals would be inclined to do), but as a road map for understanding the unfolding of events leading to the end of time. All of the references to the Antichrist, the Tribulation, the seventy weeks, the vials of judgment, the four horsemen—all of these they treat not as allegory but as prophecies of coming events. And when evangelicals juxtapose these prophecies with current events—the establishment of the State of Israel in 1948, for example, or the Six-Day War in 1967—that merely reinforces their faith in these prophecies.

Most readers find the Bible, however, both the Hebrew Scriptures and the New Testament, a wonderfully complex and internally contradictory book; among evangelicals this gives rise to myriad interpretations regarding the end of time. Vicious internecine battles have been waged, for example, over the sequence of events leading to the end of time. Will Jesus return before, during, or after the seven-year Tribulation? Will the Rapture (the assumption of the true believers into heaven) occur before the Millennium or after? Although evangelicals generally believe that life on earth will be bleak during the Tribulation, they disagree over whether or not redemption will still be possible.

Most of the speculation, however, has centered on the identity of the Antichrist. Because of Protestant suspicions of Roman Catholicism, often reviled as "the whore of Babylon," the pope has been a favorite candidate throughout the centuries. In the twentieth century, many evangelicals suggested (quite plausibly) that Adolf Hitler was the Antichrist. Mikhail Gorbachev struck some as a likely candidate, in part because the birthmark on his forehead could be interpreted as the Mark of the Beast. Apparently, if you assign numeric values to the letters in Henry Kissinger's name (A = 1, B = 2, etc.) and add them up, they total 666, the Mark of the Beast. Ronald Wilson Reagan has six letters in each of his names. More recently, a complex numerology (which was circulated, appropriately enough, on the Internet) designated Bill Gates of Microsoft as the Antichrist; some claim that if you assign ASCII values to the letters of his name, "Bill Gates III," they total 666 (it also purportedly works for "Windows 95").

The Rise of Dispensationalism

All of this might be dismissed as idle speculation were it not for the fact that apocalyptic beliefs have a social dimension as well, and nothing illustrates this better than the rise of a scheme of biblical interpretation called "dispensationalism," or "dispensational premillennialism." In the early part of the nineteenth century most evangelicals were postmillennialists; that is, they believed that Jesus would return *after* the millennium, the thousand years of righteousness predicted in the book of Revelation. That conviction conferred upon evangelicals a responsibility: It was incumbent on them to bring about the millennium here on earth, right here in America. As a consequence, many of the social reform movements in the antebellum period—abolitionism, temperance, the crusade against dueling, women's suffrage—were animated, at least in part, by postmillennialist sentiments. Evangelicals took it upon themselves to construct a righteous empire, to reform society according to the norms of godliness, because only then, *after* the millennium, would Jesus return.

The carnage of the Civil War, however, began to dim hopes for the coming kingdom of God. Urbanization, the rise of industry, rapacious capitalists, labor unrest, and the influx of non-Protestant immigrants also presented contradictions. By the 1880s teeming, squalid tenements no longer resembled the precincts of Zion that evangelicals had so confidently predicted earlier in the century, so they had to revise their eschatology, their theology of the end times.

Evangelicals latched on to a scheme of biblical interpretation called "dispensational premillennialism," which they imported from Great Britain by way of John Nelson Darby. Dispensationalism posited that all of human history could be divided into different ages or dispensations and that God dealt differently with humanity in each of these dispensations. At one time, for example, all of God's promises applied to ancient Israel; now, however, we live in a different dispensation, an age in which God has a special relationship with the church.

More important, dispensational premillennialism insisted that postmillennialists had it all wrong. Jesus would return *before* the millennium, not after. Evangelicals were wasting their time on social reform. The famous evangelist Dwight Lyman Moody declared that he found no place in the Bible where God promised that the world would get better. No, the world would grow worse and worse until Jesus came to rescue the faithful and unleash judgment against their adversaries.

Dispensationalism spread rapidly among America's evangelicals, propagated by evangelists, Bible conferences, and the *Scofield Reference Bible*, which provided glosses on the entire Scriptures to help readers understand the various dispensations. It was a doctrine that perfectly fit the temper of the times in the late nineteenth and early twentieth centuries. It was a theology of despair, in that it insisted that nothing could be done to improve society other than to encourage individual conversions. Dispensationalism, therefore, absolved evangelicals of any responsibility for social reform. The world is getting worse and worse, after all, and our efforts are much better used trying to convert as many as possible so that they will not be left behind when Jesus returns.

Dispensationalism, with its insistence that Jesus might return at any moment, has served as a powerful force for evangelism among evangelicals. Billy Graham, among many others, concluded his sermons by inviting people to come to Jesus, warning that they might not have another chance— that is, Jesus might return before they have another opportunity to convert to Christianity. Anyone left behind at the Second Coming would face terrible judgment, as predicted in the book of Revelation.

At times, dispensationalist beliefs among evangelicals take almost comic dimensions. Just prior to the 1988 Republican presidential primaries, as Pat Robertson was exploring the possibility of entering the race, he met with a group of evangelical ministers in New Hampshire. In the course of the meeting one of the ministers begged Robertson not to run. His reasoning was that if Robertson became president and proceeded to make the world more godly, then that would delay the Second Coming of Jesus. No, it was better, this minister thought, to let evil run its course and to await the imminent return of Jesus.

Implications for Jews and Israel

What does a fixation with the end of time mean for evangelical attitudes toward Israel and the Jews? It makes for an odd configuration in which evangelicals can be simultaneously pro-Israel and anti-Semitic.

A literalist reading and a dispensationalist interpretation of the Bible prompts many evangelicals to insist that Jews, although they are God's chosen people, still must acknowledge Jesus as messiah in order to redeem the promises God made to ancient Israel. For many evangelicals, the fact that most Jews have stubbornly refused to do so remains a source of regret and sadness, even hostility. Some evangelicals believe that they must re-double their evangelistic efforts in order to bring Jews into the Christian fold—and only then will the apocalyptic events unfold.

Israel, however, remains crucial to the apocalyptic scheme, and most evangelicals are certain that God always takes the side of Israel in any contretemps in the Middle East. Aside from a general fascination with Israel as the "Holy Land," the place where Jesus walked, evangelicals revere the Middle East in general and Israel in particular as the theater where the apocalyptic events will unfold. As Israelis know only too well, busloads of evangelical Christians include the plains of Megiddo on their itineraries, for it is here, they believe, that the Battle of Armageddon, predicted in the book of Revelation, will take place.

The Attractions of Apocalypticism

Aside from their convictions about the literal truth of the Bible, evangelicals have many reasons for their fixation with the end of time. First, although this may seem improbable to those outside the evangelical subculture, it is a lot of fun. Evangelicals enjoy speculating about prophetic events. Just who *is* the Antichrist? Could those UPC codes in the supermarket someday be embedded on the back of your hand for use as a kind of debit card, thereby comprising the dreaded and pernicious Mark of the Beast? How do Desert Storm and the Persian Gulf War fit into the prophetic scheme? Should true believers oppose the United Nations and the European Community as harbingers of the one-world government that would facilitate the rise of the Antichrist? Some evangelicals thought the Orwellian year 1984 would herald the end of human history; later, similar predictions shifted to the year 2000. While it is true that such speculations too often lead to paranoia and conspiracy theories, most discussions of this sort are rather innocuous.

Second, a preoccupation with the end times allows for flights of fancy about the shape of a new and perfect world, a chance to start over. These visions about a new heaven and a new earth have had a deleterious effect on evangelical engagements in this world; premillennialism has served to absolve them from responsibility for social amelioration. Ever since the late nineteenth century many evangelicals have retreated into a bunker mentality, reminding themselves that this world is getting worse, that the only hope is the imminent return of Jesus, and mollifying themselves with blueprints of the heavenly city.

A fixation on the prophecies in the Bible, moreover, places evangelicals in control of history. It allows them to assert that they alone understand the mind of God; they alone have unlocked the mysteries of the Scriptures. The corollary to this smugness, of course, is that everyone else is still benighted; they are lost in darkness—and they await divine judgment—because they have refused to take the apocalyptic prophecies seriously.

Finally, and most importantly, evangelicals see the end times as a summons to conversion. We must set our lives and our hearts in order before Jesus returns, before it is too late. Is *my* heart right with God? What about my family and loved ones? That is why the approach of the year 2000 excited both anticipation and anxiety.

Part Two

Case Studies

CHAPTER FOUR

Williston Federated Church

Williston, Vermont

The white clapboard Williston Federated Church of Williston, Vermont, with its tall steeple, looks like the prototypical New England meetinghouse. Though it sits along U.S. 2, just south of Burlington, and not on a village green, it could still pass for Hollywood's notion of New England quaintness.

On a balmy August Sunday morning, following a prelude by Johann Sebastian Bach, "Jesu, Joy of Our Desiring" (the title rendered in politically correct form—"Our Desiring" rather than "Man's Desiring"—in the morning bulletin), the pastor led the congregation in a call to worship. "We have been called to walk the faithful road," he intoned, "and to choose the way of God's justice." The congregation responded with the declarations that "our God is good" and "we are here to proclaim our faith," as dictated in the Order of Worship, which had been distributed by ushers as the worshipers entered the sanctuary. The congregation then stood for the opening hymn, the Protestant classic "Holy, Holy, Holy, Lord God, Almighty," with a guitar accompaniment. The pastor, a pleasant, middle-aged man wearing spectacles and a business suit, then strode to the lectern and announced that the reading from the New Testament that morning would be Ephesians 4:25–5:2. "This letter is attributed to Paul," he explained cheerfully, "but was probably written by a follower of Paul." Several members of the congregation reached for the copy of the *New Revised Standard Version* of the Bible, located next to the *United Methodist Hymnal* in the pew racks in front of them, and followed along.

This account is based on a visit to Williston Federated Church on August 6, 2000.

Fig. 4.1. Williston Federated Church in Williston, Vermont traces its history to 1800. Courtesy of Williston Federated Church, Williston, Vt.

"This is the Word of our God," the pastor concluded, and the congregation read responsively from a paraphrased version of Psalm 130, printed in the Order of Worship. The Gospel lesson followed, the congregation standing. The pastor read from the sixth chapter of Saint John, which speaks about Jesus as the bread of life. At the conclusion of the reading, the pastor said: "This is the Gospel of the Lord."

A similar phrase would prompt a response in an Episcopal church, "Praise to you, Lord Christ," but at the Williston Federated Church, an example of a more low-church or nonliturgical strain of mainline Protestantism, the congregation silently sat down to await the morning sermon.

Liberal Protestants and Ecumenism

In a gesture of informality, the pastor stepped down from the platform and stood directly in front of the congregation to deliver his sermon. "Please join with me in the spirit of prayer," he said. "We are grateful for those who have stood for justice and compassion." The Reverend Richard H. Hibbert delivered his sermon in a folksy, conversational style. He referred to a recently published novel by Jim Ferguson, and the burden of his sermon was the importance of unity among Christians. "What kind of example do we set when Christians cannot agree?" he asked rhetorically. "What kind of example are we setting?"

The theme of unity was reflected also in the banner hanging at the back of the sanctuary: "In Union There is Strength," it read in bold letters. And then below: "Together each accomplishes more." Ecumenism, or unity, has been a recurrent theme among Christians throughout church history, but especially since the Protestant Reformation. Leaders within various traditions and denominations have sought to stanch the fractiousness that seems to be endemic to Protestantism. Martin Luther's dictum that each believer interpret the Bible for herself has led to endless splintering among Protestants and to periodic initiatives for unity.

The most recent push for unity began at the middle of the twentieth century with the formation of the National Council of Churches in November 1949 and the construction of the Interchurch Center on the upper west side of Manhattan a decade later. Since then there have been several denominational mergers, including (among others) the United Church of Christ in 1957 (from the Congregational Christian Churches and the Evangelical and Reformed Church), the United Methodist Church in 1968 (from the Methodist Episcopal Church and the Evangelical United Brethren), and the Evangelical Lutheran Church in America in 1988 (from the Lutheran Church in America, the Evangelical Lutheran Church, and the Association of Evangelical Lutheran Churches).

Williston Federated Church exemplifies this ecumenical trend in several ways; in fact it anticipated the latest wave of ecumenism by half a century. The church was established in 1800 as the Congregational Church, and eight years later a Methodist congregation started up in Williston. The two congregations federated in 1899 when it became clear that the community could no longer support two Protestant churches. This pattern has been replicated elsewhere in small New England villages. In the resort town of Stowe, about twenty miles away, for instance, the Stowe Community Church was formed in 1920 with the merger of the Congregationalists, the Methodists, the Universalists, and members of the Baptist society because residents felt they could no longer justify separate congregations.

In this way, the declining populations and the increased pluralism of

Fig. 4.2. President Dwight D. Eisenhower lays the cornerstone of the Interchurch Center in upper Manhattan on October 12, 1958, symbolizing the 1950s fusion of mainline Protestantism with white, middle-class values. Courtesy of the Interchurch Center, New York, N.Y.

small communities reverse an earlier pattern. In many rural areas, settlers established a kind of generic Protestant congregation, sometimes called a "union chapel" or, simply, "community church." As the population increased, however, denominational differentiation became possible—a critical mass of Baptists formed a Baptist church, Methodists started a Methodist church, and so on. With diminishing populations in small communities and rural areas, together with cultural pluralism and some religious indifference, many of these congregations have found that they are too small to lure preachers or to maintain their own buildings. They have elected to pool their numbers and their resources by merging their Methodist or Congregational or Baptist churches to form, once again, a unity chapel or a community church or a federated congregation.

Williston Federated Church is ecumenical in that way, but it is also ecumenical in that it maintains ties with two denominations simultaneously: the United Methodist Church and the United Church of Christ. Hibbert, the pastor, happens to be ordained in the United Methodist Church (as was his predecessor), but the congregation would be perfectly free to choose, the next time it searches for a minister, a Congregationalist (a member of the United Church of Christ).

Protestant Musical Styles

Christian unity was very much on Hibbert's mind as he delivered his sermon. He stressed the importance of kindness and learning to speak the truth in love. "Our life in community should reflect the transformation that takes place within each of us," he said, concluding with an admonition: "Come and be one in the Spirit, one in the love of God."

As Hibbert returned to the platform to take his seat, the guitarist stood and strummed the opening chords of "Morning Has Broken." The congregation—forty-five people, all told, including the pastor—joined in. The guitar is a concession to the customary drop-off in attendance that afflicts most Protestant churches during the summer, but it is also part of an attempt to update the service to attract younger worshipers. While the *Methodist Hymnal* and the *New Revised Standard Version* of the Bible fill the racks in front of each worshiper, larger, more unwieldy copies of *Maranatha! Music Praise Chorus Book* (Expanded Third Edition) lie on the pews themselves. Williston Federated Church, like most mainline Protestant churches in America, has been slow to adapt to changes in musical styles, in part because most of those changes have emanated from the evangelical sector of Protestantism. Evangelical congregations almost universally have adopted a more casual musical style, sometimes referred to as "praise music." The use of this "praise music" takes many forms, from chorus books (like those on the wooden pews at Williston Federated Church) and a taped symphonic accompaniment to guitar music, with the lyrics projected onto a wall or an overhead screen. Some evangelical congregations have elaborate setups and state-of-the-art sound systems to facilitate this music, and mainline congregations are only now trying to catch up to the trend.

No change, however, comes without risks. Many older congregants, as a rule, favor organ music and older, more traditional hymns over the new praise music, although some try gamely to keep up with the times. Any wholesale move toward choruses and praise music runs the risk of alienating them. On the other hand, younger congregants find the old hymns distant and austere and even unsingable ("Wonderful Grace of Jesus," for instance, with a melody that soars into the upper register); they prefer the simpler melodies of the praise songs.

Some congregations, like the one in Williston, have tried to walk a middle road—singing a traditional hymn like "Morning Has Broken" to the chords of a guitar. Other churches even conduct separate Sunday morning services, one with contemporary music and the other with traditional hymns. The Federated Church has followed this tack, offering an informal, contemporary service at 8:15 A.M. on Sundays from September to June, and a traditional service with hymns and choir at 10:00 A.M. on Sundays year-round. The risk in such an arrangement, of course, is a congregation divided, usually along generational lines.

Protestants and Prayer

Following "Morning Has Broken," Hibbert stood and asked for prayer requests from the congregation and then offered an extemporaneous prayer. "We hold before you all those we have named today," he began, adding his intercessions "for all who struggle, for all who grieve, for all who are in pain." Extemporaneous prayer is another characteristic of Protestantism. Although more liturgical Protestants, such as Lutherans and Episcopalians, follow prescribed prayers, low-church Protestants traditionally have preferred extemporary or spontaneous prayer (the Puritans called it "ejaculatory prayer"). Some Protestants, notably the Pietists of the eighteenth

Fig. 4.3. Richard Hibbert, in clerical garb, is pastor of Williston Federated Church. ©
Walter Erickson III. Courtesy of Williston Federated Church, Williston, Vt.

century, believed that even the Lord's Prayer should not be recited because it was too liturgical and "popish." Hibbert's prayer derives from the Protestant low-church tradition. "Help us to learn to treat your creation with respect," he offered, concluding with an "Amen."[1]

The guitarist sang a Shaker traditional piece, "Bow Down Low," during the offertory, and the congregation sang a politically correct version of the *Doxology* ("God" instead of the pronouns "he" and "him") as the ushers brought the offering plates to Hibbert at the front of the sanctuary. The congregation sang one final song, "The Gift of Love," before the pastor dismissed the gathering with a benediction.

Williston and the Larger World

Richard Hibbert, a graying man with a goatee and an earring in his left ear, graduated from Wesley Theological Seminary, a United Methodist school in Washington, D.C., in 1971. He came to the Williston congregation from a Methodist church in Plattsburgh, New York, in 1998. Although he likes being in Vermont, he acknowledged that the Williston Federated Church faces a number of challenges as it begins its third century. "We've been struggling with how to reach unchurched people," he said, noting that the congregation has not kept up with the area's growth in population. "We ought to be stronger than we are."

Williston, Vermont, sits at the southern edge of Burlington, the state's largest city and home to the University of Vermont. Burlington is hardly a metropolis, even by the standards of the most rural state in the union, but suburban sprawl has crept into Williston over the last decade. The town now has a population of 6,000 to 7,000, and whereas the Williston Federated Church was once the only Protestant game in town, Hibbert estimates that there are now seven or eight other congregations, all of which he characterizes as "fundamentalist and evangelical." The Federated Church claims a membership of 460 (although less than 10 percent attended the Sunday worship service). "The evangelical churches are more outreach-oriented," he said.

Hibbert finds those numbers even more striking when he factors the congregation's demographics into the equation. "The core of the congregation is older, too established," he acknowledged, "and that makes it harder for us to institute new forms of worship." He said that one of the serious questions at the church was, in his words, "Are we really open to growth and new people?"

The church's literature suggests a resoundingly affirmative answer: "The Williston Federated Church is a community which seeks, welcomes and gathers people to share the Gospel of God's love, enables people to find fullness of life through Jesus Christ, goes into the world to live lovingly and justly as servants of Christ, and responds actively to human need."

The brochure goes on to list the congregation's affiliation with such organizations as Women Helping Battered Women, Salvation Army, Ronald McDonald House, Burlington Emergency Shelter, and Habitat for Humanity.

A congregation's affiliations say a great deal about its theological and political orientation. An evangelical church might share connections with Habitat for Humanity and the Salvation Army, but it might also support a local or a national pro-life organization as well as several missionaries and evangelists. Indeed, for the most part, the Religious Right notwithstanding, evangelical churches emphasize the importance of missions and evangelism, the task of bringing others into the Christian fold. More liberal churches, on the other hand, tend to concentrate their efforts—or at least their rhetoric—on social reform, often expressed in the nostrum "peace and justice" or "peace, justice, and inclusiveness." While evangelicals emphasize the importance of going into all the world to preach the gospel, liberals talk about going into the neighborhoods to work for justice. All generalizations are perilous, of course, but evangelical Protestants for more than a century have been concerned more with individual salvation and eternal destiny, while liberal Protestants have devoted their efforts to social and physical well-being in this world, which includes issues like hunger relief, homelessness, and inclusivity.

"The community of faith at Williston Federated Church invites all persons into its life of worship, fellowship and service," Hibbert writes in his pastoral column in the church brochure. "Our life in faith is open to everyone and we welcome the gifts brought to us by all those who choose to unite with us in faithful living."

In the state of Vermont in the year 2000 Hibbert's words were especially freighted. Following a 1999 ruling by the state supreme court, the legislature passed and the governor signed a bill legalizing "civil unions" for same-sex couples, which went into effect July 1, 2000. The whole process energized—and, to a large degree, polarized—both liberals and conservatives in the state, and it also attracted a great deal of outside attention. The notorious gay-basher Fred Phelps, a fundamentalist minister from Topeka, Kansas, for instance, conducted a brief demonstration on the statehouse grounds in Montpelier during the summer of 1999. During the 2000 election year the Republican nominee for governor, Ruth Dwyer, drew heavily on opposition to civil unions to fuel her unsuccessful campaign against incumbent Democratic governor Howard Dean, who had signed the bill into law.

How has all of this affected Williston Federated Church? Hibbert noted proudly that he had been among the original group of clergy to sign a statement in favor of civil unions. "I'm one of the more radical ones," he said with a smile. Although he characterized the congregation as "more progressive" than the evangelical churches in town, Williston Federated Church did not formally take a stand on the civil union issue. In a gesture that would be fairly typical of liberal Protestantism, however, the congregation made what Hibbert characterized as "a statement of openness and inclusivity."

CHAPTER FIVE

Abyssinian Baptist Church

Harlem, New York

"Great and wonderful are thy deeds, O Lord God the Almighty," the minister intoned. The congregation replied: "Just and true are thy ways, O King of the ages."

Following this call to worship, pastor and congregation said the Lord's Prayer, whereupon the pastor invited everyone to join in singing the processional: "Let us lift our voices to the glory of God as we sing with the choir 'Revive Us Again.'" The organ began in a lilting, gospel style, and everyone sang "We praise thee, O God, for the Son of Thy Love, For Jesus who died and is now gone above." The choir, dressed in maroon robes, walked down the aisles of the Akron-style sanctuary, a horseshoe-like floor plan with a balcony that all but encircles the pulpit. The choir filed through doors on either side of the platform, up the stairs, and reappeared in the choir loft directly above the preacher and the other clergy. "Hallelujah, Thine the glory! Hallelujah, amen! Hallelujah Thine the glory! Revive us again."

"We thank you for guiding our feet to the household of prayer," the pastor said for the invocation. "Come by here."

Calvin O. Butts III, dressed in a gray academic gown with crimson chevrons to indicate his doctorate, is an imposing presence behind the pulpit. He has a rich baritone that, especially with the improved sound

---

This account is based on several visits, but it derives principally from a visit on June 24, 2001.

Fig. 5.1. Abyssinian Baptist Church, founded in 1808, moved to its present location in Harlem in 1923. Underwood & Underwood/Corbis.

system in the newly renovated Abyssinian Baptist Church, fills the room. In the tradition of many other African American preachers, there is little question that Butts, the senior pastor, is in charge of the gathering—the unflappable, no-nonsense master of ceremonies who runs the service (and the congregation itself) with a firm, albeit benevolent, iron hand.

The Baptist Tradition

"We read Scripture responsively so that it will settle into our hearts and into our minds," Butts said before leading the congregation in a responsive reading on the subject of baptism. Abyssinian, like many other black congregations, is a Baptist congregation, which means (among other things) that it subscribes to adult (or believer's) baptism, rather than the infant baptism practiced in the Roman Catholic Church and in many mainline Protestant denominations. Many Baptist churches have a built-in water tank for the full immersion of those being baptized; Abyssinian's is behind the lectern, built into the marble platform. In lieu of infant baptism, Abyssinian, like other churches in the Baptist tradition, offers a blessing for babies on the second Sunday of each month; parents will bring their young children to the altar, and one of the ministers will say a prayer of dedication reminiscent of Hannah's dedication of Samuel in the Hebrew Bible. Baptism itself, however, is reserved for those who have made a profession of faith, something that Baptists believe is beyond the capacity of infants.

The Baptist tradition dates to the Anabaptists of the sixteenth century, who were persecuted, and even executed, for their convictions. In America, the Baptist tradition is generally traced to Roger Williams in Rhode Island. After Williams was baptized by Ezekial Holliman in 1639, Williams in turn baptized Holliman and a small band of followers. In part because they were a minority faith and in part because of Williams's abiding suspicions about the entanglements of church and state, Baptists agitated for the disestablishment of religion in New England and, later, in the new nation, a conviction that was codified in the First Amendment. Until the late 1970s, when the Southern Baptist Convention began its collusion with the Religious Right, Baptists insisted on religious liberty and the separation of church and state. Indeed, it has been one of the hallmarks of Baptist identity throughout American history.

Outsiders have questioned whether this principle of separation really exists among African American Baptists, because so many black churches have been involved with programs of social welfare. Abyssinian, for instance, runs a summer day camp, a credit union, and other services in Harlem. Its newsletter for summer 2000 included an article entitled "What You Should Do If Police Stop You," a response to the widespread practice of racial profiling. During the morning service Butts acknowledged from the pulpit an organization that the church supports called Na We Yone, which provides social services to refugees from Sierra Leone, and he also called the congregation's attention to a liquor store sign adjacent to a charter school on Lenox Avenue. Unless the sign comes down, Butts hinted, the owner of the sign would face collective action from members of the congregation.

These activities, together with the fact that many of the elected officials from the African American community are also clergy, has led some critics to charge that the line of separation among black Baptists between church and state, religion and politics, is nonexistent. While it is true that black churches often take stances on political issues and sometimes endorse candidates for elective office, either implicitly or explicitly, that criticism misses

Fig. 5.2. Calvin O. Butts, a forceful orator in the African American tradition, is the senior pastor of Abyssinian Baptist Church. Courtesy of Dr. Calvin O. Butts III.

the point. Historically, the reason that the church and the social order have been so entwined among blacks is that, going back to the days of slavery, the church was the only social institution that provided any autonomy for African Americans. Consequently, the only avenue for the expression of leadership within the black community was the ministry, which is why the black preacher has played such an outsized role among African Americans, from Nat Turner and Denmark Vesey to Martin Luther King Jr., Jesse Jackson, and many members of the Black Congressional Caucus in Washington.[1]

Calvin Butts and several of his predecessors at Abyssinian also fit this profile. Adam Clayton Powell Sr. became pastor in 1908 and guided the congregation through the Great Depression, instituting a free food kitchen, a retirement home, and an unemployment relief fund, along with classes in literacy, nursing, dressmaking, and business. His son and successor as pastor at Abyssinian, Adam Clayton Powell Jr., continued these programs; he also became New York's first black member of Congress. The venerable Samuel Proctor succeeded the younger Powell; Proctor saw himself as a transitional figure at Abyssinian—a calming, avuncular presence after the tumultuous tenure of his flamboyant and controversial predecessor.

Butts was an assistant pastor under Proctor, waiting for his opportunity to lead the congregation. Butts has resurrected the tradition of social action at Abyssinian, agitating for affordable housing, the removal of cigarette billboards, and an end to police brutality, among other issues. His political views frequently placed him at odds with Rudolph Guiliani, when Guiliani was the city's mayor, and some speculated that Butts would someday mount his own campaign for elective office.

The Church at Prayer

"Pray also for our city, state, and nation," Butts proclaimed as the service moved into its time of prayer. The pastor shared several prayer requests, including one from a fifteen-year-old boy with a brain tumor. "When you pray for those that you know," Butts told the congregation, "call them by name." He also enjoined them to "Pray much for me that God will be merciful as I pray for you," and he suggested that "if all is well with you, please pray the prayer of thanksgiving."

A deacon, a young man nattily dressed in a business suit, then stood to offer prayer on behalf of the congregation. "Help us to be the kind of

Fig. 5.3. A flamboyant and controversial figure, Adam Clayton Powell Jr. (1908–72) symbolized the close connection between religion and politics in the African American community. While serving as pastor of Abyssinian, he also represented Harlem in Congress. Bettmann/Corbis.

church," he prayed, "that practices inclusion, not exclusion." He prayed for the youth of the community, who "don't know what they're searching for." He enumerated the requests that Butts had mentioned and added, "Bless those who are in prison." The choir followed the prayer with "I Have Decided to Follow Jesus," sung quietly and meditatively.

Abyssinian has several choirs, and on this morning the Gospel Choir sang "My Relationship with You Is All the World to Me," a rousing song that illustrates W. E. B. DuBois's famous remark that black religious life is characterized by three things: the music, the preacher, and the frenzy. When Butts returned to the pulpit, he said, "Let the church say amen!" He moved into the announcements, including the midweek prayer meeting, "our hour of power."

"Our members continue to travel," Butts announced to the congregation. "They send us cards from all over the world." He read greetings from Jamaica, South Africa, South Carolina, southern Spain, southern Italy ("We'll tell the pope you said hi"), Mexico, Senegal, and England.

Middle-Class Black Protestantism

This extensive travel attests to the fact that Abyssinian is largely a middle-class congregation. The church was founded in 1808 by a group of educated, prosperous merchants from Abyssinia (modern Ethiopia). They had been outraged when they attended church one Sunday and were seated in the slave loft. In response, they started Abyssinian, which is the second-oldest Baptist congregation in New York City and the first to be nonsegregated.

The church moved from downtown to Harlem in 1923, where it was part of the famed Harlem Renaissance of black arts and culture. Although Harlem does not lack for churches, Abyssinian stands out as a flagship for African American Protestantism, drawing members not only from the neighborhood but from the suburbs and the surrounding boroughs as upwardly mobile members move out of Manhattan.

Abyssinian also attracts visitors from around the world, many of them drawn by the church's history and notoriety, many drawn by the tourist guidebooks, which feature the church prominently. Butts asked them to stand during the course of the announcements and offered a warm welcome, which the congregation joined with applause.

The Centrality of the Sermon

The Bible readings for the morning came from three sources: Genesis 12, 2 Kings 6, and Matthew 27. "May the Lord bless the reading of the Word," Butts concluded. The choir sang "King Jesus Is A-listening When I Pray," a spiritual sung a capella.

"Let the church say amen," Butts declared as he returned to the pulpit. "I truthfully don't want to be long this morning." The congregation shifted, waiting expectantly. "I want to preach on the subject of high visibility," he began. The sermon, using examples from the Scriptures, emphasized the importance of taking the long view, the perspective of "high visibility." In the Genesis passage, Abraham gives Lot the choice of land; Lot chose what was apparently the better tract, but it was near the evil city of Sodom. Things turned out badly for Lot and his family, Butts said, but Abraham's choice was a solid one. "Lot had the low visibility of lust," he added, "while Abraham had the high visibility of a man of faith." Butts continued, his voice booming to drive home the point. "Many of us know that the lust of the eyes can betray us," he said. "All that glitters is not gold. And sometimes, beloved, it pays to wait until the visibility is high."

Butts is a master preacher, someone who is in demand throughout the country. He preaches at other churches, at conferences, and at such places as the venerable Chautauqua Institution. Although his style differs somewhat from the call-and-response sermons in many black churches, the preaching excellence at Abyssinian and the centrality of the sermon are fairly typical of African American Protestants. At Abyssinian Baptist Church the sermon is clearly the centerpiece of the worship service; all of the other components—the congregational singing, the choir, the announcements, the offering—revolve around the sermon. And in a place with a long tradition of superb preachers, the congregation expects that the sermon will be good.

Butts did not disappoint. His sermons reflect an extraordinary biblical literacy, and he leavens his preaching with humor—sometimes, as on this morning, with barbed humor aimed at George W. Bush. In explaining the passage from 2 Kings, Butts noted that a rival king "wanted to *bush*wack the king of Israel." He paused briefly, then added: "He wanted to am*bush* the king of Israel." Again, Elisha took the longer view; he chose high visibility, as did Jesus in Matthew 27.

"It is men and women of high visibility who have truly saved the world," Butts said, driving toward his conclusion. "Men like Abraham, Elisha, and Jesus." Jesus could have come down from the cross, the preacher thundered, but he took the long view for the benefit of humanity. "Don't let low visibility cause you to abandon your principles," he said. "Stand tall for the principles of God."

The congregation responded to the preacher with amens and murmurs of assent. Butts was eager to give his sermon a more contemporary inflection, invoking the examples of Malcolm X and Martin Luther King Jr. King, he said, could have chosen an easier course, perhaps political office. "He spoke the truth about what he believed," Butts said, "and they killed him for it."

With the congregation hanging on every word, Butts approached his conclusion. "Live life with high visibility," he said, "through Jesus Christ our Lord."

Congregational Response

In the time-honored tradition of Baptist churches almost everywhere, Butts followed his sermon with an invitation. This provides an opportunity for members of the congregation to respond by walking forward to the platform, where the preachers wait to greet them. Generally, the invitation is framed to accommodate any of three responses: salvation, baptism, or affiliation with that particular congregation. "We'd love to have you as a part of our fellowship," Butts said before joining the other clergy at the foot of the platform as the congregation sang "The Solid Rock."

One woman came forward; she was greeted with a hug by a female pastor. The ushers, women dressed in white uniforms and wearing white gloves, collected the offering. Butts thanked the Lord for the blessings of this life and for "this little colony of heaven called Abyssinian." The congregation sang the Doxology ("Praise God from whom all blessings flow"), Butts offered another prayer, and the congregation, pastors, and choir sang the recessional hymn, "Wonderful Words of Life."

It took some time for the congregation to disperse. Already a long line snaked along 138th Street, around the corner, and down an entire block of Adam Clayton Powell Jr. Boulevard, waiting for the next service.

CHAPTER SIX

New Life Family Fellowship

Santa Fe, New Mexico

New Life Family Fellowship meets in a converted warehouse on Pacheco Road in Santa Fe, New Mexico. Bumper stickers on automobiles in the parking lot on a Sunday morning reflect the sentiments and beliefs of members of the congregation. One read "Christ Died For You." Two vehicles had "JESUS" imprinted on facsimiles of New Mexico license plates. A beat-up older car with a rearview mirror held together with duct tape had a sticker that read "No Jesus, No Peace. Know Jesus, Know Peace." Another read "Survival of the Fittest" and depicted a large fish, "ICTHYS" (which stands for Jesus Christ, God's Son, Savior), devouring a smaller fish, "Darwin."

The greeters at the door smiled, extended their hands, and chirped, "Good morning! God bless you!" At a few minutes after ten o'clock members of the congregation filed into the low-ceilinged auditorium. It is decorated, rather infelicitously, like a teenage girl's boudoir, with light mauve carpeting and dark mauve curtains behind the stage. Unlike a more traditional church, New Life Family Fellowship has no church pews. Instead, the congregation uses freestanding chairs which this morning formed a semicircle facing the stage, but they can be reconfigured for other types of services or church functions. As the 10:15 start of the service approached, the pastor, a bearded man dressed in a sharkskin suit, circulated through the room, stopping by visitors to introduce himself. "Hi," he said, extending his hand. "I'm Gene."

This account is based on a visit to New Life Family Fellowship on March 11, 2001.

Fig. 6.1. New Life Family Fellowship in Santa Fe, New Mexico, was founded in 1980.
Courtesy of New Life Family Fellowship.

"New Wave" Evangelicalism

New Life Family Fellowship was founded by Gene Druktenis and his wife, Daryl, as Faith Fellowship on May 7, 1980. Several years later they left Santa Fe for Oklahoma, but they later felt "called" to return to New Mexico and to the church, which eventually took the name New Life Family Fellowship. This congregation is an example of one of the many strains of evangelicalism in America, and it might be classified as part of the "new wave" of American evangelicalism, with its emphasis on family programs (as reflected in the congregation's name), its unwillingness to affiliate with any denomination, and its casual, enthusiastic worship which prizes the participation of the congregation.[1]

Fig. 6.2. Daryl (left) and Gene Druktenis (right) founded New Life Family Fellowship, moved to Oklahoma, and then returned to lead the congregation once again. Courtesy of New Life Family Fellowship.

At about 10:15 Scott Tibbets, the assistant pastor, a young man dressed in a shirt and tie and wearing an acoustic guitar, approached the lectern. "We have a lot to praise Him for," he declared, while the screen behind him displayed "New Life to the Max." Fanned out across the stage on either side of the assistant pastor was something that has become a fixture in many evangelical churches at the turn of the twenty-first century, something they call a "praise band" or a "worship team." Here at New Life Family Fellowship the worship team consists of seven vocalists (five women and two men), an electric guitar, a bass, two keyboards, and drums. Everything is amplified through a sound system that would bring a herd of bison to its knees.

The praise band sang "God Is Awesome in This Place." Tibbets strummed his guitar between songs and said, "Glory to God! Alleluia! We do thank you and praise you this morning." Some members of the congregation clapped; others had their arms outstretched toward heaven. "We trust you, Lord God," the assistant pastor continued, his exhortations directed alternately to God and to the congregation. "He dwells in the praises of his people. Amen? Isn't it good to know that Jesus is in you? Amen?" The word "amen" inflected as a question was an invitation for the congregation to respond, and this congregation responded with "amens" of their own, arms upraised in a gesture of openness to the Holy Spirit. The next song was "Jesus Is All I Need," and many members of the congregation by now had countenances that could fairly be described as rapturous. "You are the Almighty God," the assistant pastor prayed "O, how we love you and how we thank you for your precious Holy Spirit in this place."

The Holy Spirit

The Holy Spirit is arguably the most divisive figure in the history of American Protestantism. The third "person" of the Trinity, according to Christian doctrine, the Holy Spirit was bestowed on the early church at Pentecost, after Jesus had ascended into heaven. The event was recorded in the second chapter of the Acts of the Apostles. The Holy Spirit was to be the comforter, according to the New Testament, sustaining believers in their faith, and its coming in Acts 2 was met with enthusiasm, the early Christians speaking in unknown languages and so giddy that observers accused them of drunkenness.

For much of church history Christians paid little heed to the Holy Spirit, at least its more enthusiastic manifestations. During the Protestant Reformation Martin Luther fretted about the *Schwermer*, the "enthusiasts," who claimed direct communication from God through the Holy Spirit. The major eruption of pentecostal fervor occurred at the turn of the twentieth century, originating in Topeka, Kansas, but especially during the Azusa Street Revival in Los Angeles, beginning in April 1906. Those given the gift of speaking in tongues believed that God had bestowed the Holy Spirit in order to restore modern believers to the purity and the enthusiasm of the first-century church.

Not all Protestants agreed. Most, in fact, looked askance at the unbridled religious enthusiasm of Azusa Street and other pentecostal worship. They accused pentecostals of fraudulence and of conjured emotions, and they also accused pentecostals of divisiveness because of the implicit—and some-times explicit—inference that pentecostals were somehow the true or the most authentic Christians, with their claim to spiritual gifts. In addition, nonpentecostals seized on the stereotype that many of the early converts to the movement tended to be drawn from the lower classes.

Although nonpentecostals sought to perpetuate that stereotype, pente-costalism spread widely throughout the twentieth century, both geograph-ically and across class and racial barriers. Some of that diversity is reflected in the composition of the congregation at New Life Family Fellowship. The Sunday morning service drew Native Americans, Anglos, and Hispanics. The presence of the last bespeaks the growing popularity of pentecostalism both in Latin America itself and among Latin communities in the United States, especially in the Southwest.

Praise Music

Tibbets and the praise band segued into another song, "You Are Awesome in This Place, Mighty God." Three children were sprawled on the carpet near the back, playing contentedly with a truck and toy soldiers. One of the hallmarks of pentecostal or charismatic worship is its informality, which is evident in the choice of music—the praise band rather than traditional anthems—and in the "family friendly" atmosphere. Because the worshipers are open to the movement of the Holy Spirit, their worship tends to be less structured and more accommodating to individual expressions, whether it be a sudden outburst of glossolalia or a child's battle between the good guys and the bad guys.

"Let's worship this morning," Tibbets beckoned, and many in the con-gregation responded by speaking in tongues, a gentle ululation that sounds like gibberish, usually done with eyes closed, arms and head raised to heaven. "Be glorified in this place, Lord God," he said. "How we love you, Lord Jesus." After several minutes the speaking in tongues gradually sub-sided, and the congregation was seated. Gene Druktenis, the senior pastor, finally took the microphone and asked the congregation to greet one an-other. He then offered various announcements, including notice about a petition intended for state legislators, that protested the teaching of evo-lution in public schools. He dismissed the children to a separate worship and opened his Bible to Hebrews 6.

"Neutrality is one of the worst enemies you can have in this life,"

Druktenis began, calling attention to the injunction "be not slothful" in Hebrews 6:12. "This verse of Scripture I used to avoid because I didn't like the term 'sloth,'" the pastor confessed. He went on to explain that "slothful" was not synonymous with "lazy." Rather, it connoted something that is slow or sluggish, something that has lost its momentum, its zeal, its conviction. "Slothfulness is far worse than laziness."

Druktenis then referred to the third chapter of the book of Revelation, where God condemns the church at Laodicea for being lukewarm in its spirituality. Because of their indifference God threatens to spit them out of his mouth (Revelation 3:16). "There are slothful, lukewarm people in every church," Druktenis warned, and the implication was clear: It was easy to become spiritually complacent or indifferent.

Gene Druktenis is a graduate of Rhema Bible Training Center, a school founded and operated by Kenneth Hagin in Broken Arrow, Oklahoma. Druktenis grew up in the Assemblies of God, one of the largest pentecostal denominations. He launched a successful business career, but then heard the preaching of televangelist Kenneth Copeland, and something took hold of him. Druktenis abandoned business for the ministry, taking a circuitous path that led him once to New Mexico and, after a stint in Oklahoma, back again to New Life Family Fellowship in Santa Fe.

Druktenis calls himself a "charismatic" rather than a "pentecostal." Although the two are often used interchangeably, and both believe in the Spiritual gifts, including divine healing and speaking in tongues, there is a technical difference. *Pentecostal* generally refers to those who are in pentecostal denominations, such as the Assemblies of God or the Church of God in Christ. *Charismatic*, on the other hand, refers to those "Spirit-filled Christians" who are members of either independent, nonaffiliated congregations (such as the New Life Family Fellowship) or mainline denominations that generally frown on speaking in tongues and divine healing. There is a charismatic movement, for example, in most Christian denominations, including the Episcopal Church, the Southern Baptist Convention, and even the Roman Catholic Church.

Because of the emphasis on enthusiasm and spiritual ecstasy, both charismatics and pentecostals face the challenge of what sociologists call "routinization," which was the subject of Druktenis's sermon. "Let me tell you," he continued, "once you step into the anointing, it will change your life forever."

Maintaining spiritual ardor, however, can be difficult, especially in a tradition that prizes spontaneity, commitment, and fervor. "You need to have a zeal, a passion for God," Druktenis implored. "I am a fanatic, I am an absolute fanatic about praise and worship."

Druktenis also attends to other dimensions of congregational life at New Life Family Fellowship. The church, like many other Protestant congregations, offers an array of programs to meet the needs of the congregants, including a pastor's Bible study, a children's ministry "from birth all the way up to the 6th grade," according to the church's informational brochure, and a group called Pyromaniacs for grades six through twelve. The church offers a youth group "Fun Nite" every Friday evening.

Holy Communion

Druktenis ended his sermon and moved into the next phase of the service, the Lord's Supper or Holy Communion. "We have only one requirement for communion: You must be born again," he said, echoing a persistent trope in evangelical preaching. Evangelicals derive the term *born again* from the third chapter of the Gospel of John, where Nicodemus visits Jesus by night and asks what he must do to gain admission to the kingdom of God. Jesus replies that he must be "born again." Evangelical preachers regularly invite their auditors to be "born again," to be converted, or to "accept Jesus as their personal savior." Generally, they invite the penitent sinner to "pray the sinner's prayer," which usually opens with an acknowledgment of one's sinfulness and an acceptance of Jesus' death as an atonement for one's sins. Sometimes, the preacher will offer the lines for such a prayer and the penitent will repeat them. At the conclusion of such a prayer, evangelicals believe, provided the prayer is said with sincerity, the individual is "saved" or "born again."

On this morning, Druktenis had a couple of takers. "What's going to get you to heaven," he said, "is being born again." After several people raised their hands, the preacher offered a template. "Father, I thank you that Jesus Christ died for my sins . . . thank you for saving me."

The next item of business in the service was prayer for the sick. "I need someone to stand in proxy for Diane and for Carol's cousin," Druktenis said. "Father, we lay hands on Diane right now," he began. "I pray, Father, that you will skillfully guide the doctor's hands . . . that she will walk in health."

At that point the pastor moved into the Lord's Supper or Holy Communion. Most evangelicals take a "low" view of the Lord's Supper, meaning that they are "memorialists." Unlike Roman Catholics, Lutherans, and Episcopalians, all of whom believe that the grace of Christ is actually imparted to the believer through the bread and wine of Holy Communion, evangelicals believe that the elements of the Lord's Supper merely *remind* us of the life and death of Jesus. "Thank you for the blood of our Lord Jesus Christ," Druktenis prayed after thimble-sized containers of grape juice had been distributed to the congregation. "We thank you for his sacrifice."[2] At the pastor's direction, the congregation drank the grape juice in a spirit of remembrance.

Successful Formula

Congregations like New Life Family Fellowship multiplied in the final decades of the twentieth century. As denominations have fallen out of favor with American Protestants, many have looked to independent congregations for their religious sustenance. The independent churches, in turn, because they are not accountable to outside authority structures, are able to fashion their offerings—worship services, ancillary activities, outreach projects— to popular tastes. Not constrained by denominational strictures, by creeds or confessions, by history or liturgy, these new congregations are more flexible and adaptable. Novelty becomes the byword rather than adherence to tradition. The praise bands are probably the most visible manifestation of this pandering to popular tastes, but it is evident in everything from interior decoration and seating plans to preaching styles.

New Life Family Fellowship also illustrates the timeless appeal of evangelicalism throughout American history. Evangelicalism is relentlessly democratic, offering salvation to anyone who will believe, regardless of social station.[3] At its best, it has transcended class, racial, and ethnic lines. Evangelical Protestantism, like Protestantism generally, provides a community, a place where, in music and preaching and social activities, likeminded believers can share their views about God, salvation, family, even Darwinism.

Part Three

CHALLENGES

CHAPTER SEVEN

Protestants and Feminism

Historians generally agree that the two social movements that swept America in the 1960s profoundly reshaped the nation. Just how radically the civil rights movement affected American churches is a matter of some debate—Sunday, many pundits quip, is still the most segregated day of the week. Second-wave feminism, on the other hand, has indelibly marked Protestantism. Since the 1960s, women have donned clerical collars, preached from pulpits, and retooled American Christendom's vocabulary for the divine. But the meeting of feminism and Protestantism has not been a whiggish story of progress. Some feminists say the church still has a long way to go in accommodating women's concerns. At the other end of the spectrum are critics who say feminism has gone too far, much too far; some in the evangelical camp warn that feminism is causing the downfall of Christendom, and with it, America. Among Christians, few agree about whether the changes feminism has wrought are for good or ill; there is little question, though, that feminism has changed the face of the church.

"Examined Anew": Feminist Theology

Historians of Christianity have spilled a lot of ink debating how we should read theology: Do theological treatises transform the church, or do they recognize and codify changes that are already afoot? Feminist theology, which dates to the 1970s, did both—that is, it grew out of feminists' politicization, but it also shook up the church. Indeed, in an era when those in the pews do not spend much time poring over theological tomes, feminist theology has gained a surprisingly large readership.

Feminist theologians disagree with each other about many questions. Evangelical feminists insist that feminist work must be governed by the authority of Scripture, while more liberal feminists are willing to look beyond the boundaries of the Bible or even dispense with Scripture altogether. African American and Hispanic feminist theologians have protested that most of the theological works written by white women have failed to take into account minority women's experiences. They have pioneered *womanist* theology (after the term Alice Walker popularized for black feminism) and *mujerista* theology (a *mujerista*, writes Ada María Isasi-Díaz, is "someone who makes a preferential option for Latina women, for our struggle for liberation"[1]).

For all their disagreements, most Christian feminist theologians agree on a few basics. In the words of Lynn Japinga, Christian feminists seek to "empower and encourage women by helping them to find inner strength, a clear sense of identity, and freedom from stereotypes."[2] (This declaration, with its individualistic, feel-good overtones, is fodder for the canons of more conservative Christians, who note that combating stereotypes has hardly been a historic Christian value and that Christians should help one another find Jesus, not "inner strength.")

Though many contemporary feminist theologians are Protestants, the three mothers of feminist theology—Mary Daly, Rosemary Radford Ruether, and Elisabeth Schussler Fiorenza—were Catholic. In 1968, Daly, then a professor of theology and philosophy at Boston College, published *The Church and the Second Sex*. Invoking Simone de Beauvior's landmark existentialist work, Daly criticized the Roman Catholic Church's treatment of women, focusing in particular on its refusal to ordain women. In her sequel *Beyond God the Father*, Daly asserted that the church was inherently patriarchal; it would never offer women a safe home. Although Daly left the church, declaring herself post-Christian, she had a major impact on feminist theology; her questions—Can sexism be eradicated from Christianity? Can the church be transformed from an institution that oppresses women into one that empowers them?—have cast a long shadow over Christian feminist conversation.

Elisabeth Schussler Fiorenza, another Catholic feminist, has answered Daly's questions with a greatly qualified yes. Cofounder (with Jewish feminist theologian Judith Plaskow) of the *Journal of Feminist Studies in Religion*, Schussler Fiorenza maintains that some variation of the Christian vocabu-

Fig. 7.1. Elizabeth Schussler Fiorenza was one of the pioneers in the feminist theology movement. Courtesy of Harvard Divinity School.

lary can be useful for women. One of the most radical feminist theologians, Schussler Fiorenza at times seems to lapse into a parody of feminist rhetoric: She often writes of subverting "malestream" (instead of "mainstream") scholarship. And she refers to God as "G*d": "I have switched from the orthodox Jewish writing of G-d which I had adopted in *But She Said* and *Discipleship of Equals* in order to indicate the brokenness and inadequacy of human language to name the Divine to this spelling of G*d, which seeks to avoid the conservative malestream association which the writing of G-d has for Jewish feminists." The central question of her work has preoccupied almost every Christian who has done battle in the gender wars: How should we read Scripture? Schussler Fiorenza has tried to develop a way of reading Scripture—what many have called a feminist liberationist hermeneutic—that "can keep our biblical readings from reinforcing [a] dominant patriarchal system and phallocentric mind-set."[3]

Rosemary Radford Ruether has also taken up the gauntlet Daly threw. Author of the first feminist systematic theology, *Sexism and God-Talk*, Ruether has tried throughout her career to do three things: criticize Christian tradition, noting where it has failed women and, in so doing, failed the gospel; recover women's stories; and reshape the tradition in a way that responds to women's needs.

Ruether, Schussler Fiorenza, and their devotees have attempted to reconsider every aspect of Christian theology, from the Trinity to the Incarnation. As Pamela Young has suggested, "Every theological doctrine and concept had to be examined anew in light of the growing awareness that women had been oppressed in the church at least as systematically as in other parts of society." Several theologians have asked, for example, how feminists can understand Christology—that is, how we talk about Christ. Ruether devoted a chapter of *Sexism and God-Talk* to Christology, and that chapter's subtitle bluntly expressed a major feminist concern: "Can a Male Savior Save Women?" Christology, she wrote, presents a problem because Jesus is male: "Can a feminist theology come to terms with his maleness?" Is his being incarnate as a man essential to Jesus' saving work? Can a male God save women?[4]

In pressing those questions, Ruether seeks what many feminist theologians after her have sought—and what many Christian theologians of the nineteenth and twentieth centuries sought before her. She is trying to locate the essence, the *kerygma*, of the Christian story. This is not just a feminist move; it is the primary project of modern liberal Christian theology—determining the core of the Christian story and extracting that core from peripheral details. Ruether concludes that the salvation Jesus offers does not hinge on his maleness. Rather, his prophetic message of transformation, the this-worldly social change he extends to all who will listen, comprises the essence of Jesus. This social radical is, she concludes, "a savior to whom feminists can relate."[5]

Ruether's Christology departs from tradition by focusing more on the message than the person of Christ. Traditionally, theologians have developed either "high" or "low" Christologies, the former emphasizing the divinity of Christ and the latter emphasizing Christ's humanity. Some feminists have been attracted to high Christologies, which de-emphasize Christ's maleness and instead, as Patricia Wilson-Kastner has argued, look to his resurrection as a means toward transforming society. Wilson-Kastner has suggested that the resurrected Christ embodies feminist ideals of healing and renewal. Other feminists, influenced by liberation theologians, have gravitated towards low Christologies, emphasizing Jesus as a brother, a fellow sufferer: "Jesus matters only if he was fully, and only human," Episcopal priest Carter Heyward said.[6]

Another doctrine to which feminists have turned their attention is atonement. In 1993, Christian women from around the world gathered at the Re-Imagining Conference in Minnesota. The conference, which gave women the opportunity to "re-imagine" the church, the Christian God, and themselves, was controversial, with critics saying the women had stepped outside the bounds of anything that resembled Christianity. Those charges were leveled in particular at Delores Williams, a womanist theologian from New York's Union Theological Seminary. At the conference, Williams challenged her audience to rethink the meaning of the cross. "Must we understand the cross as atonement?" she asked. Is our God bloodthirsty and vengeful, bent on extracting a price from humanity for our sins? Black women could not abide this image of God, she said. Williams argued that the cross was better understood as simply the epitome of Christ's suffering; he suffered as all humans—and black women in particular—have suffered. His offering on the cross was one of solidarity, not atonement. "As Christians, black women cannot forget the cross, but neither can they glorify it. To do so is to glorify suffering and to render their exploitation sacred."[7]

Christian feminists have focused on reading, even more than on atonement and Christology, asking a very basic question: What texts do we read? The obvious answer would be Scripture. When Elizabeth Cady Stanton published *The Woman's Bible*, she told her nineteenth-century readers that pernicious readings of Scripture were largely responsible for the sexism that pervaded America. Some of her sisters in the struggle, Stanton wrote in her introduction, said she was wasting her time trying to resuscitate the Bible; it was a hopelessly retrograde document, and she should just abandon it. But, Stanton explained, Scripture was still the most influential text in the world; even if a handful of radical American women had put away their King James Version, the Bible needed to be reckoned with.

But Schussler Fiorenza and Ruether have both answered that question—What texts should Christians read?—capaciously. They read the Bible, but they have also ventured outside the orthodox Christian canon to find texts, such as the Gnostic Gospels, that might give their feminist theologies some ballast. The Bible, they say, is not the alpha and omega of Christian theology. In *mujerista* theologian Isasi-Díaz's words, "Hispanic women's experience and our struggle for survival, not the Bible, are the source of our theology, and the starting point for how we should interpret, appropriate, and use the Bible." In other words, women's experiences become the arbiters of the canon, not the other way around. Schussler Fiorenza makes a similar point: The Bible is a foundational Christian text, but it can only carry weight insofar as it does not harm women. Such a seemingly casual dismissal of the Bible has earned Schussler Fiorenza and fellow travelers the ire and condescension of evangelicals. As Bethel Theological Seminary's Mark Strauss said, "Elisabeth Schussler Fiorenza accepts as authoritative only those parts of the Bible which support the struggle for liberation. Those passages then become the norm by which to interpret others."[8]

Speaking of God(ess?)

Since the 1970s, feminists have raised questions about language: How should the church speak about the divine? Is Jesus a "he"? Should we call the first person of the Trinity "Father" or "Parent"? Is it appropriate to speak of the single Christian as male?

Many feminists have objected to the use of the generic "he" in prayers and sermons—and even church bulletins—when referring to other Christians. There are more churchgoing women in America than men, they argue, and language about the church ought to acknowledge women's presence. Feminists have spoken about how distracting and even destructive prayers can be when the very grammar of worship implies that the worshipers are men. Lynn Japinga describes her ordination as "a profoundly male event." No women were present for the laying on of hands, and the service was shot through with male pronouns. Not only was God "He," but so were the direct objects of the prayers, which implored a male God to guide Japinga, to "govern him in the ministry that he may decently and fruitfully walk therein." A friend of Japinga's from seminary, who was present for the laying on of hands, gently squeezed her every time the service referred to the new minister as "he"—to remind Japinga that she was included in the service.[9]

Not every story tells of disorientation and pain. Women have reveled in language that explicitly includes them. Episcopalian June Steffensen Hagen recounts singing a revised, women-friendly version of Hymn 673: *And blessed is she, is she who believes.* "This hymn, I discovered, is about me! For I am *she*, never *he*."[10]

Feminists have also challenged the church's traditional language for God. Theologians note two reasons for moving away from exclusively masculine terms—Father, Son, He—for God. The first has to do with women praying: The deluge of male God-language can form a barrier to prayer. As Nancy Hardesty, an evangelical theologian, described: "The water torture begins. Like an incessant dripping on the head, the words come: *man, men, he, his, him, father, son.* . . . Instead of joining in the intercession, one begins to count the times the pastor uses 'Father' in prayer. . . . The pain and anger become excruciating."[11]

Reconsidering God-language, say feminists, is imperative not just because calling God "Father" makes some women uncomfortable. Relying on exclusively masculine language limits how Christians conceive of the infinite, boundless God. As Ruether wrote in *Sexism and God-Talk*, "If all language for God/ess is analogy, if taking a particular human image literally is idolatry, then male language for the divine must lose its privileged place. If God/ess is not the creator and validator of the existing hierarchical social order, but rather the one who liberates us from it, who opens up a new community of equals, then language about God/ess drawn from kingship and hierarchical power must lose its privileged place." Ruether argues that we should draw new language for God not from rulers, but from the oppressed; not from men on thrones, but from women and peasants. And "most of all, images of God/ess must be transformative, pointing us back to our authentic potential and forward to new redeemed possibilities." Or, as theologian Elizabeth Johnson has noted, "the tenacity with which the patriarchal symbol of God is upheld is nothing less than violation of the first commandment of the decalogue, the worship of an idol."[12]

Suggestions for new God-language are legion. Yale Divinity School's Rebecca Chopp has suggested calling God, after the Gospel of John, the Word. Hardesty has suggested that Christians return to Scripture's maternal images of God—Isaiah's figuring of God as a woman giving birth or Hosea's picture of God as a bear whose cubs have been stolen away. Many Christian feminists have advocated rehabilitating the Greek term "Sophia," which means wisdom. In the wake of the Re-Imagining Conference, which detractors tarred as an idolatrous Sophia-fest, critics came out strongly against referring to the second person of the trinity as "Wisdom" or "Sophia." United Methodist bishop Earl Hunt said the Sophia language was the most dangerous heresy to emerge in the last fifteen centuries. Feminists' defenses of Sophia were just as highly pitched: Donna Blackstock, from the Presbyterian Church (U.S.A.) Christian Education Program, said denying women the right to pray to Sophia was "spiritual rape."[13]

Women in the Pulpit

For all their enthusiasm, feminists have not made great strides in retooling how the majority of Protestants speak about God. Walk into most Protestant churches on Sunday mornings, and you will still hear people praying to the Father, Son, and Holy Spirit. But second-wave feminism has had a huge impact on the ministry: Many of the pastors leading those masculine prayers are women.

American history is dotted with women pastors. Antoinette Brown, ordained as a Congregationalist minister in 1853, was the first woman ordained in the United States. Olympia Brown became a Universalist minister a decade later, and the Unitarians began ordaining women in 1871. The Disciples of Christ ordained their first female pastor in 1888; the African Methodist Episcopal Zion Church in 1898. By 1900, there were at least 3,400 ordained women in America. The number of denominations ordaining women climbed during the twentieth century: the Cumberland Presbyterian Church in 1921, the Assemblies of God in 1935, the Presbyterian Church (U.S.A.) in 1956, the African Methodist Episcopal Church in 1960. The 1970s, however, was the most significant decade for women's ordination. Not only did Reform and Reconstructionist Jews begin ordaining women as rabbis, the American Lutheran Church and the Lutheran Church in America both ordained female ministers; the Mennonites followed in 1973 and the Free Methodist Church, North American, in 1974. Episcopalians joined in with the "irregular" ordination of eleven women in 1974 (followed by the formal recognition of women's ordination in 1976), and the Evangelical Covenant Church began ordaining women in 1976. In November 1987, the National Council of Churches elected a clergywoman as president, and seven months later, the Christian Church (Disciples of Christ) jointly ordained a mother-daughter team.

More women in clerical collars has also meant more women in seminary classrooms. In 1972, 1 in 10 seminarians was female; by 1989, the figure had risen to 3 in 10. Today over 30 percent of seminary students are women, and women come close to outnumbering men at many mainline seminaries—United Church of Christ seminary enrollment is over 50 percent female, for example, as is the student body at Harvard Divinity School. In 1995, there were over 50,000 ordained women in America (including female rabbis), and the numbers rise every year.

Although women are being ordained in record numbers, they do not always find desirable posts waiting for them after seminary. Because women are more likely to enter the ministry as a second career, they are older when they first hit the job market, a strike against them in a profession already concerned with the graying of the ranks. And many female pastors find that large, prestigious churches are reluctant to hire female senior pastors.

Fig. 7.2. In Philadelphia on July 19, 1974, Marie Moorfield became the first woman ordained to the Episcopal priesthood. Five other women were ordained during the same ceremony. Although the ordinations were considered irregular, the church retroactively approved the action. Conservatives within the denomination continued to resist women's ordination. Bettmann/Corbis.

Throughout the nineteenth and twentieth centuries, ordained women had a hard time finding posts. Florence Spearing Randolph was ordained in the African Methodist Episcopal Zion Church in 1898, but she was only assigned to congregations that were "small, poor and struggling." In 1953, the National Council of Churches studied sixteen denominations and found that where women's ordination was allowed, "few women are ordained, and only a small proportion of them become pastors of churches." The situation has not improved with the explosion of women clergy since 1970. One of the first female Episcopal priests said, "It is an honor to . . . be among the first women to be ordained as ministers of the Gospel. However, don't let these actions lull you into thinking the battle is over! I may be ordained now, but I'm not experiencing hordes of people beating on my door to get me to come and serve as their pastor."[14] One sociologist painted women's prospects in the most dire terms: "In general [women clergy find placements in] small, struggling churches in economically sluggish communities, with members who are suffering from a relative lack of personal and financial resources and who are finding it difficult to replace themselves in the congregation." A 1992 study of Presbyterian ministers in San Francisco found that "women clergy do not have the choices, the mobility, the positions, or the pay of their male counterparts."[15]

Still, despite the stained-glass ceiling, the ordination of women has slowly reshaped the mainline church. Not least, seeing a woman in the pulpit has made many women in the pews feel welcome in the church. A letter Carter Heyward received after celebrating the Eucharist is illustrative: "I did not expect to be so personally affected by your presence here," her correspondent wrote. "I was unaware of the ways that I have felt excluded from God's inner circle of love until I experienced being included—both by the obvious fact of your inclusion and by you, as God's representative, including me. Somehow I've spent my life trying to be God's son, only to realize at last that I am God's daughter."[16]

The presence of women in the ranks of the clergy has also provided new models for religious behavior and for church leadership. Congregants have noted a new style of church leadership that extends to pastoral care, especially in mainline Protestantism—more nurturing and less distant or authoritative.

Some observers have noted that women who seek ordination pursue a job—or, in ecclesiastical jargon, answer a call—that no longer means very much. Since the 1960s, sociologists say, the clergy's relevance and influence have diminished in American society and even, with an ever-increasing emphasis on lay ministry, in church life. The relationship between the ordination of women and the decline in clergy status is something of a chicken-and-egg question. Did denominations begin to ordain women because ordination no longer held the status it once did? Or did clergy garner less and less respect as women increasingly filled their ranks?

The answer, no doubt, is both. By the 1960s, increased professional opportunities for male students who might otherwise have entered the ministry began to erode the clergy's status, as did countercultural challenges to the hegemony of Protestantism more broadly. Women's ordination doubtless contributed to a process of decline that was already in motion.

Complementarians, Egalitarians, and Other Evangelicals

The stained-glass ceiling in mainline Protestant churches indicates that mainliners have not fully embraced the goals of second-wave feminism, but, for the most part, mainliners are on board with at least bumper-sticker feminism: They believe women are human beings and equal to men. Evangelicals, however, remain hotly divided over not just the "f-word," but the roles of men and women in the home and at church. In evangelical circles one can find feminists who attend Take Back the Night marches and pay dues to the National Organization of Women; devotees of Phyllis Schlafly, who argues that women's divinely ordained calling is motherhood and that feminism is the cause of all of America's ills; and everything in between.

Secular pundits portray American evangelicals in stereotypes: The men are all sexists who expect hot dinners on the table at five o'clock sharp, and the women are all doormats who embrace the causes of their own oppression. But recent scholarship has offered a more nuanced portrait of evangelicals' gender politics. Historian R. Marie Griffith has argued that although many evangelical women do not identify as feminists, they are hardly passive automatons. Not only do they share some beliefs with secular feminists (abhorrence of domestic abuse, expecting equal pay for equal work), evangelical women find "power in their submission."[17]

A small cadre of evangelicals embrace the name *feminism*. If one wanted to date the birth of evangelical feminism as a movement or institution, one might point to September 1974, when eight women from North Park (Evangelical Covenant) Seminary decided that nascent Christian feminism needed a voice. They set down on paper their thoughts and questions as women who understood feminism as not only compatible with Christianity, but a natural outgrowth of it. They collected thirty dollars for postage and sent a mimeographed packet to 200 people: *Daughters of Sarah*, a magazine for Christian feminists, was born.

Evangelical feminists are no more homogeneous than any other sampling of feminists, but they agree on some basics. They believe, for example, that women should be able to work outside the home; they support the ordination of women; and they are devoted to making the church a more hospitable place for women, whether that means reconsidering the gendered language of hymns or setting up hotlines for battered wives.

Almost indistinguishable from the evangelical feminists are the "egalitarians." Insisting that God "gifts" men and women equally, evangelical egalitarians share many of the goals of the *Daughters of Sarah* crowd—but they distance themselves from the term "feminism," which not only retains red flag status in many evangelical circles but smacks of an individualism to which many Christians do not subscribe. Gilbert Bilezekian, teaching pastor at Willow Creek Community Church, is one of America's leading egalitarian scholars; his book *Beyond Sex Roles* is the most influential statement of egalitarian evangelicalism. Bilezekian is quick to point out that he is not a feminist: "I am not a feminist. Feminism is about power, and I am about servanthood. I'm not pursuing equality for its own sake; there is no mandate in the Bible to pursue equality. But there is a mandate to [encourage] full participation of women and men on the basis of spiritual gifts, not on the basis of sex."[18]

In the opposite corner of the ring reside conservative evangelicals who explicitly repudiate egalitarianism. While acknowledging that men and women are equal in the eyes of God, they maintain that men and women are not the same. God created the sexes with different gifts, and *He* intends them to spend their earthly lives engaged in complementary, but different tasks; indeed, evangelicals in this camp are often called "complementarians."

Protestants have always been—and they remain—a people of the book, so the Bible sits at the heart of evangelical battles over gender. Both sides—complementarians and egalitarians—recognize Scripture as their authority. And both sides believe that the Bible lays out a vision for how men and women should relate to one another at home, in church, and in the world.

When evangelicals read the Bible for gender, two basic—and time-honored—reading strategies emerge. The first is reading for narrative: When one considers the Bible as a whole, as one organic story of creation, fall, and redemption, what lessons about gender—about the social meanings of biological difference and the roles men and women should play in society—emerge? The second is the cut-and-paste approach to reading. Specific biblical verses may offer straightforward, succinct lessons about gender. Can we extract those verses from their narrative context and learn something about how God wants men and women to relate to one another?

Neither reading strategy has yielded an ideology of gender that all evangelicals can affirm. Instead, brothers and sisters in Christ find themselves disagreeing about all manner of questions: What is the best way to translate the Greek word *kephale*? What is Jesus' view of women? Were men and women different from the first moment of creation, or were gender differences a result of the fall?

Egalitarians' most persuasive biblical argument is that the story of the Bible arches towards the full equality of men and women. In the Garden of Eden, say egalitarians, Adam and Eve were equal. Only after the fall— after Adam and Eve disobeyed God and ate from the tree of knowledge— did gender differences mark men and women. Women's pangs in childbirth and men's being forced to toil on earth were punishments for transgressing God's command; they were not part of the original created order. As Mary Stewart Van Leeuwen explains, "There is no mention of man 'ruling' woman before the fall; there are no rigid role-assignments along the lines of a gendered public/private split. . . . But then sin comes, and because of sin, the subordination of woman, the dominance of man, and the resulting perversion of their reproductive and stewardly responsibilities."[19] Jesus, this argument continues, redeems humanity. Part of redeeming our brokenness is restoring the proper relations between men and women, the equal relations that characterized Adam and Eve before the fall. Jesus' moves in this direction can be seen, in part, in his befriending of women and making them disciples throughout the Gospels. The world is not yet redeemed, but the church is meant to live into redemption, and part of that living into redemption is striving for a healed practice of gender.

Complementarians respond that the premise of the argument is wrong— gender distinctions, they say, did not come in with the fall but were present at Creation. Adam was created before Eve, and with that chronological order came a normative hierarchy. (They often invoke 1 Timothy 2:12–13, emphasizing Paul's conjunction at the beginning of verse 13: "I do not permit a woman to teach or to have authority over a man; she must be silent. For Adam was formed first, then Eve.")

Evangelicals, often unable to shake free from a selectively literalistic scriptural hermeneutic, have not been content to consider the larger narrative of Scripture. They have also churned out dozens of books, given thousands of sermons, and spent countless hours puzzling over a few passages in the Pauline epistles that speak about the relationship of men and women, husbands and wives.

Three passages stand at the center of debate: Ephesians 5 (in which Paul instructs wives to submit to their husbands), 1 Corinthians 11 (in which Paul writes that the husband is the head of the wife), and 1 Timothy 2 (in which Paul tells Timothy that women cannot have authority over men). On the face of it, those passages seem to be straightforward: Women and men, if equal before God, are not the same; they have different, divinely ordained roles; and those roles are, at the very least, in tension with the vision of the good life that Betty Friedan, Patricia Ireland, and Germaine Greer have been extolling for nearly four decades.

Egalitarian scholars, however, have suggested other ways to read those passages. They have argued that if Christians would simply apply age-old hermeneutic principles to those Pauline passages, they would see that no clear biblical mandate for hierarchical gender roles exists. In a 1981 article in *Daughters of Sarah*, Virginia Ramey Mollenkott instructed readers on "interpreting difficult scriptures." First, one must approach the Bible historically, "mak[ing] allowance" for a first-century mindset that might have conditioned biblical texts. Second, clear passages "should always govern our interpretation of more difficult, obscure passages." Finally, readers should weigh interpretations of specific passages to make sure that they are not in tension with "major biblical themes"; 1 Timothy 2, for example, seems to conflict with the idea that the church comprises a priesthood of all believers.[20]

Egalitarians have also broken their teeth over New Testament Greek, arguing that many familiar English translations do not convey the meaning of the original. Much ink has been spilled over Ephesians 5:23, "for your husband is *kephale* of the wife." Usually translated as head, egalitarian scholars like Bilezekian maintain that the Greek in fact carries no connotation of authority; rather, it means "source," as in the source of a river.

Complementarian scholars like Phoenix Seminary's Wayne Grudem charge that insofar as they want to historicize or weigh "clear" passages against "troubling" ones, egalitarians are bucking the authority of Scripture. And, insofar as they want to argue about translation, egalitarians are playing games with Greek. Paul's meaning is simple and straightforward, according to Grudem and other complementarians. One can try to dream up alternate translations until kingdom come, but the meaning is clear. To return to Ephesians 5:23, Grudem insists that a quick glance at the Liddell-Scott-Jones lexicon of ancient Greek will convince even the most sympathetic reader that *kephale* does not mean source; and, he argues, even if *kephale* did mean source, this alternate translation does not make much sense: How can a husband be to his wife as a source is to a river? Nor does Grudem have much patience for the egalitarian interpretation of Ephesians 5:21, one that holds that wives and husbands should be "mutually submissive" to one another, not that wives should submit to their husbands. The idea that Ephesians 5:21 is best interpreted as "mutual submission . . . can be advocated only by failing to appreciate the precise meanings of the Greek words 'for be subject to' and 'one another.' Once these ideas are understood correctly, I think the idea of 'mutual submission' in marriage will be seen to be a myth without foundation in Scripture at all."[21]

These hermeneutical debates have not remained secreted away in the halls of evangelical seminaries. They have spilled over onto the pages of the women's study Bibles available at local bookstores. Evangelicals have always been devoted to Bibles that marry Scripture with a particular interpretation, as evidenced by the *Scofield* and the *Ryrie* study Bibles that placed a dispensationalist gloss on the entire Bible not only in the translation but also in the interpretive footnotes. Today, dozens of study Bibles beckon the eager consumer. There are study Bibles for couples, for African Americans, for dads, for teens. And there are study Bibles for women. The two most popular are the *Study Bible for Women*, published by Baker Books, and the *Women's Devotional Bible*, published by Zondervan.

At first blush, the two Bibles look remarkably similar. Both are pink, with a floral design on the cover. Both claim to address the topics that "[make] up the lives of Christian women in today's world" (*Women's Devotional Bible*), including "the birth or death of a child . . . body image . . . diet" (*Study Bible for Women*) and "Love. Marriage. Work. . . . Friends. Home." (*Women's Devotional Bible*). Both boast over fifty different female contributors, including "biblical scholars, nurses, midwives, psychologists, archaeologists, housewives, classicists, and art historians, missionaries, professors, pastors, academic administrators, businesswomen, sociologists, theologians, a novelist, students, evangelists, Sunday school teachers, mothers, aunts, sisters, and grandmothers" (*Study Bible for Women*); in short, "Women just like you, who get up each morning to face a day that's full of activity and opportunity for growth" (*Women's Devotional Bible*). All in all, these Bibles seek to "address the particular needs, interests, and concerns of women" (*Study Bible for Women*), providing the reader "a Bible for, by, and about today's woman" (*Women's Devotional Bible*).

A perusal of the commentaries and devotions inside the two volumes, however, reveals significant differences between the books. The *Women's Devotional Bible* offers encouragement and cheer; if the short readings throughout the volume do not challenge women to consider new interpretations of familiar Scripture passages, they certainly serve as a pick-me-up for a reader in a tough spot. The *Study Bible for Women*, by contrast, wrestles head-on with the passages in Paul that speak to women's roles.

Both Bibles treat Ephesians 5. The *Study Bible for Women* explains that "submit" is not synonymous with "subordinate," and suggests that it is a "false assumption . . . that if wives are to submit, then husbands must be in authority over them. Not so." The commentary goes on to explain that the essence of both wifely submission and husbandly love is "a completely voluntary giving up of oneself for another, first to God and then to each other." Without challenging the authority of Scripture, the commentators in the *Study Bible for Women* have, by reinterpreting a passage historically, marshaled the text to support female subordination and male headship, suggesting that husbands and wives should be equal partners in marriage.

Such an interpretation would have been unheard of fifty, or even thirty, years ago, but teachings about the doctrine of "mutual submission"—whereby biblical injunctions to submission are interpreted not as wives submitting to husbands, but as wives and husbands submitting to God and to one another—are popular among many evangelicals today.

Jane Hansen, the president of the international Pentecostal Women's Aglow Fellowship, recently proclaimed that biblical witness has long been distorted; mutual submission, she proclaimed, is the true meaning behind Paul's teachings in Ephesians. As historian R. Marie Griffith has shown, other Aglow writers back Hansen up: One popular 1985 publication encouraged readers to "look again at this area of ministry of submissions." Ephesians 5:22, the author observed, "may seem to be a difficult position for some of us who are married women to joyfully agree with, especially in an age when misunderstanding of this verse may have caused some abuse. We need to understand, however, what God desires and how He perceives it. . . . Submission to our husbands does not make us 'second-class citizens' or those who are ranked 'lower on the totem pole' as lesser beings than the husband. As viewed by God, we have a side-by-side relationship. He looks at us as equally important, but each is designed to function for His glory, in his or her role. . . . The entire Christian life is a submitted life."

The writer, in affirming men's and women's separate roles, does not seek to eradicate all gender differences, but she does suggest a reading of Ephesians 5 that would have seemed radical three decades ago—and that still seems radical, even heretical, to many evangelicals today.

In contrast to the *Study Bible for Women*, the *Women's Devotional Bible 2* (the sequel) offers a reading designed to illuminate Ephesians 5:22–33 without engaging directly with the verses about wifely submission. Written by marriage and family counselors Teresa and David Ferguson and Holly and Chris Thurman, the devotional reading coupled with Ephesians 5 is entitled "Love is Forever": "I watched him look into the window and check his reflection. He carefully combed his hair and straightened his tie. He had to be seventy years old, yet he acted eager as a schoolboy. He was a regular visitor to the nursing home. He was meeting his wife, a victim of Alzheimer's. His wife never spoke much. But it didn't seem to matter to him that he got no response from his wife. . . . Love, a rare commitment to care for another regardless of the response."

That the *Women's Devotional Bible 2* does not tackle the difficult verses head on, focusing instead on the following verse's injunction that husbands should love their wives as Christ loved the church, will not come as a great shock to the reader familiar with the original *Women's Devotional Bible*: It neglects to deal with the passage at all.

Bible Battles

Since the proper understanding of certain Greek terms is key to both complementarians' and egalitarians' arguments, it comes as no surprise that publishing houses with the copyrights to certain Bible translations have become a site of battle. Over the last decade, some Christians have called for a gender-inclusive translation of Scripture. And in 1992, the Committee on Bible translation, which oversees the New International Version (NIV) translation, undertook a gender-inclusive version. The proposed NIVI text—the New International Version: Inclusive Language Edition—would not refer to Jesus as "Sophia" or call the first person of the trinity "Mom," but it would, where appropriate, render "men" and "brothers" as "men and women" (or "people") and "brothers and sisters"; and it would replace the generic "he" with the gender-inclusive plural "they." The ire this translation provoked among American evangelicals makes nineteenth-century debates over infant baptism look tame.

Disagreement over the proper translation of gendered pronouns in

Scripture is nothing new. William Tyndale's 1526 translation of the New Testament rendered Matthew 5:9: "Blessed are the peacemakers, for they shall be called the children of God," even though the Greek word *huioi* is literally "sons." The King James Version makes a similar move with the Hebrew of the Old Testament: *ben* and *banim* are translated as "son" or "sons" 2,822 times and as "child" or "children" 1,533 times.[22]

Since the nineteenth century, feminists have argued that both women's emancipation and an accurate understanding of Scripture require new translations. In 1837, abolitionist Angelina Grimke affirmed that the Bible came from God on high, but that "King James's translators certainly weren't inspired!" The King James translation also tripped up Lucy Stone, who was horrified when, as a child, she first read Genesis 3:16: "Your desire shall be to thy husband, and he shall rule over thee." She determined to learn Hebrew and Greek, so that she could read Scripture in the original and "see how men had falsified the text."[23]

In 1987, Nancy Hardesty's *Inclusive Language in the Church* called for a gender-inclusive Bible. As an evangelical, wrote Hardesty, she believed in the "inspiration and authority of Scripture." Above all, she wanted biblical translations to be accurate. But sometimes, a translation that strives to include women can be more accurate. The King James Bible renders Psalm 68:11 as "The Lord gave the word: great was the company of those that published it." But well over a century ago some biblical scholars noted that the translation should actually read "of the female preachers there was a great host." (The Revised Standard Version, Hardesty notes, still gives the verse as "The Lord gives the command; great is the host of those who bore the tidings," but the New American Bible offers "And women who proclaim the good tidings are a great host.") Finally, says Hardesty, when there are "several different yet accurate translation possibilities, we should opt for the one which is most felicitous to the most people."[24]

During the 1980s several Bibles quietly inched towards gender inclusiveness. The Revised English Bible of 1989 (published by Oxford and Cambridge University presses) opted for "more gender inclusive reference where that has been possible without compromising scholarly integrity or English style." The Contemporary English Version, published by the evangelical house Thomas Nelson, also gestured towards gender inclusivity, and no one took much notice when it was published in 1995.[25]

Then, in the spring of 1997, *World* magazine, a conservative evangelical weekly, ran a series of articles on the new NIV translation, charging that a conspiracy was afoot to revise the very essence of Scripture. The article kicked off a storm of controversy. Complementarian scholars insisted both that the new translation was part of a feminist plot and that gender inclusivity did violence to Scripture. Just as the conservatives have portrayed the movement toward gender inclusivity as ideologically driven, so it would be easy to caricature the complementarians as driven by a political agenda. No doubt politics plays a role for both parties, but the complementarians are also worried about safeguarding the truth and accuracy of their sacred texts.

The translation debates are technical and complicated, and space permits only a brief discussion. In short, Grudem and others rightly note that translation is about interpretation, and that translation has the power to shape and reshape one's theology. They worry that the gender-inclusive translations play down or elide altogether important Christian doctrines. Consider, says Grudem, Matthew 16:24. The NIV renders this verse: "Then Jesus said to his disciples, 'If anyone would come after me, he must deny himself and take up his cross and follow me.'" The proposed inclusive NIV would have the verse read "Then Jesus said to his disciples, 'those who would come after me must deny themselves and take up their cross and follow me." The new version, says Grudem, implies that the group has some collective responsibility for one cross; it erases the individual's singular responsibility and singular shame.[26]

Or, says John Piper, look at the NIVI's proposed translation of 1 Corinthians 15:21. The original NIV gives the verse as "For since death came through a man [*anthropos*], the resurrection of the dead comes also through a man." The gender-inclusive version would read "For since death came through a human being, the resurrection of the dead comes also through a human being." Piper says that in the new version, the "masculinity of Jesus is downplayed." But defenders say Piper's argument is poppycock: The NIVI never denies Jesus' maleness. Here, they are simply accurately translating the Greek term *anthropos*, which does not denote masculinity.[27]

In the wake of the *World* magazine article, leading conservatives like Paige Patterson and Jerry Falwell chimed in, decrying the new translation. Plans to publish the gender-inclusive translation slowly crumbled.[28]

Denominational Spotlight: Women and the Southern Baptist Convention

Beginning in 1979, the Southern Baptist Convention (SBC) experienced what moderate Baptists refer to as "the fundamentalist takeover," a change of leadership in favor of conservative Baptists unswervingly devoted to biblical inerrancy and male headship, Baptists who evinced less interest in social justice than some of their coreligionists would like, Baptists who have traded in the historic Baptist emphasis on the separation of church and state for a Moral Majority–style, right-wing political activism. A decade later, those Baptists were in firm control of the denomination and most of its seminaries.

The so-called takeover had been brewing since two of the most outspoken conservatives, Paige Patterson (then a seminary student) and Judge Paul Pressler, met at Cafe du Monde in New Orleans to discuss a long-term strategy for seizing control of the SBC.[29] In the winter and spring of 1979, Patterson and Pressler headed up a campaign in fifteen states, organizing conservatives to attend the annual convention and defeat moderates; the strategy, which included busing in voters to conventions, worked. Adrian Rogers, a conservative Baptist pastor from Memphis, Tennessee, was elected president of the SBC. No moderates have been elected president since, and the conservative presidents have appointed like-minded men (and occasionally women) to denominational committees, driving many moderates out of posts in denominational agencies and, especially, at Baptist seminaries.

It is under this new conservative leadership that the SBC has made controversial moves like calling for evangelism of Jews and boycotts of Disney. And it is under this new leadership that the SBC has tried to curb women's ordination and help husbands reassert authority over their wives.

The SBC made headlines when, in 1998, it voted to add a statement on families to its 1963 doctrinal statement, the Baptist Faith and Message. First drafted in 1925, the Faith and Message is a guideline rather than a creed. Neither individual believers nor individual churches are bound by it, although employees of Southern Baptist agencies are required to endorse the statement. The new article—the first addition to the Faith and Message in thirty-five years—defined marriage as a heterosexual, lifelong commitment. It also urged parents to discipline their children. No one was surprised to see the SBC take a stand against homosexuality or in favor of discipline. The controversy erupted over the third paragraph of the new article. After stating that "the husband and wife are of equal worth before God," the article declared that a husband "has the God-given responsibility to provide for, to protect, and to lead his family. A wife is to submit herself graciously as the servant the church willingly submits to the headship of Christ. She, being in the image of God as is her husband and thus equal to him, has the God-given responsibility to respect her husband and to serve as his helper in managing the household and nurturing the next generation."

A seven-member committee wrote the article, and it passed by an over-whelming majority in a show-of-hands vote on June 9, the first day of the SBC's 1998 convention—the same day that Paige Patterson was elected president of the denomination. The next day, Tim Owings, pastor of First Baptist Church of Augusta, Georgia, offered an amendment that would urge mutual submission. Had Owings's amendment passed, the language of the new article would have read: "Both husband and wife are to submit graciously to each other as servant leaders in the home, even as the church willingly submits to the lordship of Christ." Owings and his supporters believed this language was more in the spirit of Ephesians 5:21, where Paul urges men and women to "submit to one another out of reverence for Christ."

The Owings amendment failed. Dorothy Patterson, Paige Patterson's wife and a professor of women's studies at Southeastern Baptist Theological Seminary, and Mary Mohler, wife of Southern Baptist Theological Seminary president Albert Mohler, were the two women who served on the committee that drafted the original article. Commenting on Owings's proposed amendment, Patterson allowed that Ephesians 5:21 does call for mutual submission, but that call in no way mitigates Paul's clear instructions in Ephesians 5:22–23. Those two verses, said Dorothy Patterson, make plain that wives are to submit to husbands. "When it comes to submitting to my husband even when he's wrong, I just do it. He is accountable to God." Mary Mohler echoed Patterson's sentiment: "The whole issue comes down to a matter of Scripture," she said. "It's not my prerogative to go through and start cutting and slashing passages. . . . It is my pleasure and responsibility to submit to the leadership of my husband in our home."[30]

The article garnered attention long after the Southern Baptists left Salt Lake City. On August 26, 131 evangelical leaders placed a full-page ad in *USA Today*, telling the SBC "you are right!" Signatories included Franklin Graham and Anne Graham Lotz, two of Billy Graham's children, Promise Keepers founder Bill McCartney and his wife Lyndi, and Joseph Stowell, president of Moody Bible Institute. In July 1999, Campus Crusade for Christ, an evangelical outreach organization founded by Bill Bright, adopted the SBC's family article. And in April 2000, Paige and Dorothy Patterson, and 550 other couples, renewed their wedding vows in Brinkley Chapel, the spiritual center of Southeastern Baptist Seminary. In vows the Pattersons wrote themselves, husbands pledged "sacrificially to love [their wives] as Jesus loves His church," "to be the spiritual leader of our union, to provide spiritual example through my walk with Christ, to teach the Bible, and to pray for my family, to lead family worship," and "to avoid

Fig. 7.3. Paige Patterson, shown in 1998 with his wife, Dorothy, was one of the architects of the conservative takeover of the Southern Baptist Convention in 1979. Douglas C. Pizac/ AP Photo.

all that is pornographic, impure, or unholy." Wives promised "to make our home a place of repose and comfort," "to honor [their husbands] as the spiritual leader of our home," to "graciously submit to your servant leadership," and to "regard my responsibilities as wife and mother as priority above all else except God."

Many Baptist men and women endorsed the article. Becky Thomas, of Lenoir, North Carolina, wrote a letter to her state Baptist organ the *Biblical Recorder*, informing readers that she vowed to submit to her husband on her wedding day, and that was a vow she stood by. Feminist critics, Thomas wrote, insisted that the family article was disrespectful to women. But "the only time I feel 'not respected,'" wrote Thomas, "is when I read about women upset about this resolution. They say I must be a doormat or an idiot to submit to the man I love."[31]

Some Baptists, however, were critical. Reba Cobb, a member of Crescent Hill Baptist Church in Louisville, Kentucky, and former director of the Center for Women and Children there, worried that the language about submission would encourage battered wives to stay in abusive relationships. Robert Parham, executive director of the Baptist Center for Ethics in Nashville, said that the new article put forward a vision of the family grounded in contemporary culture, not in Scripture. When Jesus spoke of the family, said Parham, he emphasized loyalty to God above loyalty even to kin. The SBC's new statement, according to Parham, "forgot Jesus and made June Cleaver a biblical model for motherhood."

Nor did Baptist leadership across the country fall into line. In November 1998, Texas Baptists adopted a resolution on biblical equality, stating that men and women were equal in the eyes of God, that both should participate in rearing children, and that husbands and wives should "submit to one another as a witness to the world of the transforming power of servant leadership." It was a pointed rejoinder to the family article the SBC had adopted just four months before. On November 9, 1999, the Baptist General Convention of Texas voted to uphold the 1963 Baptist Faith and Message as its guiding principle; it was a pointed move that rejected the new family article without ever having to vote on the article itself. In November 2000, Illinois Baptists failed to pass a measure that would endorse the 1998 article.

Still, for all its controversy, the new SBC plank made at least two converts. In September 1998, SBC press ballyhooed about George and JoAnn Carson, who "started attending Calvary Baptist Church as a direct result of the Southern Baptist Convention's adoption of a statement on the family in June in Salt Lake City." Born-again Christians, the Carsons had fallen away from church because all the churches they attended felt "more like social groups than churches." Then, George Carson read a newspaper article about the SBC's "statement about the man being the head of the house. That just struck a chord. We knew this was right." The Carsons thumbed the Yellow Pages for a Baptist church and landed at Calvary Baptist. Finally, said George, they had found "home."[32]

Evangelicals remain divided over women's ordination. Some evangelicals maintain that callings follow the gifts of the Spirit, not sex. For example, at Willow Creek Community Church—the dazzling megachurch in suburban Chicago—women teach and preach alongside men, although men still occupy the most prominent leadership roles. Indeed, in a move that sparked tremendous controversy among fellow evangelicals, Willow Creek issued a statement requiring that all members be able to sit joyfully under a female teacher or worship leader.

Not all evangelicals have signed on. Many, drawing support from the

Pauline prohibitions of women standing in authority over men, insist that ordaining women is unbiblical. These evangelicals underscore that they do not wish women to serve in "menial, insignificant . . . positions" in the church, but simply that they cannot hold spiritual authority over men. Women, in this view, can hold positions of administrative authority, and they can teach or counsel other women; they can make announcements, lead songs, give testimony, and pray in public; but they are not to exercise "authoritative, elder-like teaching over men."[33]

Baptists have straddled the fence on women's ordination. The autonomy of the local church is a hallmark of Baptist polity, so while some churches ordain women, not all do—and a statewide association can choose to "disfellowship" a church that ordains women if the association sees fit. Individual churches in the SBC have ordained women for thirty years—in 1998, there were about 1,300 female Baptist ministers—but it has always been difficult for them to find jobs pastoring churches. In 2000, the SBC amended the Baptist Faith and Message to make that difficulty official: Though women could continue to seek ordination, they could no longer be appointed as senior pastors of SBC churches. "While both men and women are gifted for service in the church, the office of pastor is limited to men as qualified by Scripture," explained SBC president James Merritt. "That statement is extremely limited in scope as it should be. We do believe that the role of the senior pastor in a church should be filled by the male only, which is exactly what God's Word teaches. We do, however, also strongly affirm the spiritual giftedness of women and their ability, in fact, even necessity to serve the church through various means and ministry. We will continue to both stand by the truth of God's Word, but also affirm the strategic role that women play in our Baptist churches here and around the world."[34]

Not surprisingly, that decision left some female Baptist pastors dismayed. Linda McKinnish Bridges, professor of New Testament at Baptist Theological Seminary, responded by urging her fellow Baptist female ministers to "travel on, sister." "Now, my dear sister, please know that you can leave the family farm," Bridges contends. "Leave home. You will be fine. There are other places waiting for your leadership."

But not all female Baptist ministers agreed with Bridges. Jane Ann Welch, a music minister at Emmanuel Baptist Church in Overland Park, Kansas, endorsed the SBC's move in 2000. "[Women] have a wonderful opportunity to be used [on church staffs]," she said. "But I do think the Bible does refer to men in that pastoral position." In the words of Amy

Giles, who directs the children's ministry at Mulberry Baptist Church in Charlotte, North Carolina, "I think it's pretty clear in the Bible that ministers and leaders of ministry should be men. Personally, I think women should take a more submissive role."[35]

Men's Revival: Promise Keepers and Masculinity

Urging women, in church and at home, to "take a more submissive role" is just one piece of the SBC's strategy in the gender wars. Graciously submitting wives need husbands who are willing and able to lead. Conservative evangelicals wish not only to combat "militant feminism," but to revive a vigorous—perhaps even militant—masculinity.

American men, conservative religious leaders cry, are in a crisis. Women have sent men mixed messages, asking them to be strong and tender, attentive dads who pitch in with housework but also draw huge salaries and advance at work. Many conservative Christians believe there is a two-step solution to the crisis American men face. First, get men back into the churches. Second, teach them how to lead as God intends men to lead.

New Orleans–based Baptist minister Fred Luter felt a special responsibility to bring men back to church. In 1986, he accepted a call from Franklin Avenue Baptist, then a struggling church with just sixty-five members. "Out of those 65 members," said Luter, "you could count the men on one hand. I wanted to reach men." Luter tried everything he could think of to bring men to church. Eventually, Luter concluded that maybe men simply did not want to spend their Sundays at worship, but he knew men always wanted to watch sports. So he hosted a men's social at his home, watching a pay-per-view boxing match. Forty-five men turned up for the boxing match, and the next Sunday five of those men attended Luter's church. Eventually, Luter lured dozens and dozens of men back to the pews. And once they were there, he set about empowering them to lead their families and community. Luring men to Christ, he believed, would save the men and their families.[36]

Luter's concerns are as old as America. Since the late seventeenth century, women have outnumbered men on church rolls, and Christian observers from Puritans to twentieth-century department store magnates and athletes—usually male Christian observers—have bemoaned this demographic imbalance, declaring periodically that "women have had charge of the church work long enough," and plotting to get more men into the pews. Those schemes have taken the form of evangelistic lunches for Wall Street brokers, imaginative novels portraying Jesus as a businessman, and, above all, efforts to yoke Christianity to sports: During the Progressive era, churches built bowling alleys in their basements and organized baseball leagues. In the 1960s, writers like James Hefley cranked out biographies of Christian sports heroes. From the books to the bowling alleys, all of these efforts attempted to show that Christianity was not for sissies, that Christian men were manly men.

The latest incarnation of "muscular Christianity" is Promise Keepers. Founded by former University of Colorado football coach Bill McCartney in 1991, Promise Keepers is an interdenominational parachurch movement designed to bring men to church and to help churched men reestablish leadership of their families. Promise Keepers held rallies (the athletic language is not an accident) that were open only to men. Rally speakers ranged from prominent evangelists to witnessing sports stars, and those in attendance were encouraged not only to dedicate their lives to Christ, but also to reaffirm their roles as fathers and husbands. "I'm not suggesting you ask for your role back," said Promise Keeper leader Tony Evans. "I'm urging you to take it back. . . . There can be no compromise here. If you're going to lead, you must lead."

The movement has many cheerleaders. In a talk called "Bringing White Guys to their Knees: How Promise Keepers Faked Right, Ran Left and Scored Big," Larry Iannaccone, professor of economics at Santa Clara University in California, told the Religious Research Association in Houston that a Promise Keeping man was a modern woman's dream come true. "Take everything women might want their husbands to do better, and in front of it put the phrase 'Real men . . . ,' and that's what Promise Keepers advocated." And many wives say they're reaping the promises their husbands are keeping. Jeanne Parrott credits Promise Keepers with bringing to her marriage "more peace, more gentleness [and] . . . deeper respect." Valerie Bridgeman Davis, "a professor of religion and an avowed and long-standing womanist/feminist," says that Promise Keepers taught her husband Don to "take responsibility for his part of the marriage" and to forgo some of his own "ego and dreams in order to be a loving husband and loving father." [37]

Many, however, have criticized Promise Keepers. The leaders of the women's movement detected an incipient patriarchalism in the Promise Keepers' rhetoric, a criticism echoed by many mainline Protestants. Noting the affinities between McCartney and leaders of the Religious Right, these critics suspected that the Promise Keepers' coupling of the soft-breasted

Fig. 7.4. Promise Keepers, founded by Bill McCartney in the early 1990s, encouraged men to be good and faithful husbands, fathers, and churchgoers. McCartney also encouraged racial reconciliation at the organization's stadium rallies across the country. Chris Gardner/ AP Photo.

male with the assumption of male authority was merely a front for the antifeminist agenda of the Religious Right. They also saw the movement as an attempt to undermine women's ordination, a phenomenon far more common among mainline Protestants than among evangelicals, despite the fact that evangelicals had been pioneers in according equal rights to women in the nineteenth and early twentieth centuries.

While McCartney and other Promise Keepers gave their critics plenty of rhetorical fodder, it was also true that mainline Protestant leaders offered few alternatives to the Promise Keepers' ideology. Numerous social commentators in the 1990s had noted the confusion that many American men felt in the age of feminism. Promise Keepers provided both an ideology and an ethic for men of faith in the final decade of the twentieth century; mainline Protestantism supplied only a criticism of that ideology.

Feminism and American Protestantism

As with other issues facing Protestants in contemporary America, there is no consensus on the matter of feminism. Whereas some see the feminist movement as a giant leap forward in advancing women to a place of equality in society and in the church, others see biblical feminism as an oxymoron, a contradiction of both Christian tradition and the Bible itself. These divergent interpretations both claim scriptural warrant, and both sides marshal a flurry of proof texts in support of their arguments.

Despite some fundamental disagreements, however, what is indisputably true is that the women's movement has changed Protestantism over the past several decades. The growing presence of female clergy has altered patterns of church leadership and communication; the increasingly feminine composition of seminaries has changed the culture surrounding theological education and formation. Feminist theology has forced a reconsideration of traditional notions about God, and gender-inclusive language has filtered into virtually all Protestant worship, in greater or lesser degrees, both mainline and evangelical.

Finally, the women's movement (at least by indirection) has prompted men to reconsider their roles in the home, the church, and society. Not all Protestants were happy with the ideologies and the strategies put forward by the Promise Keepers movement, but for the first time in several decades the issue of men's spirituality and responsibility became a topic for lively discussion among American Protestants.

CHAPTER EIGHT

Protestants and Homosexuality

Forty years ago, a good chunk of space on the bookshelf of most seminary students, ethicists, or pastors would have been taken up by James Hastings's multivolume *Encyclopedia of Religion and Ethics*. The great reference work would have disappointed those curious about what today we refer to as sexual orientation: Between "homoiousia" and "honesty," where "homosexuality" should appear, there is no entry. Volume XI does offer a lengthy discussion of "sex," where one can read about parthenogenesis, the castration of insects, and sex transformation in crabs, but nothing on human sexuality. There is an entry on sodomy, which Hastings, quoting from the *Century Dictionary*, defines as "unnatural sexual relations, as between persons of the same sex, or with beasts." The entry surveys what Babylonians, Hindus in India, and Australian aboriginals made of the practice. There's a discussion of the Hebrews, too, which focuses on Genesis 19—the story of Lot in Sodom, whence the word "sodomy" comes. There is no mention of what Christians make of sodomy, however.

Much has changed in American Christendom since the days when the safest thing to say about homosexuality was nothing, when it was widely accepted that homosexuals should be electroshocked into normalcy. Today there is no consensus at all about homosexuality: Is it an orientation or an action? Can you be healed of it? What causes homosexuality anyway? Is it a malfunction of the hypothalamus or an affliction affecting those who grew up with overbearing mothers who refused to shave? Is it a sin? Is it something to be overcome or something to be proud of? Although there is no agreement about homosexuality, however, one thing is clear: Questions about sexuality have come to dominate many of the discussions among American Protestants. Those discussions threaten to divide the church universal, to separate evangelicals from mainliners, and to fracture individual denominations.

Sex and Scripture

Those who wonder if American Protestants still consider themselves the people of the book need only look at the role of Scripture in the debate over sexuality. As Mary Jo Osterman, editor of the gay Christian organ *Open Hands*, noted in 1993, "no issue is more fraught with tensions and disagreements in our churches today than that of interpreting biblical passages related to homosexual behavior." Christians who condemn homosexuality say there are half a dozen of those passages, and all of them are on their side.

What is at stake, say conservative Christians, is far more than who is going to bed with whom; what is at stake is the very authority of Scripture, which, the traditionalists claim, could not be clearer in its condemnation of homosexual sexuality. In the words of systematic theologian Wolfhart Pannenberg, "If a church were to let itself be pushed to the point where it ceased to treat homosexual activity as a departure from the biblical norm, and recognized homosexual unions as a personal partnership of love equivalent to marriage, such a church would stand no longer on biblical ground but against the unequivocal witness of Scripture. A church that took this step would cease to be the one, holy, catholic, and apostolic Church."

Pundits draw on an array of passages to prove that the Bible prohibits homosexual sex, but six passages crop up most frequently: Genesis 9:1–8, Leviticus 18:22, Leviticus 20:13, Romans 1:26–27, 1 Corinthians 6:9–10, and 1 Timothy 1:10. Conservative Christians often begin their discussions of homosexuality with the two passages from Leviticus: "You [masculine] shall not lie with a male as with a woman; it is an abomination" (Leviticus 18:22, NRSV) and "If a man lies with a male as with a woman, both of them have committed an abomination; they shall be put to death; their blood is upon them" (Leviticus 20:13, NRSV). The Bible could not be less equivocal, they say. Men having sex with men as they have with women—

that is, homosexual sex—are committing an abomination, one punishable by death.

Many scholars, however, have disputed that reading. Rabbinic commentators for centuries have struggled to interpret these laws. According to Saul Olyan, "Some have understood them to prohibit specifically the insertive role in intercourse; others, the insertive and receptive roles; still others all sex acts between males."[1] The Anchor Bible, the standard reference work on Hebrew Scripture, says that the Leviticus 20:13 passage, which is found in a long list of relationships that are forbidden because they are incestuous, prohibits not any homosexual intercourse, but that intercourse which is incestuous, such as homosexual sex between brothers.

The weight that the story of Sodom lends to the antigay perspective is also questionable. In the story of Sodom, Lot offers hospitality to two angels for the night.

> But before they lay down, the men of the city, the men of Sodom, both young and old, all the people to the last man, surrounded the house; and they called to Lot, "What are the men who came to you tonight? Bring them out to us, so that we may know them." Lot went out of the door to the men, shut the door after him, and said, "I beg you, my brothers, do not act so wickedly. Look, I have two daughters who have not known a man; let me bring them out to you, and do to them as you please; only do nothing to these men, for they have come under the shelter of my home."

A similar story appears in Judges 19:16–30.

Conservatives usually interpret the Sodom story as a clear-cut condemnation of gay sex. The Sodomites want to have sex with Lot's two male guests, and Lot wants to prevent the men from doing this "wicked" deed. But many Old Testament scholars disagree, insisting that the sin in question is not homosexual sex, but the Sodomites' lack of hospitality. And insofar as sex is an issue, the sin is rape, not same-sex intercourse.

Gay-friendly critics have also argued that Christians who care about reading the Bible consistently are hard pressed to use the Old Testament to bolster their arguments against homosexuality. As for the passages in Leviticus, they are fairly straightforward, but the critics point out that Levitical dietary laws are equally clear. Most Christians hold that the only explicit Old Testament moral strictures to which they are bound are the

Ten Commandments. In the words of ethicists Letha Scanzoni and Virginia
Ramey Mollenkott, if Christians are going to start subscribing to the other
603 commandments God gave at Sinai, they are going to have to stop
"eating rare steak, wearing mixed fabrics, and having marital intercourse
during the menstrual period" too.[2]

When it comes to the New Testament, Romans 1:26–27 has been the
centerpiece of the debate: "For this reason God gave them up to degrading
passions. Their women exchanged natural intercourse for unnatural, and in
the same way also the men, giving up natural intercourse with women,
were consumed with passion for one another. Men committed shameless
acts with men and received in their own persons the due penalty for their
error." Here, men were punished when they had sexual relations with other
men. In this passage, Paul discusses a group of men who refused to worship
and give thanks to God. Because they refused to worship God, He abandoned them. After being forsaken by God, they fell into morally deplorable
practices, including some sorts of same-sex sexual relationships.

Many evangelicals read this passage as a clear admonition against homosexual sex: It is, they say, plainly unnatural. (Some conservatives mis-
construe the passage altogether, claiming that God abandoned the wicked
men because they lapsed into homosexual practices. What actually happens
in the text is the reverse; the men turn to homosexual sex after God aban-
dons them.) But more liberal Protestants have suggested other interpretations. The debate concerns the word "nature." Paul may not be saying that
heterosexual sex is always natural and homosexual sex always a perversion.
He may have thought, says liberal scholar Walter Wink,

> that those whose behavior he condemned were "straight," and that
> they were behaving in ways that were unnatural to them. Paul believed
> that everyone was straight. He had no concept of homosexual orien-
> tation. The idea was not available in his world. There are people that
> are genuinely homosexual by nature (whether genetically or as a result
> of upbringing no one really knows, and it is irrelevant). For such a
> person it would be acting contrary to nature to have sexual relations
> with a person of the opposite sex.[3]

Lewis Smedes, a noted sexual ethicist who was on the faculty of Fuller
Theological Seminary until his retirement, offers a similar reading. "Who
were these people, the ones who were having sex with partners of their
own gender?" he asks.

"Temple prostitutes? Pederasts? People engaged in wild orgies? Nobody knows for sure. But it seems to me that we can be certain of who they were not; they were not the sorts of people that I am talking about in this essay—Christian homosexual persons who are living out their need for abiding love in monogamous and covenanted partnerships of love." Smedes reminds readers that "what [Paul] meant by 'contrary to nature' none of us knows for sure." Throughout history, most Christian readers, he says, have assumed that "natural" sex is sex that leads to the procreation of children.[4]

The verses from Corinthians and Timothy include words often translated as "homosexuality" in lists of immoral, forbidden behavior. Conservatives say that, like Romans, the meaning of these passages is clear: Homosexuality is every bit as forbidden as fornication, idolatry, theft, and the other sins listed in the passage. Other readers disagree, saying that the meanings of the two Greek words often translated as "homosexuals"—malakoi and aresenokoitai—are far from clear. They could mean pederasts, prostitutes, or masturbators.

Many gay Christians, though willing to go head-to-head over the meaning of Koinic Greek, say that such readings are beside the point. The question according to Mary Jo Osterman is not so much what Paul says in one or two verses in Romans, but how we read the Bible. True enough, some gay Christians concede, Paul is neither "neutral nor affirming of the homosexual behavior he found in his world."[5] But he also allowed slavery and was not too fond of women who spoke above a whisper. His two verses in Romans, this argument goes, are contrary to Jesus' overarching message of love and liberation. And gay advocates are quick to point out that Jesus himself has nothing whatsoever to say about homosexuality.

In short, the debate over homosexuality is not—as many conservative critics like to claim—a debate over Scriptural authority. Many gay mainline Protestants affirm the centrality of Scripture. The question is rather a hermeneutical one: How do we interpret Scripture? How do we deal with problems of translation? How do we decide which sections of the Old Testament are binding? How do we determine that some of Paul's dictums—like women covering their hair—are culturally bound? How do we weigh the New Testament against the Old Testament? How do we weigh Jesus' words against Paul's? In short, how do we read the Bible? In Mary Jo Osterman's words, do we treat the Bible like a "rule book" or a "written witness of a magnificent story of God's love"?[6]

The Larger Picture

Not all Protestant theological discourse about homosexuality is limited to
the cut-and-paste approach to Scriptural hermeneutics. Indeed, some of
today's most respected theologians have turned their attention to examining
questions of sexuality in a broader context of Christian theology and ethics.

Conservative Protestants are also fond of making what is called the
"created order argument." The opening of Genesis, this argument goes,
makes clear that humanity is created male and female, that the divine order
is for a man and a woman to unite together, that one of the essential goods
of that union is the procreation of children. Gay couples do not achieve
male-female complementarity, and they cannot procreate. Richard Hays,
noted ethicist at Duke, makes this argument forcefully in his study *The
Moral Vision of the New Testament*. Not only, says Hays, do all the passages
in Scripture that discuss homosexuality "express unqualified disapproval,"
but

> From Genesis 1 onward, Scripture affirms repeatedly that God has
> made man and woman for one another and that our sexual desires
> rightly find fulfillment within heterosexual marriage. . . . This nor-
> mative canonical picture of marriage provides the positive backdrop
> against which the Bible's few emphatic negations of homosexuality
> must be read.[7]

One of the most influential theological works in moving discussion
about homosexuality beyond selectively literal interpretations of Scripture
is a short essay by Rowan Williams, the (Anglican) archbishop of Wales.
Though hardly a household name in America, Williams is a leading English
theologian, rumored to be the next archbishop of Canterbury. In 1996 he
published "The Body's Grace," an essay that seeks to recover the theological aspects of desire. "The whole story of creation, incarnation, and our
incorporation into the fellowship of Christ's body tells us that God desires
us, *as if we were God*, as if we were that unconditional response to God's
giving that God's self makes in the life of the Trinity," he writes. "We are
created so that we may be caught up in this, so we grow into the whole-
hearted love of God by learning that God loves us as God loves God."
Williams argues that if one wants to tease a sexual ethic out of the Bible,
"there is a good deal to steer us away from assuming that reproductive sex
is a solitary norm." A theology of the body's grace, he suggests, opens up
space for Christian homosexuality.

This spare essay was picked up by a rising star of postliberal theology, Eugene Rogers, who teaches in the religion department at the University of Virginia. Rogers published a book that reads as an extended meditation on "The Body's Grace." Grounding his argument in trinitarianism, rather than a selectively literal interpretation of Scripture, Rogers suggests that the Spirit is undeniably at work among gay Christians, extending God's grace to them every bit as much as the Spirit once extended God's grace to Gentiles.

Rogers argues that God can use bodily relationships to sanctify couples—that is, to bind people to loving partners from whom they cannot easily escape, and God can use that discipline to catch them up into the exchange of grace and gratitude that constitutes God's own trinitarian life. In short, God can use bodies to make people morally better. Rogers tries to recover for all marriages, not just same-sex ones, the idea that marriage is for sanctification rather than satisfaction or procreation. "Gay and lesbian Christians need have no quarrel with the special aptness of the Genesis account of male and female and their procreation as normative for the *species*, as long as not everyone has to instantiate it to be in God's image." That is, the homosexuality debates have something to teach that opposite-sex couples have largely lost: what marriage is for.

Christians and Gays in the Public Square

Christians slugging it out over sexuality have made headlines over the last decade, but the issue is older than that. The Stonewall uprising—in June 1969—placed homosexuality as a political issue squarely in the view of the American public, though evangelicals did not take up the fight until the late 1970s. Then, Anita Bryant, who was a spokeswoman for the Florida Citrus Growers—her slogan was "A day without orange juice is like a day without sunshine"—and a former Miss Oklahoma, realized that homosexuals posed a menacing threat to her children, and she took action.

Bryant, a devout Southern Baptist who had accepted Jesus at age eight, was no stranger to politics. Lyndon Johnson had invited her to the White House over a dozen times, and she sang *The Battle Hymn of the Republic* and *God Bless America* at the Democratic and Republican national conventions. In January 1977, when the Dade County Board of Commissioners considered passing an ordinance that would prohibit discrimination against homosexuals, Bryant was horrified. She wrote letters to the commissioners and attended the meeting at which a vote would be taken. Bryant was not

Fig. 8.1. In 1977 Anita Bryant, a former Miss Oklahoma, led a successful campaign to repeal an ordinance in Dade County, Florida, that prohibited discrimination based on sexual orientation. Bettmann/Corbis.

alone; other opponents of the measure turned up at the meeting, including Charles Couey, pastor of the South Dade Baptist Church, who read aloud Romans 1:22–32. (He was not the only Christian who could cite Scripture. A state legislator in Florida read portions of Leviticus aloud on the Tallahassee senate floor.)

The ordinance passed, but Bryant did not accept defeat. "When the homosexuals burn the Holy Bible in public, how can I stand by silently?" she asked in 1977. She founded Save Our Children, Inc. and set to work collecting signatures for a referendum to repeal the county ordinance. Bryant—described by one reporter as "one who believed in blueberry and apple pie, not to mention God, country and the difference between men and women"—captured the attention of the media, attracting the attention of journalists across the South and earning a spot on the cover of *Newsweek*. Bryant's campaign was successful. On June 7, 1977, by a margin of more than two to one, the citizens voted to repeal the ordinance. "Tonight the laws of God and the cultural values of man have been vindicated," said Bryant.[8] At the center of Bryant's campaign (as the name of her grassroots organization suggested) were children. They needed saving not from their own sinful natures, as Jonathan Edwards might have mused, but from predatory homosexuals who would either convert them to their wicked ways or, worse, molest them. Where homosexuality lurked, Bryant and others believed, pedophilia was close behind. As Bryant said, over and over, "Homosexuals cannot reproduce, so they must recruit."

Focusing on children was, of course, a shrewd political move, and it allowed Bryant, a mother, to stand at the center of a public political battle. It also prefigured the involvement of other evangelical women, such as Beverly LaHaye, in the activities of the Religious Right, just a few years later.

Second-wave feminism had come to Dade County by 1977, but Bryant rejected its assurance that women could speak in the public square as effectively, and appropriately, as men; she had articulated her conviction that feminist reforms were by and large "fostered by women with lesbian tendencies." At the outset of her campaign against the Dade County ordinance, she confessed to her pastor, "Brother Bill," that she worried that her political role displeased the Lord. "I'm just a woman. I shouldn't be this involved." There's no scriptural model for women sallying forth into the public square, she said. But her pastor disagreed. "Anytime, throughout the Bible, when God's men didn't take their stand and were not there when God wanted them, He raised up a woman," Brother Bill assured her. "Look at Esther, look at Deborah." The model was clear—men were the preferred activists, but when no man could fit the bill, a woman would do.[9]

Not only did the Bible provide models of female activists, but American history supplied examples as well. Evangelical women had couched their political activism in maternal terms since the nineteenth century. More recently, segregationist women had entered the political sphere in order to save their children from a different sexual threat—the miscegenation that was sure to follow school integration. Soon enough, Bryant was persuaded that she not only could speak out against homosexuality, but that as a woman she had a special obligation to do so. When she contemplated the moral decay of the country, she wrote in her memoir, she felt "a particular woman's pain that he [her husband Bob Green] was unable to share with me." Her primary concern, she emphasized again and again, "was voiced as a mother."[10]

Bryant's influence—and infamy—spread throughout the country. Gay activists vilified her. When, two weeks after the repeal of the Dade County ordinance, a thirty-three-year-old gay man in San Francisco was stabbed fifteen times by a man shouting "Faggot, faggot, faggot," some laid the blame at Bryant's feet. "My son's blood is on her hands," said the victim's septuagenarian mother. At the annual San Francisco Gay Freedom Pride parade, five days after the stabbing, activists waved placards with Bryant's smiling face, alongside pictures of Hitler and Idi Amin.

Evangelicals, for their part, saw in Bryant's campaign something of a template for dealing with homosexuality. Other Christians mimicked Bryant's child-centered rhetoric, suggesting, as Jerry Falwell did in a 1981 fundraising letter, that "homosexuals do not reproduce! They recruit! And, many of them are after my children and your children."

In addition to the focus on children, three other arguments that Bryant and others popularized in the late 1970s have remained remarkably resilient. First is the idea that nondiscrimination laws grant, in Bryant's words, "special privileges to homosexuals," rather than simply guaranteeing gays and lesbians basic civil rights.[11] A second pervasive rhetorical strategy links the idea of "special privileges" to the idea of choice: Homosexuality is a choice, say conservative Christians, and if a man can choose to sleep with another man, he can also choose not to. A 1992 flyer of a conservative Christian group declared: "They want their choice of homosexuality to be given the same civil protections and preferences as being born black or Hispanic. This would be like granting affirmative action quotas to celibates or polygamists just because they claim to be born that way." A year later, David Neff, editor of Christianity Today, urged readers to "reject the civil-rights approach to gaining gay acceptance, not just because it locks homosexuals into a victim identity, but, more fundamentally, because it locks them into a homosexual identity."[12] A third commonplace in evangelical antigay campaigns is the picture of gay activists as mastermind organizers with plenty of money; childless homosexuals, the reasoning goes, must be putting their paychecks into political coffers. As Bryant put it: "The foot soldiers were housewives and mothers, religious and civic leaders in opposition to a well-organized, highly financed, and politically militant group of homosexual activists."[13]

By the time this rhetoric had been recycled during the 2000 debate over civil unions in Vermont, evangelicals were even more vehement. Said Matt Daniels, executive director of a conservative organization called Alliance for Marriage, "In addition to these legal efforts, homosexual activists have run a sophisticated propaganda campaign in order to confuse and eradicate public resistance to their radical agenda. They have intimidated and overwhelmed opponents by the sheer volume and vehemence of falsehood."[14] Gay Christian activists respond to such charges with a wish list: When this rhetoric was recycled in the 2000 debate over civil unions in Vermont, gay pastor Nancy Wilson wrote, "Oh, that we were as well organized as they fantasize."[15]

Evangelicals did not just adopt Bryant's rhetoric. Like Bryant, they saw the ballot box as the solution to the gay question, and they headed to polling places to repeal ordinances similar to the one in Dade County. In April 1978, St. Paul voters repealed a gay rights law in a 54,090 to 31,690 vote. The next month, voters in Wichita, Kansas, and Eugene, Oregon, did the same. The Oklahoma state legislature passed a law dismissing teachers who "practiced" or advocated homosexuality. After the St. Paul victory, Pat Buchanan crowed, "Like the Union Army at the second Manassas, the gay-rights movement has been routed anew in its second collision with Christian fundamentalists."[16] Buchanan's was a curious, but perhaps apt, analogy, for though the Confederates trounced the Union Army at Bull Run, they eventually went down in defeat. If the tenor of the times is any indication, Buchanan's fundamentalists were more like the Confederacy than he knew: They won a few early skirmishes, but they would lose the war.

Evangelicals would battle homosexuals and their allies at the ballot boxes for the remainder of the century. In 1987, when Oregon governor Neil Goldschmidt issued an executive order forbidding discrimination within the executive branch of state government on the basis of sexual orientation, evangelical Oregonians took action. Lon Mabon, the head of the Oregon Citizens Alliance—a group whose name creepily echoed the segregationist Citizens Councils that sprang up all over the South after the 1954 *Brown* v. *Board of Education* decision—declared that moves like Goldschmidt's would have "a dramatic effect on the moral foundation of our culture." The Citizens Alliance sponsored a referendum called Measure 8, which would repeal the executive order. On election day, Mabon and his crew won 53 percent of the vote.[17]

In October 1990, the Denver city council approved an ordinance banning discrimination based on sexual orientation in housing, employment, and public accommodations. Outraged Denverites formed Citizens for Sensible Rights and began collecting signatures for a referendum to repeal the ordinance. When the city council of Colorado Springs—a city that became home during the 1990s to dozens of evangelical organizations, including James Dobson's Focus on the Family—began to consider adding sexual orientation to its nondiscrimination ordinance, a statewide grassroots movement coalesced around opposition to the protection of gay civil rights.

Originally called the Colorado Coalition for Family Values, they adopted the shorter Colorado for Family Values after a local radio personality said the word "coalition" sounded too Marxist.

The group won the backing of some prominent Colorado Christians, including Bill McCartney, then the football coach at the University of Colorado, who had founded Promise Keepers in 1990. In 1992, University of Colorado president Judith Albino criticized him for identifying himself as a university employee in Colorado for Family Values material. At a February press conference, McCartney, wearing a Colorado University sweater, declared publicly that he had loyalties to an authority higher than Albino. "Homosexuality is an abomination of almighty God," he said. The citizens of Colorado approved Amendment 2 by a comfortable margin: 53 percent to 47 percent. In 1996, in a decision one conservative Christian called "the *Roe* v. *Wade* of the homosexual issue," the Supreme Court found Amendment 2 unconstitutional.[18]

By the turn of the twenty-first century, some conservative Christians began to worry that the old Bryant ballot tactics would not be enough. After Vermont legally recognized same-sex civil unions, evangelicals decided new strategies might be in order. Matt Daniels, of Alliance for Marriage, covered the story for *World*, a polemical, right-wing Christian magazine headed by Marvin Olasky. Daniels, echoing the strategy pursued by leaders of the Religious Right in the 1980s, urged evangelicals to cooperate with like-minded people of other faiths—Jews, Muslims, Mormons—in opposing laws like Vermont's. But, he said, "no conventional legal remedy may be able to stop the juggernaut unleashed by homosexual activists in the American courts. Deep shifts in the culture of the American legal profession—especially in the values of the professors at our nation's influential elite law schools—have virtually guaranteed the eventual demise of the legal institution of marriage at the hands of the judiciary." A constitutional amendment might be the only solution, he said.[19]

More liberal Christian clergy, not surprisingly, approved of the Vermont decision. Mary Adelia McLeod, then the Episcopal bishop of Vermont, said, "I applaud and am encouraged by the Vermont Supreme Court's ruling." While the church was not "of one mind" about blessing same-sex unions, said McLeod, "the interests of the state in licensing civil marriage and those of the church in the blessing of a marriage are quite different. The civil rights flowing from marriage primarily concern property, inheritance, and the responsibilities and privileges of couples in matters of privacy, insurance, custody of children, and decision-making about one another's welfare.

These are issues faced by both heterosexual and homosexual couples."
Peace activist and preacher William Sloane Coffin, writing in the *Rutland
Daily Herald*, was equally enthusiastic. "Montpelier is being flooded with
thousands of out-of-state letters filled with inflammatory rhetoric and spu-
rious homophobic assertions, many of them written by Christians who use
the Bible much as a drunk does a lamppost—more for support than for
illumination." The Bible has more to say about polygamy than about same-
sex marriages, wrote Coffin. In short, he said, the decision to legalize same-
sex unions was a triumph, for "no human being should ever be patient with
prejudice at the expense of its victims."[20]

Some evangelicals have offered more nuanced approaches to the problem of homosexuality and the public square. The Bible may make plain that
homosexual sex is sinful, they allow, but it does not have very much to say
about county-level antidiscrimination ordinances. In a 1999 issue of *Christianity Today*, four leading evangelical thinkers—including Richard Mouw,
president of Fuller Theological Seminary, and Mary Stuart Van Leeuwen,
professor of psychology at Eastern College and noted evangelical feminist—participated in a forum about homosexuality and the polity.

Though all four participants accepted the premise that homosexual sex
was incompatible with Christian morality, they advanced some notions that
might sound fairly radical in the evangelical world. Van Leeuwen said that
domestic partnerships were a key issue. Perhaps, she suggested, evangelicals
could support state-recognized domestic partnerships if those partnerships
were not framed in sexual terms: a sister and a brother and a friend living
together and running a family farm for thirty years; two women who lived
together in a condominium in Bennington, Vermont; college roommates
who, ten years down the line, bought a house together and shared grocery
bills. These groups, said Van Leeuwen, constituted "economic commu-
nit[ies]. Should they or should they not get the benefits or tax breaks of
being an economic community? . . . The state has a compelling interest
and Christians have a compelling interest in people's emotional and economic commitments to one another. If people can demonstrate that they
are emotionally and economically committed to one another, then they
should have some of the tax benefits in that particular culture that would
be given to a married couple."[21]

Another participant in the forum, Covenant Theological Seminary's
David Jones, added, "It's not the state's business whether they're chaste or
not." Van Leeuwen did not suggest the state call these relationships marriages; she simply suggested that, as we shrink the welfare state, we need

to find new, practical, and compassionate ways of helping people stay economically afloat—and domestic partnerships might be one plan evangelicals could support.[22]

The issue of sexual identity has divided Protestants profoundly in the years surrounding the turn of the twenty-first century. Although liberal, or mainline, Protestants have tended to be more accepting of homosexuality, the issues of gay ordination and same-sex unions nevertheless threaten to divide mainline denominations. Evangelicals, though generally opposed to homosexuality, likewise are divided about how to address the matter in the public square.

Tales of Two Trials: Jimmy Creech and Walter Righter

For Protestants, homosexuality is not an issue limited to civil society. Ministers and laity must also determine the standing of gays and lesbians within the church. Inside the church, the discussion usually coalesces around two questions: ordination and marriage. Most Protestants do not quarrel over whether or not homosexuals—sexually active or celibate—should be church members or serve on, say, the overseas missions committee. But churches do have vicious public debates over whether noncelibate gay Christians should be ordained and whether the church should recognize lifelong, same-sex commitments with some sort of marriage ceremony.

Evangelicals are fairly adamant in their opposition to both proposals, but mainline Protestants are divided. Even gay mainliners cannot agree: In 1992, two gay activists debated in the pages of *Open Hands*. John Linscheid, who himself once sought ordination, said that gay Christians must "abandon the push for gay and lesbian ordination" and move beyond the "tendency to see ordination as the Holy Grail of the gay and lesbian Christian movement." Ordination, he said, accepted a heterosexual emphasis on hierarchy, something foreign to gay Christian sensibilities. It bought into heterosexual power structures (with a slightly different slant, Linscheid might have been an evangelical looking askance at worldly ways). Iliff School of Theology doctoral candidate Jeanne Knepper disagreed, declaring simply that "ordination is important," because the refusal to ordain gays and lesbians feeds society's general antigay prejudices and drives homosexuals from the community of faith. Sure, there are reasons to wonder at the wisdom of the ordination struggle, Knepper admitted: The battle, filled with rejection, was painful, and the emphasis on ordination is, on some level, about hierarchy.

But, she concluded, "this struggle to make the church more inclusive serves the lavender community, the community of faith, the individuals called to ministry, and the movement of God's will. It is a good and holy work. We must support it."

If gay activists are not unanimous in their support of ordination, governing bodies of the mainline denominations are even more fractious. For three decades, denominational decision makers have been slogging out questions about homosexuality. In 1971, the Texas Conference of the United Methodist Church suspended Gene Leggett when he announced that he was gay. In 1972, the United Church of Christ—which has been the most gay-friendly of the mainline denominations—ordained William Johnson, an openly gay man. In 1974, the United Methodist Church Council on Youth Ministry adopted a resolution stating that homosexuality should not be a bar to ordination. In 1977, Episcopal bishop Paul Moore ordained Ellen Barrett, a lesbian (and copresident of the Episcopal gay activist group Integrity), as a priest. Two years later, the Episcopal General Convention declared that "There should be no barrier to the ordination of qualified persons of either heterosexual or homosexual orientation whose behavior the Church considers wholesome"—but it then asserted that marital fidelity and sexual chastity are "the standard of Christian sexual morality." Therefore, it is "not appropriate for this Church to ordain a practicing homosexual, or any person who is engaged in heterosexual relations outside of marriage."

In 1972, the United Methodist Church stated that it did not recommend "marriage between two persons of the same sex." In 1976, the Methodist General Conference reaffirmed the 1972 position, and drafted language prohibiting Methodist churches from funding programs that sponsored or supported homosexual activity. The General Conference also declared that "a relationship between two persons of the same sex" could not constitute marriage. Two years later, a Methodist bishop refused to reappoint Paul Abels, a gay pastor, to his New York City church. The Methodist annual conference overrode the bishop's decision and reappointed Abels. The following year, Joan Clark, a Methodist deaconess who worked for the Board of Global Ministries' Women's Division, was fired after she acknowledged that she was gay.

In 1980, the General Assembly of the Unitarian Universalist Church urged UU churches to "settle" openly gay people in pulpits, but the call had little effect; gay Unitarian Universalists still had trouble getting jobs. In 1981, the Disciples of Christ ordained two open lesbians, Debra Peevey and Christine Leslie. The next year, Methodist leaders filed charges against Melvin Wheatley, a Methodist bishop who appointed a gay pastor to a Denver pulpit; the charges were later dropped. In 1984, the Methodist General Conference enacted "fidelity in marriage and celibacy in singleness" and then expressly prohibited ordination of "self-avowed, practicing homosexuals." In 1987, the first official same-sex Quaker marriage ceremony was performed in New York.

The next decade saw little letup. In January 1990, charges were filed against two Evangelical Lutheran Church in America churches, Saint Francis Lutheran and First United Lutheran churches in San Francisco; the churches had ordained three openly gay men and women. The next year, the American Baptist Church, at its biennial meeting, voted down a statement that called on Baptists to refrain from statements about sexuality that "might be based upon our cultural values rather than the values of Jesus." Instead, it adopted "A Statement of Concern Addressing Homosexuality and the Church," which explicitly condemned the gay "lifestyle," the establishment of "gay churches," and the ordination of homosexuals.

And on it went, the 1990s bringing vote after vote, declaration after declaration. Each year sees a new wave of denominational squabbles, a new round of denominational votes, a new round of headlines, and, sometimes, even church trials.

Walter Righter seemed an unlikely man to land in *Time* magazine. The kindly bishop, who resembles a cross between Santa Claus and an absent-minded college professor, probably would not have flirted with notoriety had media darling John Shelby Spong not called him out of retirement. Spong, the recently retired Episcopal bishop of Newark, has long inspired outrage in some corners (and won adulation in others) for his provocative books, which declare, as the title of one puts it, *Why Christianity Must Change or Die*. Spong fancies himself a latter-day Luther: The German reformer once proclaimed "Here I stand; I can do none other. So help me God"; Spong arrogantly called his memoir *Here I Stand*. Luther nailed *Ninety-five Theses* to the cathedral door at Wittenberg; Spong published his "twelve theses" in a book (and they quickly made the rounds on the Internet). In these theses, Spong called for abandoning a "theistic" conception of God, referred to the doctrine of atonement as a "barbarian idea . . . that must be dismissed," and said there is "no external, objective, revealed standard writ in Scripture . . . that will govern our ethical behavior for all time."

Orthodox Christians were appalled, but what really irked Spong's antagonists was his "Statement of Koinonia." Spong drafted the Koinonia

Statement—*koinonia* is Greek for fellowship—at a 1994 meeting of the Episcopal Church's general convention. The house of bishops of the Episcopal Church had been directed by an earlier general convention of the church in July 1991 to prepare a pastoral teaching on the subject of human sexuality prior to the seventy-first general convention which met in late August and early September 1994. At that convention, a statement on homosexuality came to the floor, a statement that pleased neither conservatives nor Spong and his allies. A group of conservative bishops from the Southwest issued the so-called Province VII statement (because the bishops behind the document were from the Episcopal Church's seventh province), declaring that "Sexual relationships between members of the same sex are also a denial of God's plan, and cannot be condoned by the Church." These conservative bishops managed to tack so many amendments on to the "Pastoral Teaching on Homosexuality," Spong recounted in *Here I Stand*, that gays and lesbians in the church felt "devastated—they felt beaten up and abandoned by the Church they were just beginning to trust."[23]

Spong professed to be so distraught over the Province VII statement that he roused his sleeping wife in the middle of the night and asked her to type a statement he had drafted in response. Eighty-eight American bishops eventually signed the Koinonia Statement, which declared that some people are created homosexual and others heterosexual, that the church should support gay or lesbian Christians not called to celibacy in their "faithful, monogamous, committed, life-giving, and holy" relationships, and that the church should ordain noncelibate homosexuals.

Spong, in his relentless efforts to push the Episcopal Church to the left, had made several bad decisions. In the late 1980s, for instance, he ordained Robert Williams, a noncelibate gay man, to the priesthood; when Williams's ordination became public, there was a media frenzy, and Williams proved unable to handle the attention. In the fall of 1989, while giving a speech in Detroit, Williams was asked, "Do you really think Mother Teresa's life would be enhanced—" "If she got laid?" Williams interrupted. "Yes! I am saying that everyone's life is significantly enhanced by sexual activity and significantly diminished by the lack of it." But the fracas that erupted in the wake of Williams's unfortunate comment failed to convince Spong to stop ordaining homosexuals.

In 1989 Spong asked Righter, then the retired bishop of Iowa, to come to Newark and serve as suffragan bishop, assisting Spong in the diocese. Righter agreed, and in September 1990 he ordained Barry Stopfel, another gay Newark candidate for holy orders, to the diaconate. In January 1995

Righter was spending a leisurely morning at home with his wife when he received a call from then presiding bishop Edmund Browning, who delivered some disquieting news: Ten bishops had prepared formal charges against Righter, accusing him of heresy. It was the first Episcopal heresy trial since 1923, when the retired bishop of Arkansas, who had claimed that Communism made Christianity irrelevant, was branded as a heretic.

Righter's musings about the trial were not always astute. "We were all certain there was another agenda besides heresy," he wrote in his memoir. "[A]n agenda that had not become completely apparent to any of us yet."[24] The agenda may not have been clear to Righter, but it was pretty clear to everyone else: Were the presenting bishops concerned only with heresy, they could have skewered Spong long ago for one of his cavalier dismissals of theism. They were concerned not with heresy per se, but with homosexuality, and the obscure, sometimes bumbling Righter made an easier target than the popular, media-savvy Spong, who was more than happy to let Righter take the heat from church conservatives.

The trial ended in defeat for the presenting bishops. The heresy committee—a committee, Righter noted, that everyone used to think was an

Fig. 8.2. Barry Stopfel, an openly gay man, was ordained to the Episcopal diaconate by Bishop Walter Righter, who later faced ecclesiastical charges of heresy. Righter was eventually acquitted, and Stopfel resigned his parish in 1999, citing the toll of publicity on his "psyche and spirit." Rich Kraus, The Star-Ledger/AP Photo.

easy appointment, since it never met—handed down a majority decision finding Righter not guilty of heresy. "The Court today is not giving an opinion on the morality of same gender relationships," the decision carefully noted. It was instead offering a finding on a narrower issue: There is no essential teaching concerning the ordination of noncelibate homosexuals. The court drew a distinction between "core doctrine," which is unchangeable, "the essence of Christianity and necessary for salvation," and doctrinal teaching, which, like the church's teaching about remarriage after divorce, can change over time. There was no core doctrine on homosexuality, the court said. One member of the court, Andrew H. Fairfield, the bishop of North Dakota, dissented. Citing the familiar biblical passages, from the Garden of Eden down through Paul, pointing to the Book of Common Prayer and the teachings of the church as clarified at the general convention, Fairfield concluded that "the doctrine of the Church . . . proscribes the ordination of non-celibate homosexual persons."[25] Righter went back to New Jersey to write his memoir, Barry Stopfel continued in his ministry, and Spong continued kicking up dust wherever he went.

Not all ministers have fared so well. Jimmy Creech was pastor of a Methodist church in Warsaw, North Carolina, in 1984 when the United Methodist Church added a statement to its Book of Discipline about homosexuality: Practicing homosexuals could not serve as ministers in Methodist churches, the statement declared, as homosexuality was "incompatible with Christian teaching." Creech did not think much of it until one of his congregants turned up at his office, letter of resignation in hand. Why was he leaving the church, Creech wanted to know? Because, the congregant replied, he was gay, and he would not stay in a church that condemned him for it.[26]

A few years later Creech moved to Fairmont United Methodist Church in Raleigh, North Carolina, and he became active in the Raleigh Religious Network for Gay and Lesbian Equality. In June 1988, in anticipation of the North Carolina Gay and Lesbian Pride Parade, Creech sent a letter to area clergy. He acknowledged that sexuality was an issue fraught with tension and asked local ministers to "be as positive and supportive as you are able." Creech himself marched in the parade, which he later described as "one of the spiritual highs of my life."

Members of Creech's congregation were not quite so thrilled. The next day members of a Bible class at the church handed him a letter. "In His Scriptures God has made it clear that homosexuality is an abomination in His sight," they wrote. Embracing homosexuality "or those who practice it" is "an insult to God, that should be avoided, even the appearance of it."

Creech realized a fight was ahead, and he held an impromptu meeting to discuss homosexuality with any congregants who were interested in learning his views on the matter. At the meeting he explained why the scriptural take on homosexuality was not nearly as clear as the members of the Bible study seemed to think: When God punished the citizens of Sodom, Creech insisted, he was not reacting to their sexual habits but to their failure to show hospitality to strangers in their midst. As for the laws in Leviticus, he said, those were no more binding on Christians than the laws forbidding crabs, shrimp, and lobster.

Members of the Bible study were not persuaded, and they launched a coup. In an attempt to force his ouster, they tried to break the church's budget, refusing to contribute a dime to the church until Creech left. Other members of the Raleigh Religious Network for Gay and Lesbian Equality raised money, with local churches and synagogues pitching in funds, but by the spring of 1990 Creech decided that he and the church had reached an impasse. When members of Fairmont Methodist petitioned the bishop to have Creech reassigned, he conceded.

Creech's commitment to gay and lesbian rights within the church, however, did not end. Eventually he accepted a call to First United Methodist Church in Omaha, Nebraska. On September 14, 1997, he performed a covenant service for two women, who have been called Mary and Martha by the press. Creech had performed at least a dozen same-sex covenanting ceremonies, but this was the first wedding Creech celebrated after the 1996 Methodist general conference decision explicitly forbidding its ministers to participate in such ceremonies. The statement read: "Ceremonies that celebrate homosexual unions shall not be conducted by our ministers and shall not be conducted in churches." [27]

Creech readily defied the decision. "I am doing this as part of my understanding of the Church, of Jesus, and what all people need to do," he declared. "I cannot imagine as a pastor saying 'no' to two people who say they want to make a commitment to each other in the context of their faith." [28]

The Methodist hierarchy did not take kindly to Creech's insubordination. In March 1998 he was brought up before a church court in Kearney, Nebraska. He was acquitted, but the trial had consequences nonetheless. Unofficial groups in the Methodist Church on both sides of the issue responded. "The jury decision in the trial of Jimmy Creech is a glimmer of God's grace," said Mark Bowman, executive director of the Reconciling

Congregation Program, in a March 16, 1998 statement. Conservative groups calling for "renewal" in the Methodist church had rather different reactions. The Confessing Movement, which was organized in 1994 to "call the United Methodist Church to theological and doctrinal integrity . . . [and] to lift up the centrality of Jesus Christ as Son, Savior and Lord in our preaching and teaching of the Gospel," said they felt "disappointment and consternation" about the decision. So too, apparently, did Creech's bishop, who informed Creech he would not reappoint him to the church. Creech left his pulpit at First United Methodist. (When Don Bredthauer, a Creech supporter and associate pastor of First Church for ten years, was appointed as senior pastor in Creech's stead, over 300 members of the 1900-member church broke away and founded their own church.)

The following April, Creech, back in North Carolina, co-officiated the covenanting ceremony of Larry E. Ellis and James H. Raymer. Methodist district superintendent Jim McChesney brought a complaint against Creech, and that fall he was tried again. He spoke of his second trial in prophetic terms. "This trial belongs to everyone: to all lesbian, gay, bisexual and transgender people and their families against whom this trial is an act of violence," he said, "to all who love justice and want to end the persecution of gay, bisexual, lesbian and transgender people by The United Methodist Church and other Christian churches; and, to all who grieve The United Methodist Church's renunciation, in the cause of bigotry, of Christ's unconditional love and welcome extended to all people."[29] Indeed, Creech believed the trial was the death throes of his church's unjust stance on homosexuality. "There is a saying from Africa that a man cries the loudest just before death," he told *Out* magazine shortly before the trial. "I see the resistance in the church as sort of that last cry. We have the opportunity to correct a very serious mistake that was made in the Middle Ages, when gay and lesbian people were attacked by the church."[30]

On November 16, 1999, Creech renewed the vows of Larry Ellis and Jim Raymer. The following day, a thirteen-member Nebraska church court unanimously declared him guilty of violating Methodist teaching and stripped him of his ordination.

Creech again made headlines in 2000, when Mary and Martha, the lesbian couple he had married in 1997, split up because one of them became a man. The defrocked Creech insisted that he did not regret performing the ceremony. "The crucial standard by which any relationship is judged is what is given and received between the couple," he said. "It's not the duration, but it's the depth and quality of it [that matters]." His antagonists,

not surprisingly, pointed to Martha's sex change as further evidence that
their marriage was not only a charade, but a mockery of a holy institution.
"To begin with, marriage is between one man and one woman and anything
else is not acceptable," Patricia Miller, executive director of the Confessing
Movement, told reporters. "This just reinforces that these relationships are
not appropriate." For his part, Martin (née Martha) saw God's hand in the
whole saga. "I don't think God has us go through things without a plan,"
Martin told *The Advocate*. "I am who I am today because of my female
past. And I continue to have a lot of faith in God. The church laws are
made by man. God's law is a lot higher."

Fissure in a Church

Many mainline denominations are slowly sifting into two piles—parishes
that are explicitly gay-friendly, and those that are not. One can see this at
work in the Welcoming Church movement, which one gay United Church
of Christ pastor has called "one of the most exciting and enriching developments of the church in our lifetime." To become a Welcoming Church,
an individual congregation goes through some study series about homosexuality and Christianity. Congregants might study the biblical passages
relating to homosexuality, invite gay and lesbians members to share their
stories, and host guest speakers on topics of particular concern, like the
causes of homosexuality or the current state of scientific studies about sexual
orientation. After a period of study, the church votes about whether to
become part of the Welcoming Church movement. Each denomination has
its own particular language for this step—a United Church of Christ church
adopts an "Open and Affirming" resolution, a Presbyterian church joins up
with other "More Light" churches, American Baptists become "Welcoming
and Affirming Baptists," Lutheran churches declare themselves "Reconciled
in Christ," and so on. Then the congregation joins the larger, ecumenical
network of Welcoming Churches; over 900 churches have joined up.[31]

But figuring out how to approach questions about sexuality is not always
as smooth as icing. Some denominations seem to be weathering the storm,
but others are more fissiparous. Perhaps more than any other mainline
denomination, the Episcopal Church threatens to fall apart over homosexuality. This is hardly surprising; the Episcopal Church has always been
home to Christians of extremely divergent political and theological views.
The Episcopal fold boasts died-in-the-wool evangelicals, parodies of theo-

logical liberalism like Spong, and everything in between. The church has navigated the stormy waters of controversy and dissension before. When, in the 1970s, the church admitted women to the priesthood, not a few disgruntled Episcopalians, clergy and lay, left the church to found their own, schismatic denominations.

The Righter trial did not solve matters for the Episcopal Church. To the contrary, national and international Episcopal gatherings have been dealing with the issue ever since. At the 1997 general convention, the church formally apologized to gays and lesbians "for years of rejection and maltreatment." Church leaders also voted to study further the question of blessing ceremonies for same-sex unions, and, after three votes in the house of bishops, they extended health insurance to domestic partners. The measure passed by a 93 to 90 count.

The following year, Anglican bishops from around the world met at the Lambeth Conference, held once a decade in Canterbury, the spiritual center for 70 million Anglicans throughout the world, including members of the Episcopal Church in the United States. When a long-awaited resolution on homosexuality came to the floor for a vote, the rhetoric was heated. A Pakistani bishop asked sarcastically if, at the 2008 Lambeth Conference, the bishops would vote to approve blessing cat lovers and their pets, and a Nigerian bishop tried to heal Richard Kirker of his homosexuality by laying hands on him. The bishops voted 526 to 70 (with 45 abstentions) for a resolution declaring that homosexual practice is "incompatible with Scripture" and that the church "cannot advise the legitimizing or blessing of same-sex unions, nor the ordination of those involved in such unions." The Lambeth Conference has no authority in the Anglican Church—the vote was more a straw poll than a binding policy. Nonetheless, the Lambeth action prompted swift rejoinders.

Left-leaning bishops obviously were not pleased with the result. Bishop Catherine Waynick of Indianapolis told the conference that, in the past, the church had thought it had the correct answers to moral problems such as slavery but centuries later had to repent. She said, "Our call is not to correctness but to love."[32] Observers noted that bishops from Africa had overwhelmingly supported the resolution, and rumors abounded that the votes of bishops from the developing world had been bought.

Conservative American bishops, like the nine who presented Righter for heresy, cheered the outcome. Conservative priests who led churches in dioceses with more liberal bishops were caught in a bind. Could they remain obedient to bishops who, in the clergy's opinion, openly disregarded both

Scripture and the position of the church? Judith Gentle-Hardy was rector of the Church of the Holy Trinity in Marlborough, Massachusetts, when the bishops voted at Lambeth. "When bishops and clergy preach a false gospel that has utter disregard for God's intentions for the use of the gift of human sexuality, this is no slight matter," Gentle-Hardy told *Christianity Today*. "Some bishops think unity and fellowship is more important than truth, as opposed to the fact our oneness with the Lord and his truth is what creates unity and fellowship."[33]

Gentle-Hardy's bishop, Thomas Shaw, had signed Spong's Koinonia Statement. Gentle-Hardy declared in a letter to Shaw that she no longer recognized his episcopal oversight because of his public endorsement of teachings about sexuality that Gentle-Hardy considered heretical. That Gentle-Hardy's actions smacked of Donatism, which Augustine dispatched in the fourth century, did not seem to bother the priest, who eventually struck out on her own, leaving the diocese and founding her own church.

Schism has not stopped there. Tom J. Johnston was a priest in Little Rock, Arkansas. He, like Judith Gentle-Hardy, was at odds with his bishop, whom Johnston considered too liberal on sexual matters. He decided, therefore, to take his whole church out of the American Episcopal Church and transfer the church to the Church of Rwanda so that he could receive episcopal oversight from a conservative archbishop. The bishop of Arkansas, for reasons never made clear, allowed him to do this; because Johnston had the nominal approval of the bishop of Arkansas, his move was technically not a violation of the letter of canon law, though he certainly violated the spirit of Episcopal polity.

Like-minded Episcopalians were inspired by Johnston's success. In 1999 a group of conservative Episcopal clergy sent an open letter to Anglican bishops around the world, claiming that theologically orthodox priests were increasingly marginalized in the American church and were forced to receive episcopal oversight from heterodox—or heretical—bishops. The petitioners hoped fellow conservatives elsewhere in the world would step in, like the archbishop of Rwanda, and offer them new ecclesiastical homes.

On January 29, 2000, two more priests, Charles H. Murphy III and John H. Rodgers Jr., followed suit. At a cathedral in Singapore, they were ordained by Emmanuel Kolini, archbishop of Rwanda, and Moses Tay, archbishop of South East Asia. Murphy was rector of All Saints Episcopal Church in Pawleys Island, South Carolina, and the leader of First Promise, a conservative Episcopal group founded in 1997; Rogers was a leader in the Association of Anglican Congregations on Mission, a group "of orthodox Anglican congregations fulfilling the Great Commission to reach and teach the lost, planting churches which will plant churches, and working to build a biblically orthodox Anglican Province in the United States of America."

Frank Griswold, the presiding bishop of the Episcopal Church in the United States, said he was "appalled." He admitted that "there are significant disagreements among us regarding human sexuality," but insisted that irregular and possibly noncanonical consecrations were not the way to solve the problems. George Carey, the archbishop of Canterbury, agreed. Before the consecrations Carey asked the archbishop of South East Asia not to proceed. When Tay disregarded him, Carey said the consecrations were "irresponsible and irregular and [will] only harm the unity of the [Anglican] Communion."

These contretemps within the Episcopal Church—and, by extension, within the Anglican communion—illustrate the volatility of homosexuality among Protestants at the turn of the twenty-first century. While evangelicals and the Roman Catholic Church have managed to stave off questions of ordination and same-sex unions with blanket statements of condemnation, those Protestant groups that have sought some measure of accommodation have been wracked by dissension and division.

Gay Christians Off the Beaten Path

Not all gay Christians have to contend with battles over ordination and marriage ceremonies or worry that their denomination will fall apart over issues of sexuality. While they may be concerned about the struggles their fellow gays and lesbians in Presbyterian, Methodist, Episcopal and other mainline churches have to fight, Christians who have entered explicitly gay-friendly churches know they will not risk sending anyone to ecclesiastical court for ordaining them.

The largest, oldest such church is the Universal Fellowship of Metropolitan Community Churches (MCC). MCC was founded in 1968 by Troy Perry. Its origins were humble: a group of gay Christians who met in the lower floor of the Huntington Park Women's Club in California. They ran into hostility; when the Women's Club learned they were not just any church group, the MCC had to find a new home. Perry ran into heterosexuals who taunted him, spouting Scripture against homosexuality. Perry turned such encounters into lessons in biblical exegesis:

She said, "If I had my way all of you perverted individuals would be locked up, in jail, and the key thrown away!"

I said, "Madam, that's a wonderful Christian attitude you have."

She looked me over, backed off a step, and I thought she was going to hit me again. She said, "Young man, do you know what the Book of Leviticus says?"

I told her, "I sure do! It says that it's a sin for a woman to wear a red dress, for a man to wear a cotton shirt and woolen pants at the same time, for anyone to eat shrimp, oysters, or lobster—or your steak too rare."

She said, "That's not what I mean!"

I said, "I know that's not what you mean, Honey, but you forgot all those other dreadful sins, too, that are in the same book of the Bible."

She said, "Do you know what Saint Paul said?"

Again, I said, "I sure do. He said for women to be silent, not to speak."[34]

MCC today boasts over 40,000 members and 300 congregations.

Mel White, the MCC "Minister of Justice," has entered a public donnybrook with outspoken antigay evangelicals. White was once the golden boy of the Religious Right. He was a ghostwriter for books by leading evangelical pastors and evangelists, including Billy Graham, Pat Robertson, and Jerry Falwell. He emceed Youth for Christ rallies; he taught communications at Fuller Theological Seminary. Then he came out of the closet.

White had known he was gay for years. Early on in his marriage to his college sweetheart, he confessed. Linda took the news in stride and asked White what he wanted to do about it. That much was clear to White: He wanted to be a good Christian, stay married, and somehow be cured of his same-sex predilections. He worked hard at it, praying, studying Scripture, seeing godly therapists. But he could not shake his attraction to men, and he entered into an intense same-sex love affair. Eventually, White and his wife divorced, amicably. (In her preface to his autobiography, Linda testifies to what a "good man" her ex-husband is; they both tried hard to make their marriage work, but could not.)

White pieced his life back together after the divorce. While attending an Episcopal church, he met, and became romantically involved with, Gary Nixon; White was a vestry member and Nixon a choir singer. White eventually took a public stand against what he saw as evangelicals' bigoted

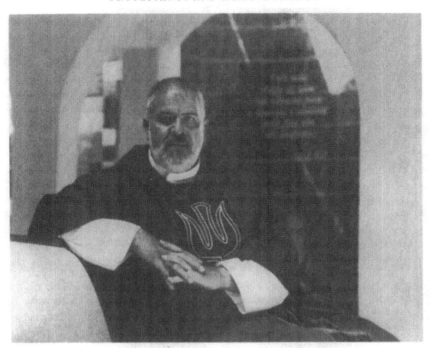

Fig. 8.3. A former evangelist for the Church of God (Cleveland, Tennessee), Troy Perry founded the Universal Fellowship of Metropolitan Community Churches. Courtesy of The Universal Fellowship of Metropolitan Community Churches.

misuse of Scripture. On June 5, 1999, White wrote an open letter to Jerry Falwell: "I've been reading your autobiography again," the letter began. "It still moves me. And I'm not just saying that because I wrote it." White went on to say he was particularly moved by Falwell's about-face on segregation: Once a committed segregationist, Falwell was baptizing African Americans by 1968. Falwell had told White that it was individual encounters with cherished black friends that had come to change his mind, finally, about civil rights. Falwell repented, recognizing the error of his ways. Well, White asked in the open letter, "Has it ever crossed your mind that you might be just as wrong about homosexuality as you were about segregation? . . . In the 1950s and 60s, you misused the Bible to support segregation. In the 1990s you are misusing it again, this time to caricature and condemn God's gay and lesbian children."[35]

Falwell was neither persuaded nor amused. Asking readers to "pray for Mel to have a true encounter of deliverance with Christ," he responded with an open letter of his own. He reminded White that Christ could and did heal homosexuals of their same-sex urges. "I have been used by God

Fig. 8.4. Mel White, an evangelical and former ghostwriter for Jerry Falwell and Pat Robertson, came out of the closet, was ordained in the predominantly gay Metropolitan Community Church, and launched a crusade to encourage evangelicals to be more accepting of homosexuality. The News & Advance, Mark L. Thompston/AP Photo.

to lead many practicing and committed homosexuals to Christ," he wrote. "I have also helped lead many Christian young people out of this lifestyle. . . . I personally know former homosexuals who have been delivered from the gay lifestyle." Falwell expressed the hope that White would join the ranks of those former homosexuals.[36] That has not happened. White has, however, written Falwell three more open letters, confronted another former client, Pat Robertson, and continued in his activism.

Gay Christians like Perry and White have not just gravitated toward gay churches and denominations like MCC. Some gay Protestants have also devised their own Christian rituals. Arguing that prayers should reflect the experiences of those praying, they have "take[n] a more active role in creating and choosing our rituals." As Methodist pastor Gregory Dell put it, "If liturgy is, as its derivation suggests, the *ergos* (work) of the *laos* (people), it ought to reflect a collaborative and corporate style in its creation as well as its practice."[37]

Activists argue that gays and lesbians, excluded by many churches from the sacraments of ordination and baptism, need a sacrament of their own. Some have suggested that baptism should be reclaimed as a gay ritual, underscoring that as babies, long before anyone can discriminate against them because of sexual orientation, gays and lesbians are received as members of the body of Christ. Others have suggested that gay Christians need a coming-out ceremony. In the words of Matthew Fox—the defrocked Roman Catholic priest—"the sacrament of coming out" is a "kind of letting go: a letting go of the images of personhood, sexuality, and selfhood that society has put on one in favor of trusting oneself enough to be oneself."[38]

Like baptism, coming out is a rite of introduction, one witnessed by others. In a coming-out ceremony written by Methodist pastor Rebecca Parker, friends and family welcome the newly uncloseted gay Christian and "proclaim the sacred worth of every child of God." Glaser, then director of the Lazarus Project, a Los Angeles, Presbyterian-based ministry of reconciliation between the church and the gay and lesbian community, has argued that "coming out is not a singular event, but one that anticipates repetition (as Communion) or reaffirmation (as Baptism)." Like the Christian who is baptized, a gay person who comes out dies to his old life and is born anew. Coming out resonates with the sacrament of reconciliation (as homosexuals "repent of the closet") and of the anointing of the sick, insofar as it provides healing. Glaser insists, however, that coming out is most like communion: "Both involve a sacrifice and an offering that creates an at-one-ment or communion with God and with others."[39]

Others have argued that gay Christians need to recapture the sacred nature of eating together: "The eucharistic meal becomes an act of defiance against homophobic oppression." Just as the breaking of bread reminds worshipers of Jesus' body, broken in the service of the Lord, so "queer Christians commit themselves to breaking their bodies in loving service to each other and to the struggle for God's justice-doing."[40]

Glaser and fellow travelers believe that new, gay-friendly rituals benefit not just gay Christians, but the entire church. He suggests creating rituals like "A Call to Repentance: Confessing Homophobia and Heterosexism," in which a congregation is led in a liturgy, which reads in part: "We confess that we have sinned in thought, word, and deed, in acts of commission and omission, against our lesbian sisters and gay brothers, and against our bisexual and transgendered sisters and brothers. Lamb of God, who takes away the sins of the world, have mercy on us." In a "Litany of a Supportive Community," people say "We will love you and accept you. We will not judge your decision, as we ask you not to judge ours." A "Liturgy of Affirmation" concludes with this spin on the dismissal that traditionally concludes a service: "And now may the Wildly Inclusive God—Creator, Savior, Spirit—who loves all aspects of the beautifully created rainbow of human sexual orientation, hold us and keep us until we meet again."[41]

Christians who have had enough of 1970s-style feminist liturgies may wince at the Carter Heyward-esque Wildly Inclusive God, but gay Christians—again echoing early feminist critics—say their unique spiritual insights, reflected in the prayers they write, have a thing or two to teach the church. What some activists call a lavender sensibility infuses gay liturgy, even when individual prayers do not mention sexual orientation. A lavender eucharistic service, published in *Open Hands* in 1992, for example, makes no mention of sexuality, but it is explicitly "nonhierarchical." In place of a "leader" leading the "congregation," this service calls for "One" to lead the rest of the "People." Liturgist Elizabeth Stuart says that gay liturgies offer a connection with oppressed people and are generally more "honest" than the standard fare; some gay marriage ceremonies, she notes, recognize the fragility of romantic unions and do not attempt to have people stay in them forever.[42]

It is precisely such sentiments, of course, that make lavender liturgies fodder for conservative Christians' canons: Not only does gay marriage violate Christian heterosexual norms, it apparently also violates Christian expectations of lifelong monogamy.

The Elusive Center

Protestantism has survived in America—indeed, it has flourished—in large measure because of its ability to adapt to changes in social and cultural circumstances. At times, as in the nineteenth-century controversy over slavery or the twentieth-century debates over abortion, those adjustments have been painful, prompting theological contortions and heated rhetoric on both sides of the issue. No issue over the last half-century has prompted more debate than human sexuality, from gender roles and the ordination of women to gays and lesbians and their place in the church.

Homosexuality has divided American Protestants more profoundly than perhaps any other issue. Protestant liberals see the use of gender-inclusive names for the deity, the ordination of women, and now the acceptance of gays and lesbians as a steady march toward progress and a fulfillment of the New Testament warrant of equality. Conservative Protestants, on the other hand, view these same developments as a slippery slope toward heresy.

CHAPTER NINE

Protestants and Social Justice

When Clara McBride Hale opened her doors to drug-addicted babies, she got more than she bargained for: Her five-room apartment in Harlem became home to twenty-two babies within two months, and she cared for over six hundred babies before she was through. God "kept sending them," she said, "and He kept opening a way for me to make it."

Don Martin, a physician in Hagerstown, Maryland, says his life was transformed by an adult Sunday school class on the Sermon on the Mount. He left the class convinced that he was called to serve the poor, so he gave up his nineteen-year private practice and began to work at Christ House, a temporary shelter for the homeless sick in Washington, D.C.

When Howard Janifer was sent to an AIDS hospice, he was prepared to die. Miraculously, he recovered. Janifer moved out of the hospice, but he returned twice a week to care for other men dying of AIDS. When asked how he could bear the physically challenging and emotionally draining work, Janifer replied, "The same way Jesus laid there with nails in his hands. If he could do that for me, why couldn't I do this for another man?"

Ted Wardlaw, senior pastor of Atlanta's Central Presbyterian Church, occasionally squabbles with the Atlanta police force. About once a year, a downtown police officer notices the hundred or so homeless men lined up outside the church and asks Wardlaw, "Can't you find another place for those guys to stand?" "Those guys" are waiting to enter Central's Outreach Center and Night Shelter. The Outreach Center is often the first stop of

Atlantans in distress, from drug addicts and the mentally ill to homeless people and low-income families. The Center often helps fifty people a day, listening to their problems and making appropriate referrals to other social service agencies. Wardlaw says he can find another place for them to stand, but he refuses. "The fact that we take seriously what it means to live the Cross and to talk about it, to believe in God, and to believe that we will be united with him and with each other some day," says Wardlaw, is what is at stake in Central's thriving urban ministry. "This place not only goes about trying to do good, but it's also about struggling to get an eschatological glimpse in the middle of the city of what the world will look like when God is finished with it."[1]

Hale, Janifer, Wardlaw, and Martin: different denominations, different regions, different races, different educations, different sexes. What they share is a concern for social justice grounded in the gospel.

American Protestants have always evinced a concern for the society and the world around them. Nineteenth-century evangelicals sought to end drinking, prostitution, and, in the North, slavery. Christians in the city built YMCAs and Salvation Army outposts to tend to the needs of the poor. Missionary forays sought the conversion of souls, but missionaries also set up medical clinics to minister to physical needs, and a survey of hospital names in mid-sized American cities—Iowa Methodist Hospital, Saint Luke's Presbyterian—indicates that Protestants have institutionalized their concerns for the well-being of individuals. Social justice activism for American Protestants became much more diffuse in the twentieth century, ranging from poor relief and economic boycotts to abortion counseling and advocacy for gay and lesbian rights. However, a shared commitment to social justice has not united Protestants of different political or theological temperaments. Indeed, at the beginning of the twenty-first century, differences about how to heed the gospel's mandates to build a just world have caused more division than harmony.

The History of Protestants and Social Justice

By placing service at the heart of the Christian mission, Wardlaw, Hale, Martin, and Janifer participate in a long and venerable history. Taking their cue from the New Testament and from Martin Luther's determination to "re-form" the church and, by extension, society, Protestants throughout American history have sought to recast American culture according to the norms of godliness.

In the first days of the nation, the founding fathers determined that religion and politics should be separate, but having disestablished religion with the First Amendment, religious groups found new expressions for social action in the form of voluntary associations. While disestablishment provided the legal basis for voluntarism, the Second Great Awakening fueled the engines of reform. Revivalists, who were overwhelmingly post-millennialist in their theology, came to believe that they could inaugurate the kingdom of God here on earth—more particularly, here in America—by dint of their reforms. Especially among northern Protestants, the antebellum era witnessed an unprecedented effort to regenerate American society. Protestants organized societies to abolish slavery, curb rampant alcohol abuse, provide education for women, reform prisons, and outlaw dueling. If those reforms could be effected, Protestants believed, the millennial kingdom (one thousand years of righteousness predicted in Revelation 20) would appear, thereby paving the way for Christ's return. The intensity of those reform efforts in the antebellum period led to the Civil War, pitting brother against brother and, more often than not, Protestant against Protestant.

For Protestants in the North, the carnage of the Civil War began to dim hopes of the millennial kingdom that they had so confidently predicted earlier in the nineteenth century. The growth of the cities, burgeoning with non-Protestant immigrants and with labor unrest, no longer resembled the precincts of Zion. In the face of these dashed expectations conservative Protestants gradually abandoned postmillennialism for premillennialism and, in so doing, forsook the task of social reform in favor of individual regeneration. Liberal Protestants stepped into the breach with a theology of reform that came to be known as the Social Gospel. Working side by side with the reformers of the Progressive era, the "Social Gospelers" yoked biblical witness together with the power of a newly expansive state to bring about the redemption of sinful social institutions rather than merely sinful individuals. They worked to defeat corrupt political machines, institute child-labor laws and the six-day workweek, and clean up the slums. After Black Tuesday and the onset of the Great Depression in 1929, the enormity of the social problems all around, both rural and urban, overwhelmed Protestant reform efforts. Franklin Roosevelt's New Deal offered an "alphabet soup" of agencies and programs to meet social needs and to lift the nation out of the Depression. In so doing, the government assumed many of the social reform responsibilities that the churches, no longer able to address the magnitude of the problems, had once shouldered.

In the decade following World War II Americans finally turned their attention to racism. Not that they did so willingly. Many white Protestants were content with the status quo, but black Americans, inspired in part by the rhetoric of freedom coming from the Allied struggle against fascism in the Second World War, began to demand that America finally live up to the ideals of its charter documents. Some advances had been made, both symbolic and substantive: Black entertainers such as Paul Robeson and Billie Holliday attracted audiences and influenced white performers such as Elvis Presley and Buddy Holly; and Jackie Robinson broke the color barrier in major league baseball when he took the field as a member of the Brooklyn Dodgers on April 15, 1947.

The biggest impetus for reform, however, came from the government. On July 26, 1948, Harry Truman issued an executive order desegregating the armed forces. On May 17, 1954, the United States Supreme Court issued its portentous *Brown* v. *Board of Education* decision, ruling that separate facilities for blacks and whites, the entrenched practice in the South, were inherently unequal and therefore violated the Constitution. In the following decade, a political movement exhibiting a rare blend of local and governmental activism emerged. Thousands of ordinary black Southerners wrought a social revolution that was aided by federal law—the Civil Rights Act of 1964 and the Voting Rights Act of 1965.

One of those "ordinary" black Southerners was Rosa Parks, a diminutive seamstress from Montgomery, Alabama. On December 1, 1955, Parks refused to move to the back of the bus on her way home from work. She was promptly arrested, whereupon the city's restive African American community, led by its clergy, chose to resist the entrenched patterns of racism in Montgomery. At an organizational meeting several days later, the black clergy unexpectedly turned to the new, twenty-six-year-old pastor of the Dexter Avenue Baptist Church, situated only a block away from the state capitol. "Well, if you think I can render some service, I will," the reluctant minister, Martin Luther King Jr., replied.

The struggle for civil rights required the cooperation of many individuals and entities, ranging from King, Birmingham minister Fred Shuttlesworth, and John Lewis of the Student Nonviolent Coordinating Committee, to the Southern Christian Leadership Conference and politicians who finally listened to the insistent calls for racial justice. But the civil rights movement would have been unthinkable without the rhetoric and the leadership of Protestant ministers—black and, eventually, white. King's eloquent calls for justice echoed not only the Old Testament but also the ideas of Walter Rauschenbusch, "father of the Social Gospel," whom King had read while

Fig. 9.1. Three black ministers, Fred Shuttlesworth, Ralph David Abernathy, and Martin Luther King Jr. (left to right), march for civil rights in Birmingham, Alabama, on Good Friday, 1963. From the collections of Birmingham Public Library Archives.

a student at Boston University. The rhetoric of King and others sustained the activists during their struggle, and the strains of spirituals and gospel music coming from the lips of Fanny Lou Hamer and others inspired and comforted them.

The Varieties of Activist Experience

Since the heyday of the civil rights movement, American Protestants have participated in many social justice initiatives. In the 1980s, evangelicals, inspired in equal measure by Jesus' blessing the peacemakers and heady memories of anti-Vietnam protests, backed nuclear disarmament and pacifism. Peaceniks found theological ballast in the writings of Christians like theologian John Howard Yoder and Old Testament scholar Walter Bruggeman, who, in a Bible study on Isaiah 52, reminded readers that "The baptized disciples of Jesus disengage and stand tall . . . because we know our place is not in the midst of the war-making energies of our society."[2]

Christian pacifism was most vibrantly expressed during the Gulf War, when Protestant pacifists argued that anyone who called the Prince of Peace "Lord" could not support the military strikes in the Middle East. Patricia J. Rumer, general director of Church Women United, a New York City–based group, exemplified a doveish Christian response to the conflict when she asked the world to make "no more widows from war." Retelling the story of the unjustly treated widow in Luke 18, Rumer called on world leaders to ensure that women everywhere would be able to live abundant and long lives.[3] Many Christians disagreed, pointing to the centuries-old tradition of Just War theory and arguing that sometimes Christians have an obligation to support their country in war.

World hunger has inspired Christians to write, fast, or donate. Ronald Sider, a member of Evangelicals for Social Action and author of *Rich Christians in an Age of Hunger*, urged Christians to take biblical teachings about wealth to heart and work to transform "economic relationships among [God's] people." A group of Christians formed Bread for the World, whose agenda was to "act on the crucial matter of influencing policy decisions on hunger"; in its first decade, Bread for the World attracted 45,000 members. Socially conscious Sunday school manuals directed teachers to design justice-oriented arts and crafts projects for Christian youngsters: Children could build African huts out of construction paper while their teacher "emphasize[d] the living conditions of people in India or Africa who must stay in such buildings."[4]

Another major concern for many Protestants has been urban renewal. In 1993, black activist John Perkins, writing in the pages of the socially conscious evangelical magazine *Prism*, tartly wondered if "the church at large has adopted the notion that the inner city should just heal itself." Black and white Christians, said Perkins, have fled the city, and those who have remained are parishioners of "commuter churches," who live in suburban bliss but heroically trek into the city once a week for prayer and praise.[5] Perkins accurately describes the choice of many city churches: As drug rates climbed and income levels plummeted, many churches decided to head to the hills (or at least the subdivisions).

Nonetheless, a number of American churches remain rooted in urban centers and work with local communities to heal the ills that plague cities. Take, for example, Atlanta's Central Presbyterian, which sits across from the state capitol building on the same spot it has occupied since its founding in 1858. As the title of a history of the congregation indicates, Central prides itself on being "the church that stayed" long after most other downtown churches fled the city. Or consider New Song Community Church, a PCA church founded in Baltimore, Maryland, in 1986, nestled in the Sandtown-Winchester neighborhood of west Baltimore—home to thousands of unemployed African Americans. The congregation took over a townhouse and turned it into an education center for local children, developing a preschool, a middle school, an after-school program, and a summer camp. The church also founded a health care center, worked with Habitat for Humanity to provide affordable housing, and established a corporation called EDEN JOBS to educate and train the unemployed. Clevelanders are proud of Olivet Institutional Baptist Church. Founded in 1931, Olivet has historically been committed to social justice, offering practical assistance to job seekers during the Depression and opening its doors to Martin Luther King Jr. before the civil rights movement had gained widespread acceptance in the area. At Sunday worship, church members listen to sermons that urge them to yoke their faith with activism and rouse them to go forth into the world and work for Habitat for Humanity, assist in ministry for the deaf, lead Girl and Boy Scout troops, and serve the elderly. But the church's crowning achievement has been in the arena of health care. Under the leadership of Otis Moss Jr., who became the pastor in 1974, the church began to reexamine health care. Moss understood decent health care as "a basic human right and a moral imperative rooted in our Christian faith." Olivet worked for over ten years to build a facility that would link the church and the hospital in their efforts to provide holistic healing and preventive health care. On November 15, 1997, Olivet members gathered for the dedication of the Otis Moss Jr.–University Hospital Medical Center.[6]

Just as the Bible influences Christians' conversations about gender and sexuality, so too Scripture informs Protestant approaches to social justice. Socially conscious Christians draw on the Old Testament passages about justice—such as Amos's vision of justice rolling down like a mighty river and Micah's famous instruction to do justice, love mercy, and walk humbly with God. They find inspiration in the New Testament, as well, in the words of James, who enjoins the rich to care for the poor and cautions that faith without good works is meaningless, and in the overarching tenor of Jesus' ministry to the oppressed and marginal. Among the synoptic Gospels—Matthew, Mark, and Luke, which tell many of the same stories, though sometimes with slightly different emphases—Luke is a favorite of Christian social activists. In particular, activists dwell on the Lukan redaction of the Beatitudes, in which Jesus praises the poor (in Matthew's version of the Beatitudes, Jesus praises the poor in spirit). One author, in a Lenten meditation on the Beatitudes, asks readers to consider whether "my desire for poverty of spirit is congruent with my lifestyle." Other authors claim that the Beatitudes—with their blessing of peacemakers—call Christians to pacifism. "Can we chance all we are on the beatitudes?" asked one impassioned Christian. "Can we follow the nonviolent Jesus?"[7]

What is striking about Christian social activism of the last generation, however, is not merely the many different movements Christians have supported, but the wide variety of Christians who have been involved. Common caricature paints mainliners as do-gooding bleeding hearts and evangelicals as too focused on "me and Jesus" to care much about eradicating inequality. Those stereotypes dissolve under scrutiny. Jim Wallis has argued that American Christians from diverse denominational and theological backgrounds have been able to make common cause serving the poor. During the last quarter century, he wrote, ecumenism has happened "in soup kitchens and homeless shelters more than at tables of theologians trying to find unity on the meaning of the Eucharist." Mainliners, to be sure, are sometimes more comfortable discussing social causes than the task of evangelizing unbelievers. But as churches like Atlanta's Central Presbyterian demonstrate, many mainliners understand their soup kitchens and drug rehabilitation clinics as expressions of obedience to Christ's call. For their part, evangelicals have emerged as activists, ready and eager to transform the world. Recognizing that throughout the nineteenth century, their forebearers were at the front of American reform efforts, evangelicals in groups like Sojourners and Evangelicals for Social Justice have insisted that anti-abortion activism is not the only type of political work they can and should undertake. For example, in recent years evangelicals have received high marks for their increased concern for the poor. When asked, in 1999, if evangelicals agree that assisting the poor should be a priority for Christians, Asbury Theological Seminary's Christine Pohl answered in the affirmative. She qualified her yes, though, by nothing that even if in theory evangelicals believe assisting the poor is important, most "generally use our very substantial resources for other purposes." Keith Wasserman, director of Good Works, Inc., echoed both Pohl's optimism and her caution, applauding evangelicals for their growing efforts in "relief work"—providing food and clothing for the needy—but noting that they have not, on the whole, attacked the structural causes of poverty and oppression.[8]

After Civil Rights: Racial Reconciliation

For all the diverse expressions of concern for justice, the civil rights move-ment—which united religion with a mass political movement in a way that is unique in twentieth-century American history—casts a long shadow over Christian reform. Since the civil rights movement, the church has been especially concerned with questions of racism. The movement is over, but activists understand that the churches still need to work to eradicate racism, which Jim Wallis has called "America's original sin."

The precise way Christians have chosen to address those questions, however, has changed dramatically. The civil rights movement was explic-itly political, and saw churchmen and churchwomen turning to the state to help right wrongs. Increasingly, Christians, especially evangelicals, have adopted an apolitical language that expects transformed hearts and trans-formed relationships—not transformed statutes—to bring about the just world God requires.

The new buzzword is "reconciliation"—racial reconciliation. Here is a brief survey of the names of recent books and current organizations devoted to addressing racism: *Breaking Down the Walls; A Model for Reconciliation in an Age of Racial Strife*; *He's My Brother: Former Racial Foes and Strategies for Reconciliation*; *The Coming Race Wars?: A Cry for Reconciliation*; the Twin Cities Urban Reconciliation Network; Chicago's Urban Reconciliation En-terprise; the John M. Perkins Foundation for Reconciliation and Develop-ment; and so on. In 1996, Promise Keepers devoted itself to racial recon-ciliation. During the 1990s, *Christianity Today* published numerous articles on the issue, but most of them advocated "getting to know people of other races" and befriending them rather than integrating neighborhoods or working against discrimination in any systematic fashion.[9]

Some Christians' commitment to racial justice has gone beyond hugs and rhetoric, though they work in a framework of friendship and recon-ciliation. David Anderson and Brent Zuercher, a black and a white Christian who jointly wrote a collection of letters about racism, stated as their aims "the action of restoring friendship or harmony and the action of settling or resolving differences." Reconciliation involves a "macroelement," but it "starts with and must happen first between two individuals."[10]

Spencer Perkins, son of African American activist John Perkins, and Chris Rice, a white "Vermont Yankee," lived together in an interracial intentional community in Jackson, Mississippi, until Perkins died of a heart attack in 1998. Perkins and Rice argued that the church—and America— needs more than integration; it needs healing. Integration, they rightly noted, was the strategy of one particular political movement—the civil rights movement of the 1950s and 1960s. "*Integration* is a political and social concept," they wrote. "The *beloved community* spoken of by biblical and contemporary prophets is a much higher calling." Perkins and Rice want blacks and whites to spend time together. They want white suburbanites to borrow lawnmowers and screwdrivers from their black neighbors. They credit socializing between the races with leading to justice, suggesting, for example, that "it is no accident that Republican Jack Kemp and Democrat Bill Bradley were for two years their parties' most passionate voices for racial healing": The two former sports stars learned about the importance of racial justice from their years sharing locker rooms with black athletes.[11]

Some anti-racist activists have pointed to Pentecost as a holiday that is especially compatible with fostering racial reconciliation. Described in Acts 2, the first Pentecost was a literary and theological reversal of Babel. At Pentecost, the Holy Spirit descended on members of the early church and enabled them to speak in foreign tongues. A crowd gathered, amazed, because "each one heard them speaking in his own language." The holiday's theme of bridging difference, say Protestant activists, should inspire Christians to get to know people of different races. As Michael Verchot put it, Pentecost draws people from all backgrounds into one community. On Pentecost, many Protestants convene Bible studies on Acts 2, Galatians 3, Ephesians 2, and other passages that show that God's spirit can unite people. Pastors preach sermons on interracial dialogue; they ask parishioners to take a cue from the model of the early church and spend time with people whose background, pedigree, or skin color is different.[12]

This idea of togetherness certainly seems to have biblical imprimatur— Jesus himself spent much of his time with women, lepers, and other outcasts with whom Jewish carpenters did not usually associate—and it has taken hold in contemporary Christendom. But not all Christians are satisfied with the reconciliation movement. Sociologists Michael Emerson and Christian Smith have blasted white evangelicals for a theological-cum-political strategy that focuses so much on individual friendship and reconciliation that it admits no real structural change.[13] Ethicist David Gushee has argued that friendship is well and good, but it is no substitute for political change. "The concept of reconciliation is empty of content," said Gushee, "unless it is built upon the sturdy foundation of justice. If reconciliation is understood as the repair of broken relationships and the restoration of trusting and intimate community between persons or groups, then justice is its first step. There can be no racial reconciliation unless there is first the redress of race-based or race-linked injustice, just as there can generally be no reconciliation between alienated persons or groups until or unless previous and current wrongs are constructively addressed."[14] Some ministers have wondered if the Religious Right is, in fact, genuine when it calls for reconciliation. Herbert D. Valentine, Executive Presbyter of the Baltimore Presbytery of the Presbyterian Church (U.S.A), said, referring to Pat Robertson's support of Jesse Helms and David Duke, "We might be more willing to accept their claims at face value were it not for the Christian Coalition's repeated willingness to work with racists." Frederick James, retired bishop of the Second Episcopal district of the African Methodist Episcopal Church, echoed the point, insisting that calls for reconciliation meant little if those doing the calling also supported political programs that were at odds with the needs of black America. In particular, James pointed to the Religious Right's antistatism: "The leadership of the Christian Coalition . . . sought to dismantle legal services for the poor. . . . Reed and Robertson supported cuts in Medicare and Medicaid, supported cuts in Social Security, and pushed for the harshest forms of welfare reform versions which, even more than the present law, punish children because their parents are poor."[15]

Charitable Choice: Faith-Based Social Programs and the Federal Government

All Christians, however, agree that individual Christians and individual churches should be feeding the hungry and clothing the naked—and helping them to feed and clothe themselves. For example, many liberal Protestants opposed the sweeping changes of the 1996 Welfare Reform Act. Methodists, Lutherans, and Congregationalists in cities across the nation participated in rallies and flooded their representatives in Congress with mail protesting the scaling back of welfare. But once the bill was signed into law, those Christians—and many who had supported ending welfare as they knew it—rechanneled their energies toward assisting the citizens whom the bill would affect directly. In Kentucky, churches ran vans to help newly employed women get to work. In Minneapolis, they gave and lent money to women who wanted to start in-home day-care services. In Richmond, Raleigh, and Seattle, churches offered job training services, and in

programs like Faith and Families (Mississippi), Hope Makers Job Partnerships (Minnesota), and One Church, One Family (Delaware), they helped
workers learn job-retention and money management skills. National organizations rolled up their collective sleeves as well: In September 1997,
the National Association of Evangelicals gathered leaders from fourteen
denominations for a program designed to help church leaders deal with the
transformations welfare reform would bring. The Center for Public Justice
convened three similar conferences.[16]

When it comes to government participation in social reforms, however,
Christians find themselves in vehement disagreements. As sociologist and
minister Tony Campolo has said, Christians may understand that you cannot "spiritualize the beatitudes," but "controversy rears its ugly head when
it comes to public policy."[17]

One of the cornerstones of the 2000 presidential campaign was charitable choice, the notion that the federal government should funnel relief
money through religious organizations to those in need. Candidates argued
that faith-based organizations already conducted effective relief work; with
an infusion of federal money, they would be able to improve and enhance
their efforts. At the same time, the government would be able to shed some
of its burden for social welfare.

Both of the major candidates for president, Albert Gore and George
W. Bush, endorsed the proposal, albeit with minor differences. In an interview during the campaign, Bush supported the idea and added that faith-
based programs work in part because of their spiritual emphasis. "There
are faith-based organizations in drug treatment that work so well because
they convince a person to turn their life over to Christ," he said. "And by
doing so, they change the person's heart. A person with a changed heart is
less likely to be addicted to drugs and alcohol."

Bush and others looked to Eugene Rivers, pastor of the Azusa Christian
Community, a pentecostal congregation in the Dorchester neighborhood of
Boston. Rivers, who was converted at age thirteen while listening to Billy
Graham on the radio, had developed a program called the Ten Point Coalition, a multifaceted initiative involving religious and governmental agencies aimed at training community leaders and strengthening family bonds.
Rivers's plan was so successful that it became a model for how faith-based
initiatives could relieve the government of the responsibility for social welfare while simultaneously augmenting church programs.

Charitable choice was not new to the Bush administration. Passed in
the 1996 Welfare Reform Act, the plan allowed religious groups to get

federal funds for social services without requiring them to conceal their religious character. But the Bush administration has made charitable choice a priority, hiring John J. DiIulio Jr., a maverick Democrat and a professor at the University of Pennsylvania, as head of the new Office of Faith-Based and Community Initiatives. DiIulio, an expert in corrections policy, had become convinced of the potential of churches to prevent rampant crime, especially in the African American community. The United States, he noted, has some 65,000 black churches with 23 million adherents. These churches, he concluded, "are outperforming many secular alternatives in terms of primary and secondary crime prevention." Bush's appointment of DiIulio drew widespread praise, even from those who took a dim view of faith-based funding. Until he stepped down during the summer of 2001—citing health problems and family demands—DiIulio was the point man who lobbied Congress to pass Bush's proposal to give more money to faith-based groups. He guided a watered-down version of the bill through the House, but was not able to persuade the Senate to consider the bill before he resigned.

Free federal dollars would seem like a hard thing to pass up, but to the surprise of many, including President Bush, Protestant leaders in America were fiercely divided about the wisdom and benevolence of charitable choice. Though many Christians—not to mention Jews, Hindus, and Muslims—were eager for the financial help, some prominent evangelicals have come out against the Bush administration's plan. Jerry Falwell worried publicly about the faith-based programs when he figured out that they would subsidize not only Christians, but other religious groups as well. He seemed especially exercised about the possibility of Muslims and Scientologists receiving funds. Other conservative leaders—most notably Pat Robertson and Richard Land, head of the SBC's Ethics and Religious Liberty Commission—voiced a different fear. With government dollars come government rules; if Washington starts funding church-based social projects, then Washington will be in a position to regulate those programs. The white conservative evangelicals' concern echoed debates about the First Amendment; the separation of church and state was instituted not so much to protect government from religion but to protect religion from government.

Land and others have criticized the Bush administration for its blithe assumption that religious organizations can deliver social services without being religious. In fact, says Land, Christians cannot comply with that— and do not want to. Land believes that the gospel is not some add-in that can be removed from a Christian soup kitchen or pregnancy center. He also fears the reach of the state. "Partnering with the government in this way will increase your exposure to government intervention in your ministries," he wrote. "Is working with the government to obey our biblical mandate to help the poor, the hungry and the hurting worth that exposure? That is a question each church, synagogue, temple and mosque must decide for itself. As for me and my house, I would not touch the money with the proverbial 10-foot pole."[18] Contemporary evangelicals—in contrast, say, to the evangelicals of the 1940s—may be politically engaged, but the politics of many is about rolling back the state and the reach of politics. That has never been made clearer than in current debates about the extent to which the state should be involved in social programs.

Many local Christian leaders agree. When it surveyed ninety-six members of the Association of Gospel Rescue Missions, *World* magazine found that three out of five of the affiliated missions organizations would not apply for government funds if they became available. And if Washington insisted that religious organizations "segment" their activities into those that were "religious" and "nonreligious" in order to qualify for funds, 81 percent of the groups surveyed said they would not seek government dollars. As a representative of a Philadelphia group said, "Evangelical faith-based organizations cannot segment their programs into 'religious' and 'nonreligious' aspects. Christ is the center of all we do." "Can I say that only parts of my life are religious?" echoed a missions organization in Rock Island, Illinois. "I hope not."[19] Barbara Johnson of the Capitol Hill Crisis Pregnancy Center—an anti-abortion crisis facility that keeps statistics on how many of its clients convert to Christianity every year—said that, even for a substantial funding offer, she could not separate her Christian witness from the rest of her work at the center. "We're a package deal," she said. "If you want this to work, you can't leave that part out. We'd be like any other social service agency, and we'd have their results."[20]

African American churches, too, have argued over the merits of faith-based funding. In April 2001, a group of black clergy attended a Washington conference called "Black Churches and Political Leadership in the New Millennium." Of the attendees, 21 percent strongly supported government funding of faith-based programs, while 39 percent strongly opposed it.[21]

Many African Americans want the very thing Land and his allies fear: robust state involvement. An NAACP resolution on charitable choice stated that "the NAACP opposes any and all faith-based and charitable choice initiatives which do not include traditional and well-established employment rights, civil rights and antidiscrimination protections which can be enforced by our nation's courts." Representatives of the Congress of National Black Churches, an umbrella organization for eight historically black denominations, have said they feel, in the words of AME Bishop John Hurst Adams, "somewhere between alarm to caution to militant opposition." Reverend C. Mackey Daniels said that "this initiative can only be seen as another effort to muffle the prophetic voice of the African-American church."[22]

For his part, Rivers, whose political philosophy is something of a cross between William H. Seymour and William Julius Wilson, has long supported faith-based programs. But he shares with some of his coreligionists the sense that white evangelicals, in their anti-statism have not been the friends of black people. When Land, Falwell, and other white evangelicals came out against the Bush administration's plan, Rivers charged racism. Rivers identified a "racial logic" in their response; since they realized the Bush initiative would help African Americans in inner cities, they walked away from the table. Rivers points to the so-called Samaritan Project: In 1997, the Christian Coalition pledged to give $10 million to black churches, but nothing more came of the promise than a press conference. When DiIulio stepped down, Rivers said African Americans could forget about benefiting from charitable choice. "Without John J. DiIulio, there is no substantial commitment to the faith-based initiative beyond underwriting the interests of white evangelicals and the white mainline denominations. The black and brown churches that serve poor people have no place at the Bush administration's table beyond being exploited with ceremonial rituals."[23]

At the turn of a new century, American Protestants were as concerned with social justice as they ever have been. But social justice ideals were torn between, on the one hand, those of the Progressive era and the civil rights movement, which pushed the state to do more in the interests of justice, and, on the other hand, a conservative political movement that wants the church to push the state away from the arena of social welfare. Conservative white evangelicals suggest that the integrity of the church is at stake; their interlocutors agree, but suggest that "integrity" is manifest less in the church's freedom from state regulation and more in the lives of America's poorest citizens—those whom Jesus called "the least of these."

CONCLUSION

The Promise of Protestantism in the Twenty-first Century

At the turn of the twentieth century George A. Campbell Jr., editor of a small periodical called *The Christian Oracle*, published in Chicago, thought that the turn of the calendar was so propitious that he wanted to change the name of his magazine. "We believe that the coming century is to witness greater triumphs in Christianity than any previous century has ever witnessed," Campbell wrote in his editorial announcing the name change, "and that it is to be more truly Christian than any of its predecessors." Henceforth, the editor declared, the magazine would be called *The Christian Century*.

The magazine, as it turned out, was purchased in 1908 by Charles Clayton Morrison, who transformed *The Christian Century* into the mouthpiece for liberal, or mainline, Protestantism throughout the twentieth century. With the approach of the twenty-first century, however, the magazine's name caused the editors some embarrassment. The influx of non-Protestant—and non-Christian—immigrants following changes to the immigration laws in 1965 made the United States appear quite a bit less Christian in 2000 than it had in 1900. Although the federal government had added "under God" to the Pledge of Allegiance and "In God We Trust" to the currency in the 1950s, America seemed much more secular at the end of the century than it had at the beginning.

The *Protestant* Century?

The question of whether or not the twentieth century in America was a *Christian* century, however, may not be as simple as it seems. At first glance, the answer would seem to be no, but the fact remains that, depending on the polling data one consults, approximately 80 percent of Americans who express a religious preference call themselves Christians. Although there is no question that the influx of Buddhists, Hindus, Sikhs, Muslims, and representatives of other religious traditions has altered the religious landscape in America—now dotted with Islamic mosques, Hindu temples, Sikh gurdwārās—the United States remains an overwhelmingly Christian nation. And despite the increased assimilation of Catholics into American culture—symbolized by the election of John F. Kennedy, a Roman Catholic, to the presidency in 1960—Protestantism remains the religious expression of the majority in America.

One cannot deny, however, that the *mainline* Protestantism that *The Christian Century* espoused was not the ascendant form of Christianity at the turn of the twenty-first century. Indeed, despite the self-confident predictions that evangelicalism would wither and die, mainline Protestantism suffered the greatest decline. Even though mainline Protestantism continued to embody the aspirations of middle-class Americans, as it had in the 1950s, Americans' allegiance to its denominations dropped precipitously in the final decades of the twentieth century (as did the number of subscribers to *The Christian Century*). At the same time, evangelical churches and denominations grew in numbers, donations, and cultural influence. Evangelicalism, with its time-honored ability to adjust to the cultural idiom, offered certainty—a clearly articulated theology and morality—in an age of moral ambiguity symbolized by the Vietnam War, the sexual revolution, the emergence of the counterculture, and Richard Nixon's duplicity.

As evangelicals articulated clear ideas about God, the Bible, and morality, mainline Protestants sought desperately to stanch the bleeding, initiating all sorts of renewal programs to lure their members back to church. In an effort to regain touch with their constituents, several denominations moved their offices out of New York City and into the hinterlands—the United Church of Christ to Cleveland, the Lutherans to Chicago, and the Presbyterians to Louisville, Kentucky. The Episcopalians even declared the 1990s their "Decade of Evangelism," an event that passed almost entirely without notice, both within and outside of the denomination.

Curiously, the strategy they most often employed was arguably the strategy that had caused their decline in the first place: ecumenism. The ecumenical movement has a long history, dating back at least to the Protestant Reformation, but the most successful religious movements in American history have been *exclusive*, not inclusive. At the same time that Americans were looking for theological definition, mainline Protestants chose to minimize further their doctrinal and institutional differences in the name of Christian unity. By the turn of the twenty-first century it had become increasingly difficult to distinguish a Presbyterian from a Methodist or a Congregationalist, thereby undermining even more any vestigial loyalties that Americans had to one denomination or another.

As Protestants moved into the twenty-first century, they could not be as sanguine about their cultural hegemony or their internal unity as they were a hundred years earlier. Despite the challenges facing Protestantism today—the task of theological definition, the responsibilities of working for social justice, the calls for change from feminists and gay rights advocates—Protestants in America can derive some comfort from the fact that the movement is healthy and thriving. Examples of vitality abound, from creativity at the pulpit to an intellectual renaissance among evangelical Protestants, offering promise for the future.

Renewal of Preaching

When Fleming Rutledge stands up to preach, people listen. She is an elegant woman with a powerful, orthodox message about the saving work of Jesus Christ. She is also an Episcopal priest, and if you want her to come preach at your church, you will have to book her months in advance. Crowds around the country flock to hear Tony Campolo, a sociologist at Eastern College and a preacher who deftly mixes humor and passion into his sermons. Another revered preacher is William Willimon, the dean of the Duke University Chapel. An ordained Methodist minister, Willimon has served at Duke since 1984. He has written some fifty books, but he is most famous for his preaching. He made Baylor University's 1996 list of the twelve most effective preachers in the English language. So did Episcopal priest Barbara Brown Taylor, Baptist Gardner C. Taylor (whom *Time* magazine once called "the dean of the nation's black preachers"), Dallas Theological Seminary's Charles Swindoll, and, not surprisingly, Billy Graham.

Preaching has always stood at the center of the Protestant church experience in America. Puritans in colonial New England heard an average of fifteen thousand hours of sermons during a lifetime—as compared with, for example, fifteen hundred hours of lectures a college student hears in the course of earning a four-year college degree.[1] From Cotton Mather's seventeenth-century musings on "The Wonders of the Invisible World" and Devereux Jarratt's eighteenth-century words on "The Nature of the

Love of Christ" to Dwight Moody's postbellum sermon "On Being Born Again," sermons have been the stuff of Protestant spirituality (not to mention some of the great works of modern literature). And, as Martin Luther King Jr. demonstrated at the March on Washington, the sermon's role in American life extends beyond the church and the revival tent.[2]

Although one is likely to hear a few grumbles as parishioners across the country head to the after-worship coffee hour on Sunday mornings, American Protestants still know how to deliver sermons that have the power to bring people to faith. Protestant preachers today also deserve kudos for their willingness to take risks. Many preachers are experimenting with what one commentator has called different homiletical "plots." For example, Eugene Lowry, who teaches preaching and communication at Saint Paul School of Theology in Kansas City, Missouri, has developed a technique that, unfortunately, he calls "Preaching from Oops to Yeah." The moniker may be infantilizing, but Lowry's homiletical plot is actually sophisticated and effective. He begins by naming some problem or point of tension that arises from his text; then he analyzes the problem; then in the "Aha" stage of the plot he "reveals insights from the gospel that point to ways in which God's love and call for justice can resolve the tension and difficulties articulated earlier in the sermon; fourth ("Whee"), he offers an imaginative recreation of the gospel; and finally, he unfolds the future that grows out of the gospel message.

His sermon "A Knowing Glimpse," on Luke 24:13–35, the story of the road to Emmaus, illustrates his technique. Lowry opens by asking an offbeat question: Just what are those two men doing on the road to Emmaus anyway? Then, Lowry admits that when he first read Emmaus, he simply did not believe that the two men did not recognize the risen Jesus as soon as he appeared at their side. "How could they not know it was he?" Then (this is the "Aha") Lowry admits that he does not "wonder anymore," because of something that happened to him at a birthday party twenty-five years before. Eventually, Lowry explains the old, familiar story—Jesus' breaking of bread at the travelers' table, and with that breaking of bread a breaking of "the veil of their ignorance"—in a way that seems fresh and alive. In the fragments of broken bread, the strangers got a "fragmentary glimpse" of the risen Jesus, a glimpse that turned their lives around 180 degrees. And ("Yeah"), we too might get a glimpse, and it might revolutionize our lives, just as it revolutionized the lives of the strangers on the road to Emmaus.[3]

Preachers today are also more willing than ever before to draw on personal experiences in illuminating the gospel—a trend, perhaps, that is both a cause and an effect of our ever more voyeuristic talk-show culture. Kathy Black, Gerald H. Kennedy Professor of Preaching and Worship at California's Claremont School of Theology, opened one dramatic sermon, called "Why Me?", with a story about suffering: "I was a wonderful dancer. A celebration to end four years of high school. He was with his girlfriend and they were double dating with his football buddy." The prom ends with a car accident and the death of one of those couples. Black goes on, offering a litany of senseless suffering: a divorced mother diagnosed with brain cancer; a young woman diagnosed with schizophrenia; a troop of Girl Scouts who swam every summer in a lake contaminated with toxic waste runoff. Then Black ups the ante, revealing that "My own disability . . . was a result of this toxic exposure, [and it] manifests itself in what I call 'spells.' For me, a 'spell' means I lose all muscle tone and basically become paralyzed." The sermon is not just an exercise in solipsism, though. Black circles around to the gospel, to stories in Matthew and Mark about Jesus' healings, and she concludes by urging her audience to "be God's agents of healing in our hurting world."[4]

Preaching today is noteworthy not only because pastors are exploring new forms for their sermons, but also because of the content of their sermons. Today's preachers often engage theology in the pulpit, and not only that, they often demonstrate its meaning there. Preachers like Yale Divinity School's Serene Jones use the sermon to respond to larger philosophical trends. Jones's "A Church of Good Friday" has been called an example of postliberal preaching, because it does not evaluate the church's claims on standards derived from outside the church (especially derived from the Enlightenment), an exercise especially provocative at Easter time. Instead of asking who was responsible for Jesus' death, or whether Jesus was really raised again, Jones discusses Good Friday from the perspective of a friend who only recently became a Christian and who, for the first time, was stumbling through the process of figuring out what it meant to belong to a community "that founds its identity upon a tale of genuine murder." To read the Good Friday story, Jones suggests, we should not look for where we are in the story—do we identify with Pilate, or the disciples, or Mary? Rather, we should ask what Jesus sees when he looks out from the cross. In this way, Jones narrates the church in the church's own vocabulary, on the church's own terms, while avoiding the problem of tautology (as Ronald Allen puts it, "The community should accept a Christian version of life because that version is at the center of Christian language and community") that so often plagues postliberal preaching.[5]

If ivory tower–based preachers like Jones take preaching as an opportunity to introduce audiences to new philosophical trends, many pastors
perform rather simpler—but even more important—theological work on
Sunday mornings. They introduce their audiences to the basics of the gospel. Indeed, hecklers who insist that the Protestant mainline has abandoned
Christianity for feel-good therapy better suited to a twelve-step meeting
need only listen to Barbara Brown Taylor or Fleming Rutledge preach.

Rutledge has moved from a parish post in New York to a ministry of
evangelistic preaching across the country (in large part, some have observed, because of that pesky stained-glass ceiling—the Episcopal Church
may welcome women priests, but not, apparently, as rectors of large urban
churches). Listening to Rutledge is like listening to Dwight L. Moody or
Charles Finney, except that Rutledge's sermons, while every bit as evangelistic as her forebears', are also unmistakably contemporary. As the title
of one of her books, *The Bible and the New York Times*, suggests, Rutledge's
concern is to show how the gospel speaks to the conundrums of modern
life, not to make the Bible relevant, but to bring out the Bible's timeless
truths. She is especially sensitive to the late-twentieth- and early-twenty-
first-century plague of doubt (as the title of her second book, *Help My
Unbelief*, suggests). She makes sophisticates feel okay about believing something as old-fashioned as the Bible. As *Christianity Today*'s Michael Maudlin
put it, "Her preached words reassure me that I am indeed on the right path,
that wisdom and traditional Christian faith belong together, that I can have
a big view of God while simultaneously reading sophisticated pundits and
opinion journalists."[6]

Taylor, who once served All Saints' Episcopal Church in Atlanta and
Grace-Calvary in Clarkesville, Georgia, now holds the Harry R. Butman
Chair in Religion and Philosophy at Piedmont College in Demorest, Georgia. Her published collections of sermons disprove the generally sound
bromide that sermons have short shelf lives and should not be anthologized.
Taylor's sermons are distinguished because she has a gift with words, she
laces her preaching with autobiographical nuggets, and, as those who have
been privileged to hear her in person know, her delivery makes the whole
of each sermon greater than the sum of its parts. It is tempting to say that
the Holy Spirit is present during her preaching. Most striking is the con-
sistency with which she preaches Christ crucified. She does not soften Jesus'
words to make them go down easily.

Take her sermon on Luke 13:1–9. Like Black, Taylor took suffering as
her theme. She told the story of a woman whose five-year-old daughter
had a brain tumor. The mother understood the tumor as God's punishing

her for smoking so much. Brown said that most of us react to tragedy that way, making sense of calamity by "wondering what we did wrong." But, she said, "Jesus doesn't go there." He does not set up simple equations whereby bad things happen to bad people as punishment for their misdeeds (and, by implication, bad things do not happen to righteous people). "No, Jesus says, there is no connection between the suffering and the sin. Whew. But unless you repent, you are going to lose some blood too. Oh."[7]

Taylor speaks of "sin," a word, some observers have charged, not heard very often in mainline churches.[8] Sin is one of Taylor's favorite themes. She wants Christians to use sin, and other hard words, because, she says, "Abandoning the language of sin will not make sin go away." Sin is real, she tells her flock over and over, and the only true response to sin is the cross.[9]

Spiritual Direction and the Recovery of Liturgy

Preaching the Word of God remains at the center of American Protestantism, but Protestants are also turning toward devotional practices they once derided as Catholic. Increasingly, Presbyterian and Baptist churches across the country are celebrating Holy Communion weekly, rather than once a month or once a quarter, as in the past. Protestants all along the theological spectrum are delving into liturgical prayer and spiritual direction. (Spiritual direction is a variant of the centuries'-old Catholic practice of submitting to the spiritual guidance, or direction, of another, usually a seasoned believer considered to be more mature.)

Spiritual directors, who might be cynically described as personal trainers of the soul, are experts in prayer. Often, but certainly not limited to, members of the cloth, spiritual directors meet with their "clients" in a therapy-like setting to pray together and help the client in his or her prayer life. Although the practice of spiritual direction should not be overstated, especially among evangelicals, noted Christian novelist Susan Wise Bauer wrote: "We buy books, in part, because of our reluctance to take prayer out of the closet: Most of us don't have (and wouldn't welcome) the interference of a spiritual director—an experienced Christian who helps us to pray and lends a hand in interpreting the answers." But the practice is growing, and those Christians who partake swear by it. "My spiritual director is really essential to me," said Georgia Sweeny, an Iowa Methodist who has been meeting with her spiritual director for two years. "I couldn't do it without her. My prayer life is just so much richer than before."

Sweeny's sentiments are echoed by evangelicals all across the country, who marvel that it "took so long for us evangelicals to catch on to the wisdom of this discipline," as Sweeny put it. A typical meeting with a spiritual director would begin and end with prayer; the meat of the meeting would consist of either praying together or discussing a given prayer technique. *Lectio divina*, a Benedictine approach to prayer that involves letting the words of Scripture speak directly to the person praying, is a favorite among American spiritual directors. But evangelicals investigating the practice of spiritual direction for the first time are increasingly making "soul healing" prayer central to spiritual direction.

Spiritual direction is not the only historically Catholic practice that contemporary Protestants find appealing. Mainline and evangelical Protestants alike have found a new appreciation for formal liturgy at the turn of the twenty-first century, practices once shunned as papist nonsense. The publication of a spate of prayer books for the liturgically challenged—most notably Robert Benson's *Venite* and Phyllis Tickle's three-volume lectionary—is just one sign of Protestants' turn to liturgical prayer. Tickle explains that Christians have been saying fixed prayers, at fixed hours, since antiquity. "But that was something we Protestants lost," says Tickle. "Catholics, of course, kept it up, but Protestants got away from the habit of saying regular prayers at regular hours." The recent Protestant rediscovery of the divine hours, she says, has a lot to do with Christians meeting Buddhists. "Christians began to learn from their Buddhist neighbors about spiritual practices like meditation, and they began to ask, Doesn't Christianity offer any spiritual practices?" Yes, says Tickle enthusiastically: liturgical prayer.

Tickle says it is important for Christians to engage in Christian practices. Sitting Zen is all well and good, but if you use Buddhist maps to navigate spiritual terrain, you are probably going to wind up in Buddhist places, "and that is not where mama and grandmama were when they prayed."

The recovery of Christian spiritual disciplines like liturgical prayer and *lectio divina* has to do not only with meeting Buddhists, but attenuating some of the centuries'-old Protestant suspicions of Catholicism. "My grandmother would be rolling over in her grave if she knew what I was up to," says Charles Bagden, a Southern Baptist whose copy of Tickle's *Divine Hours* sat on his bedside table with a Bible and a Len Deighton novel. "She taught me to pray, and she taught me to pray well," says Bagden. "She taught me I could be intimate with God, that I could talk to Jesus like a friend and tell him anything." Bagden insists that he will never give up that type of prayer.

But he says that "conversational, pull-your-chair-up-and-pour-your-heart-out style of praying isn't everything, and it isn't enough. Praying the liturgy regularly forces a discipline to one's prayer, so that you do not always pray about the issues on the top of your head. Without the liturgy it is easy to get stuck in a rut. You might always ask God to help you through things, but leave off praising Him, or leave off praying for the needs of the poor. With the liturgy guiding you, you can't forget to do those things."

Many Protestant congregations, even those with decidedly low-church pedigrees, are also appropriating liturgy in their worship. In so doing, they not only connect with historic creeds and traditions, they attract a new generation of churchgoers, many of whom have grown weary of the contemporary worship styles that dominate the baby-boomer megachurches. The endless search for novelty and the emphasis on entertainment in these new-style congregations has robbed Christianity of its history, even its dignity, liturgical advocates believe. "In most of our churches, people don't sing anymore, because it's performance," laments Robert Webber, a professor at Northern Baptist Theological Seminary.[10]

The return to liturgy among Protestants implies that some of their longstanding suspicions toward Roman Catholicism and Eastern Orthodoxy have abated. Protestant congregations unabashedly appropriate elements associated with these historic traditions—creeds, prayers, liturgies, even, at times, vestments and incense—while they remain grounded in Protestant theology. Protestant liturgical renewal also signals a movement away from a faith beholden to Enlightenment rationalism. "We are currently experiencing a revolution in communication whereby we are moving from verbal to symbolic means of expression," Webber, an Episcopalian, explains. "The symbolism is part of the text of worship."[11]

The countercultural character of this liturgical renewal appeals to the younger generation. "The liturgical style is more serious about mystery," according to Dean Borgman, who teaches at Gordon-Conwell Theological Seminary. "This is attractive to Gen-Xers because mystery provides a more satisfactory solution than the cognitive explanations of suffering, tragedy and the cross. Protestants tend to explain these things, and postmodern folks don't accept the explanations. The mystery suggests that things aren't supposed to be explained."[12]

A New Generation

Protestants in America have always taken seriously the task of evangelism. Evangelicals share their name with the term "evangelize," which means to spread the good news. As recently as the 1950s, even the National Council of Churches had an evangelist, Charles Templeton, on its payroll.* From Charles Finney's "new measures" to the Salvation Army's Hallelujah Lasses' boisterous songs, from Dwight Moody to Billy Graham, reaching the next generation has always been central to the designs of American Protestants. As sociologist Arlene Sanchez Walsh said, "Evangelical Christianity has an almost limitless ability to harness its message to nearly every facet of popular culture: bobby-soxers, hippies, cholos, tattooed, body-pierced college students searching for God—if there is a song to be co-opted, a style to be transformed, a ministry will seek to do just that."[13]

Recognizing that only about 30 percent of Generation-Xers attend Sunday worship, churches are frantically trying to get a line on "Gen-X spirituality" and boldly trying to minister to them. Tom Beaudoin, an Xer who also happens to be a former altar boy and a Ph.D. candidate in religion and education, became the guru of Gen-X spirituality with his 1998 book *Virtual Faith: The Irreverent Spiritual Quest of Generation X.*[14] Beaudoin characterizes Xers with three i's: irreverence, irony, and anti-institutionalism. One sees the irreverence in everything from Xers' taste in music to their taste in body art, all of which flouts the standards and mores of their elders, just as their parents' generation did in the 1960s. As for the irony, Beaudoin points to Xers' "employment of sexuality in pop culture," which, far from signifying how far Xers have fallen into promiscuity, instead points to "How deeply GenX desires God." Finally, says Beaudoin, Xers exhibit a strong streak of anti-institutionalism—something else, presumably, they got from their parents. This distaste of institutions has not just pushed Xers out of denominations; it is giving birth to a whole new theology.

"A new sort of GenX liberation theology is emerging," says Beaudoin, "but it is not primarily about the poor, who are normally the focus of liberation theology. Instead, it begins with the liberation of Jesus from the clutches of the Church."[15] *Virtual Faith* was just the splashiest of numerous books and articles that alerted church leaders to the need to think creatively about how to get Xers to church. And churches responded not just by thinking, but by building all sorts of programs designed to attract those between twenty and their early thirties. Lutheran churches that have developed Gen-X ministries include, for example, Saint Paul's in Tracy, California (which holds its "Com21" Ministries worship service at 6:00 P.M. on Sundays), and Zion Lutheran Church in Anaheim ("Fuel" meets at 6:30; "If you don't think you belong in church," their savvy motto proclaims, "then you belong here"). For those "born after 1960," Triumphant Cross Evangelical Lutheran Church in St. Clair Shores, Michigan, holds a special evening service that meets in the church gym. Lakeville, Minnesota's Hosanna! Lutheran Church runs Higher Grounds Ministries for "singles and newlyweds in [their] 20s–30s." Lutherans at The Well in Pineville, North Carolina, are remodeling an old church into a coffee shop/worship site with couches, chairs, and tables. Trinity Lutheran Church in Cleveland operates The Alternate Grind, a Friday evening coffeehouse, at a former cigar bar in Cleveland's warehouse district.

Protestants disagree among themselves about these Gen-X ministries. Not everyone, for example, shares Beaudoin's "irreverent" assumption that Gen-Xers are, in their bones, opposed to anything institutional. Some Xers, in fact, are attracted to liturgy, one of the most institutional expressions of Christianity.[16] And not all Christians believe that these generational strategies should be encouraged. Dieter Zander used to head up Axis, the Gen-X ministry for Willow Creek Community Church, suburban Chicago's megachurch; now Zander says he has some questions about the wisdom of trying to build "a church [for Xers] within a church. . . . Creating new churches within churches leads to the hall of mirrors question: When will it ever stop? The potentially endless proliferation of new subgroups begins to look like it is based on nothing more substantial than catering to new styles. That kind of shallowness won't last." Zander now helps start churches in San Francisco, where, he says, "both 'youth' and those who are older have characteristics we have often associated with Gen Xers . . . it's clearer than ever that these are cultural, not merely generational, characteristics."[17]

Andy Crouch, editor of *Regeneration Quarterly*, has questioned not just the wisdom of generationally specific worship services, but of the very category "generation," which, he says, "is a convenient fiction born of equal parts historical accident, marketing genius, and over-simplification. Like every construct, it is a useful tool for those who maintain it—mostly, those whose businesses require a segmented market and those who make their living at cultural commentary and prognostication." But, he says, generational segmentation may not be useful for the church; indeed, it may be downright destructive. After all, Christians are a people whose sacred Scripture reminds readers, "The eye cannot say to the hand, 'I have no need of you,' nor the head to the feet, 'I have no need of you'" (1 Cor. 12:21 RSV).[18]

Still, for all the controversy they have inspired, Gen-X ministries seem to work—if success means reeling in new converts. Xers are proving true one of the slogans they grew up with: If you build it, they will come. One young woman, for example, attended the Committed Christian Fellowship, an Xer movement born in a surf shop and affiliated with Calvary Chapel, and was impressed. "It gave me a new view of God," she said. "Everyone was just like this neo-postmodern Christian punk rock. . . . It kinda gave me a new outlook on [Christianity] . . . it's like you think one way about something, and then someone comes around and like, they'll show you another way to look at it. It's refreshing."[19]

The ministry to Generation X provides an example of the adaptability of American Protestantism to cultural changes. Born out of a desire to evangelize, Protestants have been willing to reinvent and to reinterpret their tradition to successive generations, taking full advantage of market forces. In the nineteenth century evangelicals organized Sunday schools as a means of reaching the younger generation, and in the twentieth century they turned to various forms of electronic media. Despite the critics who decry innovative methods as pandering, this strategy has served Protestantism—especially evangelicalism—well for three centuries; it seems likely that it will continue to produce results into the twenty-first century.

Protestant Engagement with Popular Culture

The religious use of popular culture has a utility for Protestants beyond reaching the younger generation. One could talk about this renaissance in the visual arts—pointing, for example, to the dark, eerie paintings of North Carolina's G. Carol Bohmer. Her rejection of anything reminiscent of Precious Moments inspired one reporter to warn that "Anyone who likes their Christian images served up in safe Sunday School settings beware."[20] Or one could point to developments in contemporary Christian music: Jars of Clay, with their distinctive sound that has "crossed over" to the popular music charts; Jennifer Knapp, whose throaty voice and folksy rhythms have garnered her unapologetically Christian tunes Grammy nominations and have earned her a spot at Lilith Fair; and Julie Miller, whose haunting lyrics about a man who makes "old things" like broken hearts "new" could be mistaken for a stirring love song, until one realizes her direct object is Jesus, not a boyfriend. One could even point to a new presence of Protestants on television. Kristin Chenoweth, whom critics say was the only good thing to come out of the Broadway disaster *You're a Good Man, Charley Brown,* has starred in an eponymous NBC series about a Southern Baptist actress trying to make it in New York. In shows like *Seventh Heaven,* upstanding, white-bread ministers dish up family values and some watered-down version of faith. Christian expositions of the faith have also appeared on the silver screen; motion pictures like *The Spitfire Grill* and *The Apostle* provide only two of several examples.

Protestants—especially evangelicals—have also taken on cultural criticism, with writers like William Romanowski and Rodney Clapp suggesting that insularity and condemnation are not the only responses to the culture wars. Evangelicals should not merely attack, ignore, or parrot the larger culture; they should engage it from a distinctively Christian perspective. Clapp's aptly named *Border Crossings,* referring to the borders between Christian and secular things, examines Winnie the Pooh, *The X-Files,* and John Coltrane, struggling to find a Christian response.[21] Many devotees even claim that *The Simpsons* is profoundly religious.[22]

The most robust arena for faith in popular culture has been fiction. Protestants in America have long been ambivalent about novels. In the nineteenth century, many evangelicals took up the new genre with enthusiasm—it was yet another tool for propagating the gospel, after all. Seeing fiction's value as less artistic than moral, evangelicals produced some of the most important fiction of the day, perhaps most notably Harriet Beecher Stowe's *Uncle Tom's Cabin.* But a stock trope in these sentimental Christian novels was that reading novels was perilous; the novels, with their tales of seduction and vice, were veritable slippery slopes of sin that could lead female readers in particular to trade a path of virtue and righteousness for a life of sex and consumerism.

From the Civil War to the 1960s, according to literary historian Willard Thorp, almost every fall and spring saw at least one best-selling novel "whose *main* concern is to present a sermon in the guise of a story."[23] In the twentieth century, Protestant novelists included such noteworthy names as John Updike, Madeleine L'Engle, and Frederick Buechner, and the last few years have seen a new wave of evangelical fiction. Though still recognizably Christian—and recognizably conservative—Christian writers and publishers are taking a few more risks. As Susan Wise Bauer wrote in *Christianity Today,* "in 1999, some consciously Christian fiction (from evangelical houses) and some genre fiction (mostly from Catholic houses) shunned Bible lessons, talked about sex, occasionally swore, and quite often failed to convert anyone."[24] Critics in *Publishers Weekly*, *Regeneration Quarterly*, and elsewhere are dignifying the new Christian novels with the label "literary fiction" and saying that, if the Christian Booksellers Association (CBA) has not yet found the next Chekhov, it has at least found a Jane Hamilton or two. Jamie Langston Turner, who teaches English at Bob Jones University, made a splash with her 1998 novel *Some Wildflower in My Heart*, which tells the story of an autodidact cafeteria worker who is brought to Christ through the example of her cheerful, charitable coworker, Birdie Freedman. The novel, which is a tad too long and a tad too writerly, might be mistaken for an Oprah Book Club pick: It includes intimate friendship between women, childhood abuse in a dysfunctional family, and a cast of quirky supporting characters. The difference is that, in Oprah's novels, the characters always save themselves. In Turner's novels, Jesus most definitely does the saving.

Vinita Hampton Wright may be doing more than anyone to transform fiction sold by the CBA. *Grace at Bender Springs* and *Velma Still Cooks in Leeway* are not, one reader pointed out, Christian answers to postmodernism; no one will mistake them for Don DeLillo.[25] They are, like Turner's novels, small-town tales, character studies of men and women trying to figure out what it means to live a faithful life in the face of family turmoil or neighborly betrayal. In one, a young widower tries to come to grips with his losses. In another, an upstanding minister-to-be beats his wife. Wright's huge successes on the CBA market say something about Christian readers' hunger for quality fiction, but the hurdles she has faced in the CBA also reveal the industry's hesitance to take risks. In the early 1990s, Multnomah, an Oregon-based press, signed up her first novel, *Bender Springs*. A few weeks before it was to go to press, the publishing house canceled the contract. "I was never told why they canceled it. It was an executive decision, not an editorial one, but I don't know what the details behind the decision were," says Wright. "The kind of thing they said was that they told the editor from the beginning that the tone needed to be different. . . . All I could figure was the characters were just a little too dark." Wright eventually garnered a three-book contract with Broadman and Holman.[26]

The best novels to robustly express Protestant Christianity do not, in fact, come from the CBA; they come from the South. Few of today's noted Christian writers would describe themselves as being in the evangelical fold, nor would most evangelicals want to claim them. But the Christianity they write about is, without question, evangelical. The eccentric characters that populate their fictional small Southern towns are the evangelicals of the authors' childhoods, not the wishy-washy mainliners of their adult lives. The great modern Southern writers—Lee Smith, Clyde Edgerton, and others—were all reared in the church, and they all now profess some ambivalence: The church continues to have a hold on them, even as they speak of it with touches of sophisticated disdain or condescension. Lee Smith's work is unavoidably shot through with Christianity. She gives her books titles like *Saving Grace* and *News of the Spirit*, and creates characters who are profoundly shaped by evangelical Christianity. Smith was reared Methodist, and she describes a deeply religious youth, where, because sexual passion and religious passion were so inextricably intertwined, she and her beaux went to revival meetings instead of going to the movies. Smith says she "outgrew" that faith, but it is still present in her fiction. The structure of the last chapter of *Fair and Tender Ladies* mirrors Ecclesiastes.

Clyde Edgerton has left the rigors of his childhood Baptist church, but that church still pervades his novels that are set in the South, especially *Raney*, which tells about the clashes that Baptist Raney has with her husband, a kind man who would be just perfect if only he were not a liberal Episcopalian from Atlanta. "My personal religious beliefs are perhaps more slippery, less certain than those of some of the characters in *Raney*," Edgerton once said.[27]

The fiction of a lesser-known writer, Mary Ward Brown, is perhaps most illustrative. Her stories are peopled by evangelists and the evangelized, and they are set, as she writes in *A New Life*, in "the southern Bible Belt, where people talk about God the way they talk about the weather, about His will and His blessing, about why He lets things happen." The religion she invokes in her short stories is, to be sure, an evangelical one, where people know God intimately and talk not just about Him, but to Him, just as sure as they are talking to their neighbors. But Brown herself says she left that kind of religion—the fecund mix of Baptists and Methodists, of Bible and Sunday school with which she grew up in the Black Belt of Alabama—in college. "Eventually I joined the Episcopal Church and have considered myself 'churched' for forty years, but I'm probably not orthodox. I'm Christian because I live in a Christian culture, but I think I could be anything. If I lived in the Far East, I would get down on the ground and bow to whatever they bow to. I think God is greater than any form of religion."[28]

Christianity, to invoke Flannery O'Connor's famous phrase, haunts the writings of Lee Smith and Clyde Edgerton every bit as much as it does those of O'Connor herself. Communicating the faith to the culture has preoccupied Christians, especially Protestants, for decades. That enterprise continues in the realms of film and fiction, and even into the academy.

Protestant Intellectual Renaissance

George Marsden cuts an unlikely figure for a crusader. He is graying, bearded, bespectacled, and often clad in tweed. But the Francis A. McAnaney Professor of History at Notre Dame is nonetheless on something of a crusade: to help Christians, in particular Christian scholars, wake up to the fact that the university is downright hostile to anything that smacks of— or anyone who subscribes to—orthodox Christianity. Marsden contends that while the university is a hotbed of identity politics, happily making room for people whose epistemology and scholarship are informed by Marxism, feminism, and so forth, there is no room for a scholar who identifies as a "Christian economist" or a "Christian literary critic." "The fact is that, no matter what the subject," he writes, "our dominant academic culture trains scholars to keep quiet about their faith as the price of full acceptance in that community."[29]

Not all Christian scholars agree with Marsden—indeed, some have pointed to Marsden's own successful career as evidence that his argument is at best overstated—but Marsden's mission highlights one of the most dramatic transformations in evangelicalism in the last decade: Evangelicals, once as wary of the academy as they were of the rest of the larger culture, are now engaging secular intellectual spheres. (And those secular spheres have taken notice, as evidenced by major stories about Christian scholarship in *Lingua Franca* and *The Atlantic Monthly*.) It is not an exaggeration to say that there is a veritable intellectual renaissance afoot among evangelicals.

"Renaissance" is the operative word, for Christian scholarship in America is nothing new. As Marsden points out, the universities that today tower before us as titans of secularism and "relativism" (a code word that for many evangelicals encapsulates everything that is wrong with the academy and American culture in general) were once bastions of Christian scholarship. Harvard, Yale, and Princeton were all founded to train ministers. Harvard's seventeenth-century "College Laws" mandated that "Every one shall consider the mayne End of his life and studies, to know God and Jesus Christ which is Eternall life." Yale's 1745 rules enjoined Yalies to "Live Religious, Godly, and Blameless Lives according to the Rules of Gods

Word, diligently Reading the holy Scriptures the Fountain of Light and Truth; and constantly attend upon all the Duties of Religion." Rutgers, founded as Queen's College in 1766 by Theodore Frelinghuysen and Dutch Pietists, took as its goal the imbuing of men with "the principles of human wisdom, virtue, and unostentatious piety."

The history of the nineteenth-century university, as concerns religion, mirrors the history of the rest of society: For much of the century, evangelical Protestantism was ascendant and unquestioned, but by the turn of the twentieth century that evangelical hegemony was being challenged from many corners. Academics grew increasingly wary of confessing Christians, and confessing Christians felt increasingly alienated from the academy.

The Scopes trial, not surprisingly, crystallized many evangelicals' anxieties about the academy: The university, after all, was doing more than any other American institution to propagate Darwinism. (It is no coincidence that in early-twentieth-century satires, such as Thomas Wolfe's *Welcome to Our City*, the character branded by small-minded small-towners as dangerously radical is the college professor with Darwinist leanings.) As evangelicals built their own subculture in the 1930s and beyond, they also built new colleges—and built up colleges founded in the nineteenth century. Notable Christian colleges that were founded during this era include Bethany Lutheran College (1927) and Westmont College (1937), with its motto *Christus Primatum Tenens* ("Holding Christ Preeminent"). In 1932, the Eastern Baptist Theological Seminary founded, as a department housed within the seminary, Eastern College; the board of trustees established Eastern Baptist College as a separate institution in 1951. The Pacific Bible Seminary, founded in 1928, became Pacific Christian College in 1964. Minnesota's Bethel Seminary, for example, was founded by the Baptist General Conference in 1871, but not until 1948 did the seminary establish Bethel College, where young Baptists could get a four-year liberal arts education. Calvin College, a Christian Reformed Church school, was founded in 1876. Initially, it was primarily a theological college; at the turn of the century, the curriculum was broadened to appeal to students preparing for careers other than the ministry. In 1906, Calvin officially inaugurated a two-year college, John Calvin Junior College, which gradually developed into a four-year school; in 1921, Calvin College awarded a B.A. for the first time. Northwestern College was founded in 1882 as a high school. It too developed a junior college program and then inaugurated a four-year liberal arts curriculum in 1961.

Christian scholarship was alive and well during the years after the

Scopes trial, even as evangelicals labored under persistent charges of anti-intellectualism. The fundamentalist-modernist debates inspired a great many minds in Christendom, but evangelical scholarly conversations were mostly internal conversations. Christian intellectuals continued to try to argue with more liberal scholars who subscribed to the German higher criticism and to Darwinism, but those conversations gradually turned into monologues, for the intellectual temper of the times had changed. Evangelicals simply did not keep up; they refused to engage the new academic debates.

That is not to say that there was no intellectual life among evangelicals in the generation after Scopes. To the contrary, leading lights like E. J. Carnell and Carl F. H. Henry were fecund and provocative scholars. Henry, for example, insisted long before it was fashionable that science and faith were compatible, and he worried about why evangelicals lacked the intellectual tradition of liberal Protestants or Catholics. But if Carnell and Henry had some desire to reach beyond the walls of evangelicalism to participate in a large intellectual conversation, they never quite went the distance. Henry advocated the founding of Christian think tanks and a Christian university, not a deep integration of Christian scholars into the larger academy.[30]

All that changed in the final decades of the twentieth century. From biologists to literary critics, evangelical Christians boldly engaged contemporary intellectual questions. What does postmodernism have to say to the church? What makes art or literature "Christian"? What should be the believers' response to poverty or to secularism? All of these are questions Christian scholars are asking.

Part of the story is institutional. In the last decade alone, the Mustard Seed Foundation, a philanthropic organization that seeks to "be stewards by participating in the expansion and realization of the kingdom of God on earth," has inaugurated a generous three-year fellowship for Christian graduate students explicitly designed to "encourage Christian graduate students to integrate their faith and vocation and pursue leadership positions in strategic fields where Christians tend to be under-represented"; Christianity Today, International, the parent company that publishes *Christianity Today* magazine, has founded *Books and Culture: A Christian Review*, which unabashedly seeks to be a sort of Christian *New York Review of Books*; Calvin College has sponsored a conference called "Christian Scholarship . . . for What?" (the title a play on social scientist Robert Lynd's 1939 address, "Knowledge for What?"); the Pew Charitable Trusts has given fellowships to dozens of graduate students who attended Christian colleges. All of that institutional energy has borne institutional fruit; one year alone saw the University of Virginia hire a Christian sociologist, Princeton Ph.D. in hand, and it saw the Princeton religion department hire a Yale graduate student whose intellectual formation included both Campus Crusade for Christ and a Rhodes scholarship. If Marsden was right about the state of the academy in the 1990s, these hires suggest that the next generation of academic superstars may be more studded with confessing Christians.

The evangelical intellectual renaissance is about more than just placing Christian scholars in posts at prestigious universities. It is about rethinking what it means to think as a Christian. Just what is at stake in these debates was articulated most forcefully in a slender book called *The Scandal of the Evangelical Mind* by historian and Wheaton College professor Mark A. Noll. The scandal, in short, was that there was no evangelical mind. Evangelicals, in their zeal to follow Deuteronomy's command to love the Lord their God with all their strength and heart, had neglected the command to love God with their mind. "[N]o mind," wrote Noll, "arises from evangelicalism. Evangelicals who believe that God desires to be worshiped with thought as well as activity may well remain evangelicals, but they will find intellectual depth—a way of praising God through the mind—in ideas developed by confessional or mainline Protestants, Roman Catholics, perhaps even the Eastern Orthodox."[31] But the picture, Noll went on, is not actually all that bleak. Evangelicals have resources for intellectual development, especially "the heart of the evangelical message concerning the cross of Christ. If evangelicals have systematically disregarded the implications of the work of Christ for the life of the mind, they nonetheless continue to talk about Jesus. In that talk is potential beyond estimation."

It would be difficult to overestimate the galvanizing effect *The Scandal of the Evangelical Mind* had on Christian scholars across the country (including the two authors of this book). It has inspired a generation to ask what Christian scholarship might look like. What is a Christian epistemology? How does being a Christian shape the way one writes about the Glorious Revolution or change the way one reads *Middlemarch?* Can one build an argument about the unity of virtues that suggests that Christians have a leg up when it comes to studying church history or theology—and how do all the counterexamples of the brilliant scholars who are not believers challenge such a theory?

Among the many academic disciplines that seem to be experiencing a Christian intellectual revival, at least two stand out. One is philosophy.

Thomas Morris, professor of philosophy at Notre Dame, has noted recently that although most of the twentieth century was devoted to "the divorce of faith and philosophy . . . there have been tremendous changes within the world of philosophy over the past couple of decades. In that short time, we have seen a dramatic and unexpected resurgence of religious belief and commitment taking place among the ranks of some of the most active practitioners and teachers of philosophy on college and university campuses all over America."[32] Alvin Plantinga, one of the most illustrious Christian philosophers, echoed the thought when he recalled starting graduate school in 1957. Positivism was ascendant, and most of Plantinga's colleagues believed that "an intelligent and serious philosopher couldn't possibly be a Christian." Today, he writes, there are hundreds of Christian philosophers, many of them producing first-rate work.[33]

One of the foundational figures in reuniting faith and philosophy in America has been Arthur Holmes, who was the chair of the Wheaton philosophy department until he retired in 1994. Holmes wanted to serve as a mentor to younger students—and, in particular, to build a department that might send Christian college grads on to graduate school. He also wanted to demonstrate that believers are no more biased or subjective than "the psychologist whose naturalistic premises influence his or her work." Both psychologists and Christians could comfortably work in the modern academy "provided that they both are open, aboveboard, and self-critical about it."[34]

The second discipline that is being transformed by an army of Christian scholars is history, in particular American history. Marsden, Noll, and others—most notably Nathan O. Hatch and Harry S. Stout, but also Joel Carpenter, Grant Wacker, and Richard T. Hughes—have wrought something of an intellectual revolution. Evangelicals, having shaped much of American history and culture, have now become increasingly influential in the writing of American history, especially American religious history.

In 1979, Hatch, Noll, and others founded the Institute for the Study of American Evangelicals at Wheaton College, and since then they have not only marshaled their own tremendous intellectual resources for the study of American religious history, but also tapped funds from foundations, especially the Lilly Endowment and the Pew Charitable Trusts. (Carpenter, now the provost at Calvin College, was head of the religion program at Pew for much of the 1990s, helping to direct money to the Institute for the Study of American Evangelicals and similar scholarly initiatives.) The results have been impressive. These scholars themselves have produced important works, and they have profoundly influenced the field of American religious history by way of academic conferences and by nurturing younger scholars. Their own success in the academy—Marsden at Notre Dame, Hatch as provost of Notre Dame, Wacker at Duke Divinity School, and Stout as Jonathan Edwards Professor at Yale—belies somewhat Marsden's claim that people of faith are unwelcome in "secularized" universities.[35]

The Christian intellectual renaissance as a success story for contemporary Protestants brings its own set of challenges, especially for mainline Protestants. Despite their towering contributions in decades past—the names Reinhold Niebuhr, Roland Bainton, and Martin E. Marty come immediately to mind—mainline Protestants are largely absent from this resurgence of Protestant intellectual life. They will have to do some hard thinking about what a robust intellectual tradition within liberal Christianity looks like. Protestants also face the challenge of co-option. As Christians are increasingly out of the academic closet, as it were, and as the academy seems increasingly receptive to rigorous Christian work, Christian scholars will have to prayerfully consider how to engage the academy without being idolatrous. Alvin Plantinga once wrote that "A *successful* Christian philosopher is not first of all one who has won the approval and acclaim of the philosophical world generally, not someone who is 'distinguished'; it is rather one who has faithfully served the Lord in the ways put before her."[36] The same can be said of all Christian scholars, from philosophers to paleontologists. That may be the greatest challenge of the evangelical intellectual revival.

Half Empty or Half Full?

Despite the challenges to mainline Protestantism in particular, Protestantism itself has been—and remains—a formidable force in American society. Institutionally, Protestantism has contributed schools, colleges, universities, orphanages, nursing homes, and hospitals to the American landscape, despite the fact that many of those institutions have traveled far down the road toward secularism. Protestantism has undeniably enriched American musical and artistic traditions in myriad ways, ranging from shape-note singers and choral music to neogothic architecture and stained-glass windows, although it must be acknowledged that some of those contributions have been derivative and others just plain bad. Protestant denominations have exerted themselves in the economic realm, in part because of the pension funds they manage but also because many operate their own insurance companies.

Like other religious traditions, Protestantism offers a kind of cradle-to-grave security, rubrics and ceremonies to mark the passages of life. The church provides baptism (or, in Baptist traditions, child dedication) in infancy, confirmation at adolescence, marriage (and, all too often, remarriage) rites, and funeral arrangements, but interspersed with all of that, many Americans turn to their Protestant churches for aid and comfort in dealing with a sick child, an alienated spouse, or the death of a loved one. In "ordinary times," however, to borrow a Catholic expression, millions of Americans continue to look to their Protestant churches—be they evangelical or liberal, pentecostal or liturgical—for meaning, community, and identity, a place to set down roots and find at least a measure of stability in a chaotic world.

Addams, Jane (1860–1935)

Protestant social activist and founder of Hull House. Jane Addams's mother died when she was three, so she was reared in Cedarville, Illinois, by her father, who was a successful miller, a Quaker, an eight-term Illinois state senator, and a friend of Abraham Lincoln. At seventeen Addams entered the Rockford Female Seminary (now Rockford College) and later studied medicine at the Women's Medical College of Pennsylvania, although poor health forced her to curtail her medical studies. On the advice of doctors she took two trips to Europe; after the first she returned to Cedarville and joined the Presbyterian Church. In the course of her second trip, which lasted from 1887 to 1889, Addams visited Toynbee Hall, an institution designed to meet the needs of London's poor. When she returned to the United States she moved to Chicago and, with her college friend Ellen Gates Starr, founded Hull House in a shabby old mansion on Halstead Street in the city's Nineteenth Ward, an area of tenements and sweatshops.

Within months Addams and Starr had transformed the building into a center of cultural activity and social outreach: a theater, a day nursery, a boys' club, and a home for working girls. The success of the enterprise attracted support from private philanthropists, and it gave Addams public exposure as an advocate for the urban poor. She worked for legislation to improve the lot of urban laborers, and she became increasingly interested in issues surrounding women; she addressed prostitution and feminine psychology in her writings.

Addams's *Twenty Years at Hull-House*, published in 1910, earned her an international reputation. During World War I she helped to form the Women's Peace Party and lobbied extensively in Europe for an end to hostilities. In 1920 Addams helped to organize the American Civil Liberties Union and was elected the first president of the Women's International League for Peace and Freedom. Her efforts on behalf of the poor, for peace, and for women were recognized in 1931 when, with Nicholas Murray Butler, she was named recipient of the Nobel Peace Prize.

By the time of her death in 1935 Hull House had expanded to cover an entire city block, with buildings centered around a courtyard. In 1961 plans were made to tear down Hull House to make room for the Chicago campus of the University of Illinois. Despite worldwide protests against such plans, the properties were sold in 1963, although the original building was preserved as a memorial to Addams. Hull House settlement work was relocated to other venues in Chicago.

BIBLIOGRAPHY: Jane Addams, *Democracy and Social Ethics* (1902); *idem, Newer Ideals of Peace* (1907); *idem, The Spirit of Youth and the City Streets* (1909); *idem, Twenty Years at Hull-House* (1910); *idem, A New Conscience and an Ancient Evil* (1911); *idem, The Long Road of Women's Memory* (1916); *idem, The Second Twenty Years at Hull-House* (1930).

Beecher, Catharine Esther (1800–78)
Lecturer, moral reformer, educator. The daughter of Lyman and Roxana Foote Beecher, Catharine Beecher was born in East Hampton, New York, and, try though she did, she could never appropriate the kind of evangelical conversion that her father expected of her. She became a moral reformer nevertheless, especially in the field of women's education. Beecher founded the Hartford Female Seminary, which trained women for work as ministers' wives and as missionary teachers who would bring Christian literacy to the frontier. Beecher, more than anyone else, was responsible for the nineteenth-century cult of domesticity, which insisted that women belonged in the home and that they should assume responsibility as the moral guardians of their families. Paradoxically, she traveled throughout the country encouraging women to do just that, and she wrote a number of devotional and advice books.

BIBLIOGRAPHY: Kathryn Kish Sklar, *Catharine Beecher: A Study in American Domesticity* (1973).

Beecher, Lyman (1775–1863)
Congregationalist minister. Born in New Haven, Connecticut, Lyman Beecher matriculated at Yale College in 1793, where he came under the influence of Timothy Dwight, who became president in 1795 and initiated an aggressive campaign to root out infidelity and Enlightenment influences among the students. Beecher was one of Dwight's first converts, and the two men became colleagues and friends. After his graduation in 1797 Beecher studied with Dwight for another year, whereupon he accepted the pulpit of the East Hampton Presbyterian Church on Long Island. Beecher came to public attention when he launched a campaign against dueling after Alexander Hamilton was killed in a duel with Aaron Burr in Weehawken, New Jersey.

Beecher moved from East Hampton to the Congregational Church at Litchfield, Connecticut, in 1810, where he became an ardent defender of establishment status for the Congregational Church, warning that disestablishment would sound the death knell for religion. Shortly after Connecticut disestablished Congregationalism in 1818, however, Beecher recanted his earlier sentiments. The voluntary principle, he concluded, had been the best thing to happen to organized religion because it forced the churches to compete openly in the free market of religion. During his Litchfield years Beecher added another cause to his crusade against vice: temperance.

In 1826 Beecher moved to the Hanover Street Congregational Church in Boston, where he hoped to combat Unitarianism at its source. Beecher also became sympathetic to the "new measures" of revivalism, much to the consternation of old-line Calvinists, who accused him of betrayal.

Concerned about the "invasion" of foreigners (Roman Catholic immigrants), especially in the West, Beecher accepted the presidency of Lane Theological Seminary in Cincinnati in 1832, where he also served as pastor of the Second Presbyterian Church. In his fundraising and recruiting trips on behalf of the seminary Beecher became more and more vociferous about the threat of Roman Catholicism. In 1834, after Beecher had spoken in Boston, an angry mob burned the Ursuline convent in Charlestown, Massachusetts; many contemporaries believed that Beecher's incendiary rhetoric had galvanized the mob.

Beecher's tenure at Lane was checkered. He tried unsuccessfully to mediate between the pro- and antislavery factions during the Lane Rebellion. Beecher himself was brought up on charges of heresy in 1835 on the grounds that he did not subscribe strictly enough to the Westminster Confession of Faith, the doctrinal standard for Presbyterians. Although he was exonerated, Old Side Presbyterians continued to regard him as suspect for his sympathies with revivalism.

BIBLIOGRAPHY: Lyman Beecher, *The Autobiography of Lyman Beecher*, 2 vols. (1961); Stuart C. Henry, *Unvanquished Puritan: A Portrait of Lyman Beecher* (1973); Marie Caskey, *Chariot of Fire: Religion and the Beecher Family* (1978).

Bryan, William Jennings (1860–1925)
Progressive-era politician, preacher, and attorney. William Jennings Bryan, the "Great Commoner," cut a wide swath through American culture as attorney, orator, editor, congressman, three-time Democratic nominee for president, and secretary of state. The inveterate populist was also a devout Presbyterian layman.

After graduating from college and law school, Bryan settled in Lincoln, Nebraska, in 1887. Three years later he won election to Congress and soon emerged as leader of the free-silver Democrats. His electrifying "Cross of Gold" speech at the 1896 Democratic National Convention, in which he railed against monopolistic business interests, won him the Democratic nomination for president at the age of thirty-six. Although Bryan also captured the nomination of the Populists and campaigned in twenty-six states, the "Boy Orator of the Prairie" lost the election to William McKinley. Four years later, a rematch yielded the same result.

After capturing the Democratic nomination again in 1908, losing this time to William Howard Taft, Bryan threw his support to Woodrow Wilson in 1912. The new president rewarded the Great Commoner with appointment as secretary of state, but as war approached in Europe Bryan dissented from Wilson's move toward engagement and resigned from the cabinet in June 1915.

The eclipse of Bryan's political career allowed him to devote his energies to such Progressive causes as prohibition, peace, and women's suffrage. He is probably best remembered, somewhat unfairly, for his final public act in Dayton, Tennessee, assisting in the prosecution of John T. Scopes, who had violated the state's newly minted Butler Act by teaching evolution in the schools. Bryan had long been suspicious of Darwinism, not so much because it challenged the Genesis account of creation but because, as a true Progressive, he feared the effects of social Darwinism. Clarence Darrow, Bryan's adversary in the courtroom, transformed the trial into a showdown between biblical literalism and scientific progress. In the

trial's most dramatic moment, duly recorded by H. L. Mencken and a pha-
lanx of journalists, Bryan took the stand himself, whereupon Darrow succeeded in making Bryan—and, by extension, all fundamentalists—look
foolish. Exhausted and humiliated, Bryan died in his sleep five days after
the trial.

BIBLIOGRAPHY: William Jennings Bryan, *The First Battle: A Story of the
Campaign of 1896* (1896); *idem, The Prince of Peace* (1909); *idem, The Mem-
oirs of William Jennings Bryan* (1925); Robert W. Cherny, *A Righteous Cause:
The Life of William Jennings Bryan*; Lawrence W. Levine, *Defender of the
Faith: William Jennings Bryan, The Last Decade, 1915–1925* (1965); Garry
Wills, *Under God: Religion and American Politics* (1990); Edward J. Larson,
*Summer for the Gods: The Scopes Trial and America's Continuing Debate over
Science and Religion* (1997).

Carter, James Earl ("Jimmy") (1924–)

Peanut farmer, governor of Georgia, missionary, U.S. president, statesman,
and humanitarian. The man who would become the thirty-ninth president
of the United States was born in Plains, Georgia, and reared in the Baptist
faith by a devout mother. Jimmy Carter attended the U.S. Naval Academy
and served in the navy from 1945 to 1953, where he became a protégé of
Admiral Hyman Rickover. Following the death of his father, Carter resigned his commission to return to Plains and take over the family's peanut
business. In 1962 he won a seat in the Georgia State Senate in a bitterly
contested election, recounted in his book *Turning Point*, that pitted Carter
against a local political machine. His first bid to become governor of Georgia, which ended in defeat in 1966, prompted a religious conversion, which
Carter recounted as being "born again."

Carter's second try for the governorship, in 1970, was successful, and
he almost immediately plotted a course that would lead to the Democratic
presidential nomination six years later. Carter's ascendance from a relatively
unknown one-term governor of a southern state through the Iowa precinct
caucuses to the nomination and to the presidency remains one of the more
legendary feats of modern-day politics. Throughout his campaign he made
no secret that he was a born-again Christian and a Sunday school teacher
in his local Southern Baptist church. To a nation still reeling from the
ignominy of Vietnam and the sting of Watergate, Carter's obvious probity
and his pledge that he would "never knowingly lie to the American people"
resonated.

Once in office, Carter faced a series of crises that would test his mettle and eventually erode his popularity—the Arab oil embargo, runaway inflation, the Mariel boat lift, the Iran hostage crisis. Many evangelicals, who had helped elect him to office in 1976, turned against him in the 1980 election, claiming that Carter was too liberal; Jerry Falwell, for instance, founded Moral Majority in 1979 as little more than a tool to defeat Carter. The 1980 presidential election featured three candidates, all of whom claimed to be evangelical Christians: Carter; John B. Anderson, who had been reared in the Evangelical Free Church of America; and Ronald Reagan, a divorced former movie actor from California. Politically conservative evangelicals threw their support behind Reagan, thereby helping to turn Carter out of office.

It has been said and often repeated that Jimmy Carter was the only man for whom the presidency was a stepping stone. While other ex-presidents have been content to dictate memoirs and to collect large fees for giving lectures or sitting on corporate boards, Carter has vigorously engaged in humanitarian activities, often under the auspices of his presidential library, the Carter Center in Atlanta. He has served as a kind of freelance peacemaker around the world, and he and his wife, Rosalynn, have been active in such causes as Habitat for Humanity.

BIBLIOGRAPHY: Jimmy Carter, *Turning Point: A Candidate, a State, and a Nation Come of Age* (1992); idem, *Living Faith* (1996); Dan Arial and Cheryl Heckler-Feltz, *The Carpenter's Apprentice: The Spiritual Biography of Jimmy Carter* (1996).

Darby, John Nelson (1800–82)

Itinerant preacher, teacher, and popularizer of dispensationalism. Perhaps no individual has had more effect on American fundamentalism than John Nelson Darby. Born in London to wealthy Irish parents, Darby graduated from Trinity College, Dublin, and practiced law for a time before entering the ministry of the Church of England in 1825. Although he enjoyed considerable success as a parish priest in County Wicklow, Ireland, Darby disliked the formalism and lack of spiritual ardor that he found in Anglicanism. In 1827 he joined a small group of people in Dublin who met for simple, nonliturgical worship and study of the Bible. Darby left the Church of England in 1831 for the Plymouth Brethren, among whom he became their most influential theologian.

Darby's ideas were shaped by an interpretation of the Scriptures called "dispensationalism," which posited that all of human history—as well as the Bible itself—could be divided into different ages or dispensations and

that God dealt with humanity in different ways during different dispensations. The present age, Darby insisted, called for the separation of the true
believers from nonbelievers in anticipation of the imminent return of Jesus.

Darby propagated these ideas through his many travels, including seven
visits to North America between 1859 and 1874. Darby's interpretive scheme
eventually caught the attention of such American evangelical figures as
Dwight L. Moody, A. J. Gordon, and James H. Brookes. The general pes-
simism implicit in dispensationalism fit the temper of America's evangelicals
late in the nineteenth century as they surveyed what they saw as the de-
generation of American society everywhere around them. Darby's ideas
assured evangelicals that this was part of a divine plan, that the world would
indeed grow worse and worse just prior to the rapture, at which time a
tribulation would punish the enemies of righteousness and the millennial
kingdom would begin.

Dispensationalism, also known as "Darbyism," was popularized
through the Bible conference movement and especially through the Niagara
Bible Conference. The publication of the *Scofield Reference Bible* by Oxford
University Press in 1909 became an even more effective means for propagating dispensational interpretations to American evangelicals.

BIBLIOGRAPHY: Ernest R. Sandeen, *The Roots of Fundamentalism: British
and American Millenarianism, 1800–1930* (1970).

Edwards, Jonathan (1703–58)

Pastor and theologian. Born in East Windsor, Connecticut, the son and
grandson of Congregationalist ministers, Jonathan Edwards became a Congregationalist minister himself and also one of the greatest minds in American history. A precocious child who ruminated about God and the natural
world, Edwards graduated from Yale College at the age of seventeen and
stayed an additional two years to study theology, whereupon he was licensed
to preach and briefly served as pastor of a Presbyterian church in New
York City from 1722 until 1723. He returned to Yale the next year as a
tutor, and after two years there he accepted a call as assistant pastor to his
grandfather, Solomon Stoddard, in Northampton, Massachusetts. He married Sarah Pierrepont in 1727 and in 1729, upon Stoddard's death, became
sole pastor of the Northampton congregation.

During the winter of 1734–35 a revival of religion swept through
Northampton, a phenomenon that Edwards recounted as a visitation of
divine grace in *A Faithful Narrative of the Surprising Work of God* (1737).
Three hundred people were added to the church. Religion, according to

Edwards, became the dominant topic of conversation among townspeople. After the revival waned somewhat, the fires were rekindled with the visit of George Whitefield in 1740, during his tour of the Atlantic colonies. By this time the revival was widespread, a phenomenon known to historians as the Great Awakening.

By the mid-1740s, however, some of the excesses associated with the revival began to discredit the Awakening itself. Edwards was placed in the awkward position of defending the revival from its enemies by rescuing it from his friends, and he engaged in a protracted pamphlet war with Charles Chauncy of Boston. Edwards's attempts to distinguish between true and counterfeit religious expressions issued in his most famous work: *A Treatise Concerning Religious Affections*, published in 1746. The revival, however, eventually took its toll on Edwards's ministry. Edwards's sharp distinction between the converted and the unconverted led him to renege on Stoddardeanism, his grandfather's practice of allowing anyone to partake of Holy Communion, not merely the regenerate. Eventually, the Northampton congregation forced Edwards's ouster in 1750, whereupon he became a missionary to the Indians in Stockbridge, Massachusetts. It was during this "Stockbridge exile" that Edwards produced some of his most important work, including *Freedom of the Will*, *The Nature of True Virtue*, and *The History of the Work of Redemption*.

In 1757 Edwards was chosen to succeed his late son-in-law Aaron Burr as president of the College of New Jersey. Shortly after assuming office, Edwards died of complications from a smallpox inoculation.

BIBLIOGRAPHY: Perry Miller, *Jonathan Edwards* (1949); Patricia J. Tracy, *Jonathan Edwards, Pastor: Religion and Society in Eighteenth-Century Northampton* (1979); John E. Smith, *Jonathan Edwards: Puritan, Preacher, Philosopher* (1992).

Finney, Charles Grandison (1792–1875)

Revivalist and theologian of the Second Great Awakening. On October 10, 1821, a religious conversion occurred that would change the course of one man's life as well as redirect the course of American evangelicalism. Until that moment Charles Grandison Finney had prepared to practice law, but he now believed that he had been given "a retainer from the Lord Jesus Christ to plead his cause." The St. Lawrence presbytery licensed him to preach in 1823 and ordained him the following year. He began preaching in upstate New York under the auspices of the Female Missionary Society of the Western District in 1824.

Early in his career Finney harbored doubts about Calvinism, not so much on theological as on pragmatic grounds; Finney was convinced that Calvinistic determinism simply did not lend itself to revivals. Instead, he preached that by the mere exercise of volition anyone at all could repent of sin and thereby claim salvation. Finney assured a people who had only recently taken their political destiny into their own hands that they controlled their religious destiny as well.

Finney experimented with many ideas for promoting revivals, including protracted meetings, allowing women to pray or exhort in public, and the "anxious bench" for wavering auditors, who could come forward and contemplate the choice between heaven and hell. These innovations eventually became known as "new measures," and they have been present in American revivalism ever since. Whereas Jonathan Edwards, the primary apologist for the Great Awakening, had argued that revival was a gracious visitation, in his words "a surprising work of God," Finney argued that it was "the work of man," that simply following the proper formula—which he provided in his *Lectures on Revivals of Religion*—would bring about revival.

Finney's revivals in Rochester and in upstate New York spread to major eastern cities. They attracted national attention as well as spirited opposition from old school Calvinists. Finney nevertheless remained adamant in his conviction about the importance of human volition in the salvation process, just as he believed in the perfectibility of both human nature and society.

A bout of cholera in 1832 prompted Finney to retire from active leadership in the western New York phase of the Second Great Awakening. He served as pastor, successively, of the Second Presbyterian Church and the Broadway Tabernacle in New York City and the First Congregational Church in Oberlin, Ohio. In 1835 Finney accepted an appointment in the newly formed Oberlin Collegiate Institute (now Oberlin College) as professor of theology, and he served as president of the college from 1851 to 1866.

BIBLIOGRAPHY: Charles Grandison Finney, *Lectures on Revivals of Religion* (1835); idem, *Sermons on Important Subjects* (1836); idem, *Lectures on Systematic Theology*, 2 vols. (1846–47); Keith J. Hardman, *Charles Grandison Finney, 1792–1875* (1987); Charles E. Hambrick-Stowe, *Charles G. Finney and the Spirit of American Evangelicalism* (1996).

Fosdick, Harry Emerson (1878–1969)
Liberal preacher and ecumenist. Born in Buffalo, Harry Emerson Fosdick studied at Hamilton Theological Seminary and then transferred to Union

Theological Seminary in New York City, where he suffered a severe mental breakdown. After four months in a psychiatric hospital and a tour of Europe, Fosdick returned to New York, where he resumed his studies at Union and at Columbia University.

After eleven years at the First Baptist Church in Montclair, New Jersey, he became professor of practical theology at Union, during which time his reputation as a preacher and a writer of popular religious literature grew. In 1918 he cut back on his teaching in order to become the preaching minister at the First Presbyterian Church in New York, where he ran afoul of the fundamentalists, who reacted to his famous 1922 challenge, "Shall the Fundamentalists Win?" Conservatives in the Presbyterian denomination led by William Jennings Bryan tried to force his ouster on charges of heresy. Eventually the Presbyterian general assembly ruled that Fosdick could retain his pulpit, but only on the condition that he become a Presbyterian and affirm the Westminster Confession of Faith. Fosdick's longstanding opposition to formal creeds precluded this, and he submitted his resignation in 1925.

Among his many admirers, however, was John D. Rockefeller Jr., who moved quickly to secure Fosdick's services as pastor of the Park Avenue Baptist Church. Rockefeller made good on his promise to build a new church for Fosdick, one that eschewed creedal requirements and doctrinal rigidity, one that would be self-consciously international, interdenominational, and interracial. The massive Gothic-style edifice of Riverside Church, on Morningside Heights in upper Manhattan, was completed in 1931; Fosdick remained its senior minister until his retirement in 1946.

Although he never fully repented of his liberalism, Fosdick retreated somewhat from religious modernism. In a 1935 sermon, "Beyond Modernism," he acknowledged the persistence of sin and guilt in the world in light of World War I atrocities. He tempered his optimism about the progress of culture and confessed to excessive intellectualism. The militarism of the Second World War so distressed him that he became one of the nation's foremost proponents of pacifism.

BIBLIOGRAPHY: Harry Emerson Fosdick, *The Meaning of Prayer* (1915); idem, *Christianity and Progress* (1922); idem, *The Secret of Victorious Living* (1934); idem, *On Being a Real Person* (1943); Robert Moats Miller, *Harry Emerson Fosdick: Preacher, Pastor, Prophet* (1985).

Fuller, Charles Edward (1887–1968)
Pioneer radio preacher. Charles E. Fuller spent his early years in the family orange business near Redlands, California. After graduating from Pomona

College in 1910, he returned to the orange groves and soon expanded his interests into real estate, leasing land for oil drilling, and trucking. Under the fundamentalist preaching of Paul Rader, pastor of Moody Church in Chicago, Fuller experienced a dramatic conversion in 1916 and began teaching an adult Sunday school class at his church, Placentia Presbyterian Church. Increasingly dissatisfied with his secular pursuits, Fuller set them aside and enrolled at the Bible Institute of Los Angeles (BIOLA), where, under the influence of Reuben A. Torrey, he learned dispensational premillennialism.

Unhappy with the emphasis on social action at Placentia Presbyterian, Fuller resigned from the board of elders and founded Calvary Church as an independent congregation in 1925. He was ordained by a group of Baptist churches associated with the Baptist Bible Union, a fundamentalist organization, and soon became an itinerant preacher. In 1930 he began broadcasting the church's worship services and a program of Bible studies over local radio stations. His congregation eventually grew impatient with Fuller's attention to radio evangelism; he submitted his resignation in 1933 and formed the Gospel Broadcasting Association to support his radio and evangelistic ministry. After experimenting with several formats Fuller settled on a Sunday evening revival service, called *Radio Revival Hour*, complete with a studio audience. By 1937 the program, renamed *The Old Fashioned Revival Hour*, was aired nationwide over the Mutual Broadcasting System, and Fuller's broadcasts were more popular than *Amos 'n' Andy*, Bob Hope, and Charlie McCarthy. "We are allied with no denomination," Fuller declared in 1937. "We are fundamental, premillennial, and our desire is to bring up no controversial questions, but only to preach and teach the Word of God."

Mutual dropped the program in 1944, however, but Fuller was able to knit together a collection of local independent stations until a new network, ABC, picked it up in 1949. The advent of television signaled a long decline for Fuller's program. His attempts to adapt to the new medium ended in failure, and ABC radio finally forced him off the network in 1963.

Fuller's other contribution to American Protestantism was in the field of education. He provided the money to begin a "Christ-centered, Spirit-directed training school" that would provide education and training for ministers and missionaries. In 1947 Fuller Theological Seminary opened its doors in Pasadena, California, under the direction of Harold John Ockenga, who also served as pastor of the Park Street Church in Boston. Ockenga and other members of the faculty, however, shared a vision for the seminary that would be somewhat at odds with Fuller's. Ironically, the school sought to shed the legacy of a narrow premillennialist fundamentalism with its mechanical insistence on biblical inerrancy, characteristics that applied to Charles Fuller's own theology.

BIBLIOGRAPHY: Wilbur M. Smith, *A Voice for God: The Life of Charles E. Fuller, Originator of the Old Fashioned Revival Hour* (1949); Daniel P. Fuller, *Give the Winds a Mighty Voice: The Story of Charles E. Fuller* (1972); George M. Marsden, *Reforming Fundamentalism: Fuller Seminary and the New Evangelicalism* (1987); L. David Lewis, s.v., "Charles E. Fuller," in Charles H. Lippy, ed., *Twentieth-Century Shapers of American Popular Religion* (1989).

Graham, William Franklin Jr. ("Billy") (1918–)

World-renowned evangelist. Born November 7, 1918, near Charlotte, North Carolina, William Franklin Graham, better known as Billy Graham, went to one of Mordecai Ham's revival meetings in 1934 and there experienced a religious conversion that shaped the direction of his life. By the time he graduated from Wheaton College in 1943 he had developed the preaching style for which he would become famous. In 1946, Graham joined the staff of Youth for Christ and later became, for a time, president of Northwestern Schools in Minneapolis, all the while continuing his evangelistic campaigns.

Graham's successful Los Angeles crusade in 1949 brought him national attention, in no small measure because newspaper magnate William Randolph Hearst, impressed with the young evangelist's preaching and his anticommunist rhetoric, instructed his papers to "puff Graham." From Los Angeles Graham took his evangelistic crusades around the country and the world, thereby providing him with international renown.

Graham, by his own account, has enjoyed close relationships with American presidents, from Dwight Eisenhower to Bill Clinton (even though Graham met with Harry Truman in the Oval Office, the president was little impressed with the young evangelist). Although he purported to be apolitical, Graham's most notorious political entanglement was with Richard Nixon, whom he befriended when Nixon was Eisenhower's vice president. During the 1960 presidential campaign Graham met in Montreaux, Switzerland, with Norman Vincent Peale and other Protestant leaders to devise a way to derail the campaign of John F. Kennedy, the Democratic nominee, thereby assisting Nixon's electoral chances. Although Graham later mended relations with Kennedy, Nixon remained his favorite, with Graham all but endorsing Nixon's re-election effort in 1972 against George McGovern. As the Nixon presidency unraveled amid charges of criminal misconduct,

Graham reviewed transcripts of the hitherto secret Watergate-era tape re-
cordings. Although the tapes provided irrefutable evidence of Nixon's various attempts to subvert the Constitution, what sickened Graham most was
his friend's use of foul language.

Throughout his career, Graham's popular appeal lay in his extraordinary charisma, his forceful preaching, and his simple, homespun message:
Repent of your sins, accept Christ as savior, and you shall be saved. Behind
that simple message, however, stood a sophisticated organization, the Billy
Graham Evangelistic Association, which provided extensive advance work
and a follow-up program for new converts. Even though he pioneered the
use of television for religious purposes, Graham has always shied away
from the label "televangelist." During the 1980s, when other television
preachers were embroiled in sensational scandals, Graham remained above
the fray, and throughout a career that spanned more than half a century
few people questioned his integrity. In 1996, Graham and his wife, Ruth,
received the Congressional Gold Medal, the highest honor that Congress
can bestow on a citizen.

Graham claims to have preached in person to more people than anyone
else in history, an assertion that few would challenge. His evangelistic crusades around the world, his television appearances and radio broadcasts,
his friendships with presidents and world leaders, and his unofficial role as
spokesman for America's evangelicals made him one of the most recognized
religious figures of the twentieth century.

BIBLIOGRAPHY: Billy Graham, *Just As I Am* (1997); William Martin, *A
Prophet with Honor: The Billy Graham Story* (1991); Larry Eskridge, "'One
Way': Billy Graham, the Jesus Generation, and the Idea of an Evangelical
Youth Culture," *Church History: Studies in Christianity and Culture*, LXVII
(1998), 83–106; *Crusade: The Life of Billy Graham*, PBS documentary
(1993).

Hodge, Charles (1797–1878)

Presbyterian theologian and leader of the Princetonians. Probably the most
famous proponent of the Princeton Theology, Charles Hodge graduated
from Princeton Theological Seminary in 1819, became an instructor there
in 1829, and was elected Professor of Oriental and Biblical Languages in
1822. From 1826 to 1828 he took a two-year hiatus to study in Europe,
where he spent most of his time in Halle, Germany, under the tutelage of
F. A.D. Tholuck, with whom he forged a lasting friendship. Hodge was
appointed professor of theology at Princeton Seminary in 1840, a post he

retained until his death. Hodge is best known for his three-volume *Systematic Theology* (1872–73) and for his work as founding editor of the *Biblical Repertory*, later known as the *Biblical Repertory and Theological Review* and later still as the *Biblical Repertory and Princeton Review*. Hodge's discursive comments over nearly four decades in the *Biblical Repertory* show the true range of his considerable intellect. He offered his Reformed perspective on everything from higher criticism to Jacksonian democracy, from science to slavery.

BIBLIOGRAPHY: Charles Hodge, *The Way of Life* (1841); *idem, Theological Essays* (1846); *idem, Essays and Reviews* (1857); *idem, Systematic Theology*, 3 vols. (1872–73); *idem, What Is Darwinism?* (1874).

King, Martin Luther Jr. (1929–68)

Baptist preacher and civil rights activist. Born in Atlanta, Martin Luther King Jr. attended Morehouse College, where he was influenced by the ideas of the school's president, Benjamin E. Mays. King elected to prepare for the ministry and attended Crozer Theological Seminary in Chester, Pennsylvania, and proceeded to a doctoral program at Boston University. During the course of his studies King absorbed the ideas of Walter Rauschenbusch, Reinhold Niebuhr, and the ethics of nonviolence of Mohandas Gandhi. King came to believe that social change was possible through passive resistance.

In 1955, the same year he was awarded the Ph.D. and while serving as pastor of the Dexter Avenue Baptist Church in Montgomery, Alabama, King led the Montgomery bus boycott, a protest against the routine segregation of Montgomery's buses. King's success as leader of the Montgomery Improvement Association emboldened him to lead other protests throughout the South and eventually in the North, where his oratorical artistry motivated thousands of protesters. He organized the Southern Christian Leadership Conference, and his "Letter from Birmingham Jail" remains a classic defense for Christian social activism. King orchestrated the famous March on Washington in August 1963, where he delivered his "I Have a Dream" speech, which functioned as a kind of manifesto for the civil rights movement.

Time magazine named King its Man of the Year in 1963, and he was awarded the Nobel Peace Prize the following year. Once his efforts helped to secure civil rights legislation King turned his attention to other social issues, including poverty and opposition to the war in Vietnam. He was assassinated on April 4, 1968, in Memphis, Tennessee, while organizing his Poor People's Campaign.

BIBLIOGRAPHY: Martin Luther King Jr., *Stride Toward Freedom: The*

Montgomery Story (1958); *idem, Strength to Love* (1963); *idem, Why We Can't Wait* (1964); *idem, Trumpet of Conscience* (1968); David Garrow, *Bearing the Cross: Martin Luther King, Jr. and the Southern Christian Leadership Conference* (1986); Taylor Branch, *Parting the Waters: America in the King Years, 1954–1963* (1988); *idem, Pillar of Fire: America in the King Years, 1963–1965* (1998).

Machen, John Gresham (1881–1937)

Presbyterian theologian. Without doubt the most famous Presbyterian among the first generation of fundamentalists, J. Gresham Machen was born to a socially prominent family in Baltimore and was educated at Johns Hopkins University, Princeton Theological Seminary, and Marburg and Göttingen in Germany. Although he never lined up fully with fundamentalism—Machen referred to dispensationalism, for example, as a "false method of interpreting Scripture"—he was leader of the conservative forces within Presbyterianism. Machen supported the ouster of Charles A. Briggs from the Presbyterian ranks in the 1890s after Briggs, a professor at Union Theological Seminary in New York, cast doubt on biblical authority. Machen accepted a teaching position at Princeton Seminary in 1906, inherited the mantle of his mentor, B. B. Warfield, and established himself as the last bastion of Princeton Theology at the Seminary.

The Princeton Theology, with its trademark adherence to biblical inerrancy and subscription to the Westminster Standards, came increasingly under attack in the 1920s. Machen sought to confront the issue in 1923 with the publication of *Christianity and Liberalism*, which argued, in effect, that the two were mutually exclusive. The Presbyterian Church (U.S.A.), however, continued to move in a modernist direction. The denomination adopted the Auburn Affirmation in 1925, which allowed broad tolerance on doctrinal matters. Machen and other fundamentalists resisted, albeit unsuccessfully; in 1929 the Seminary was reorganized to accommodate the Auburn Affirmation. Believing that the reorganization had effectively silenced "Old Princeton," Machen withdrew from the faculty and formed Westminster Theological Seminary in Philadelphia. This was merely the first in a succession of schisms. Machen organized the Independent Board for Presbyterian Foreign Missions, which led to his expulsion from the Presbyterian Church (U.S.A.) ministry. In 1936 he and other conservatives founded the Presbyterian Church of America, which took the name Orthodox Presbyterian Church in 1939. Machen caught pneumonia and died while on a trip to Bismarck, North Dakota, to rally support for his new denomination.

BIBLIOGRAPHY: J. Gresham Machen, *Christianity and Liberalism* (1923);

idem, The Virgin Birth of Christ (1930); Bradley J. Longfield, *The Presbyterian Controversy: Fundamentalists, Modernists, and Moderates* (1991); D. G. Hart, *Defending the Faith: J. Gresham and the Crisis of Conservative Protestantism in Modern America* (1994); *idem*, "When Is a Fundamentalist a Modernist?: J Gresham Machen, Cultural Modernism, and Conservative Protestantism," *Journal of the American Academy of Religion* LXV (Fall 1997): 605–33.

McPherson, Aimee Semple (née Aimee Elizabeth Kennedy) (1890–1944) Pentecostal preacher, broadcaster, and impresario. A woman of indomitable energy and enormous contradictions, Aimee Semple McPherson overcame several personal and professional setbacks to become one of the twentieth century's most intriguing religious personalities. She was born near Ingersoll, Ontario, and reared in both the Methodist and the Salvation Army traditions. During the winter of 1907–08 a pentecostal evangelist named Robert James Semple held evangelistic meetings in Ingersoll. Young Aimee Kennedy was one of his converts, and on August 12, 1908, the two were married. They settled briefly in Stratford and in London, Ontario, before moving on to Chicago, where both man and wife were ordained by William H. Durham at his North Avenue Mission on January 2, 1909.

The Semples had decided on a career as missionaries. They left for Hong Kong in 1910 with a view toward learning Chinese and then moving on to China. Shortly after their arrival in Hong Kong, however, Robert Semple contracted typhoid fever and died on August 19, 1910, leaving behind a pregnant widow not yet twenty years old. In part because of the financial strain, Aimee remained in Hong Kong until after the birth of her daughter, Roberta Star.

Aimee and Roberta returned to New York City, where they were joined by Aimee's mother, Minnie. They worked with the Salvation Army mission, and Aimee met and soon married Harold Stewart McPherson. The marriage, however, was an unhappy one. The couple settled briefly in Providence, Rhode Island, but after the birth of the couple's son, Rolf, Aimee moved back with her parents to Ontario, where she soon established herself as an effective preacher with a series of revival meetings in Mount Forest. McPherson rejoined his wife for a time, serving as an advance man for her revival campaigns, but he eventually returned to Rhode Island. The couple divorced in August 1921.

By then "Sister Aimee's" career as a preacher and faith healer had been launched. Her mother took over the advance work and administrative duties. McPherson began publishing a monthly magazine, *Bridal Call*, in 1917; she was ordained as an "evangelist" by the Assemblies of God in 1919, although she resigned that ordination three years later, after her divorce. She dressed in a white nurse's uniform and traveled in her "Gospel Auto," a car with various evangelistic slogans ("Jesus Is Coming—Get Ready") emblazoned on the sides.

The Gospel Auto attracted a great deal of attention on the drive west to California in 1918. McPherson would pull into a town, wait for a crowd to gather around the car (automobiles themselves were still a curiosity in the late 1910s), preach a sermon, and collect a few contributions. She arrived in Los Angeles in the fall of 1918 and proceeded to establish her base of operations there. In 1921 she purchased property in Echo Park, and her magnificent Angelus Temple, with seating for 5,300, was dedicated January 1, 1923. The Temple served as the fulcrum for all of McPherson's operations, including a nascent denomination, which would be incorporated in 1927 as the International Church of the Foursquare Gospel.

For Sister Aimee, Angelus Temple was a stage and a showplace; she understood that she was competing with the glamour of Hollywood across town. Her "illustrated sermons" very often were delivered against the background of elaborate sets, many of them designed by Thomas Eade, a former vaudeville performer. One Easter Sunday she appeared, dressed entirely in yellow, out of an oversized Easter lily made of plaster of Paris. On another occasion she roared onstage dressed as a cop and straddling a motorcycle. Yet again, she dressed up as George Washington and reviewed the troops at Valley Forge as synthetic snow fell all around her.

In 1922 McPherson became the first woman ever to preach a sermon over the radio, and her station, KFSG ("Kalling Four Square Gospel"), was the nation's first station owned and operated by a religious organization. She set up satellite congregations in various venues and broadcast her sermons to those gatherings. McPherson also continued her itinerations, and she established her own school—L.I.F.E. (Lighthouse for International Foursquare Evangelism) Bible College—in 1923.

McPherson's professional success, however, was not matched by personal fulfillment. In May 1926 she "disappeared" while swimming at Venice Beach. She surfaced a month later in Mexico with a story that she had been kidnapped by two drunken desperadoes, Jake and Mexicali Rose. Her return to Los Angeles was greeted by a rousing public welcome, reportedly attended by 50,000 people. Journalists and others, however, grew suspicious of McPherson's story, especially amid rumors of an affair with Kenneth

Ormiston, who had operated KFSG. Faced with legal charges of perpetrating the hoax of her disappearance, McPherson struck back with a "Fight the Devil" fundraising campaign for her legal expenses and dueled the district attorney to a draw; eventually all charges were dropped.

McPherson's troubles did not abate, however. In the 1930s she became estranged from her mother and from her daughter. She struggled with alcoholism, and on September 13, 1931, she entered into what would become another unhappy marriage, to David L. Hutton. She traveled around the world in 1936 and returned with warnings about totalitarianism, and she became an enthusiastic supporter of the war effort. By 1939 McPherson had regained some of her verve for evangelism, Angelus Temple, and her denomination.

In 1944 she appointed her son, Rolf McPherson, vice president of the International Church of the Foursquare Gospel. In September of the same year she began a revival campaign at the Civic Auditorium in Oakland, California. She preached her final sermon on the evening of September 26, returned to her hotel room, and was found dead the next morning of "shock and respiratory failure" following an overdose of medication that may or may not have been suicidal.

BIBLIOGRAPHY: Aimee Semple McPherson, *This Is That: Personal Experiences, Sermons and Writings* (1919); idem, *The Second Coming of Christ* (1921); idem, *Give Me My Own God* (1936); idem, *The Story of My Life* (1951); Edith L. Blumhofer, *Aimee Semple McPherson: Everybody's Sister* (1993); William G. McLoughlin, "Aimee Semple McPherson: 'Your Sister in the King's Glad Service,'" *Journal of Popular Culture* I (1967): 193–217.

Mears, Henrietta Cornelia (1890–1963)
Pioneer Christian educator. Best known for her long tenure as director of Christian education at First Presbyterian Church in Hollywood, California, Henrietta Mears was influential in the Sunday school movement, in the development of Christian education materials, and, perhaps most significantly, in her encouragement of several young men, including Billy Graham and Bill Bright, at early stages of their careers. Born in Fargo, North Dakota, and reared in Minneapolis, Mears attended First Baptist Church, led by William Bell Riley, and began teaching Sunday school at age twelve. After graduating from the University of Minnesota and several stints as a school teacher, Mears accepted a position as director of Christian education at Hollywood Presbyterian, where the Sunday school grew significantly under her leadership.

After surveying the existing curricular materials for Sunday schools and finding them inadequate, Mears began writing her own in 1929. She, together with Cyrus Nelson, founded Gospel Light Press in 1933 (since renamed Gospel Light Publishers) to publish her materials, which soon found wide acceptance among evangelical churches. In addition to her attention to the grade school curriculum, Mears developed a college-level program. In 1937 she negotiated the purchase of Forest Home Camp Grounds, near San Bernardino, California, for use as a spiritual retreat center, and it was here, at a place commemorated by a plaque, that Graham made his famous decision to renounce intellectual pursuits and concentrate simply on preaching the Bible.

Mears inspired many evangelical leaders in postwar America. Wilbur M. Smith once remarked that Mears's efforts amounted to "the most significant work among our nation's youth done by a woman in the twentieth century."

BIBLIOGRAPHY: Wendy Murray Zoba, "The Grandmother of Us All," *Christianity Today*, 16 September 1996, 44–46.

Moody, Dwight Lyman (1837–99)

Urban evangelist. One of the most influential preachers in American history, Dwight Lyman Moody was born in Northfield, Massachusetts, and headed east for Boston at the age of seventeen, where he worked in his uncle's shoe store. In Boston Moody attended Mount Vernon Congregational Church and was converted to evangelical Christianity by his Sunday school teacher, Edward Kimball.

In 1856 Moody headed west for Chicago, where he became a successful shoe salesman. He joined Plymouth Congregational Church, rented four pews, and filled them with acquaintances and business associates. In 1858 "Crazy Moody," as he was sometimes known because of his fervor, started a Sunday school in the slums, and two years later he quit his business to devote his energy to religious pursuits. A conscientious objector during the Civil War, Moody did evangelistic and relief work for the United States Christian Commission, traveling to Shiloh, Murfreesboro, and Chattanooga, and was among the first Union forces to enter Richmond. In 1864 he consolidated his various evangelistic efforts to form the Illinois Street Independent Church (now Moody Church), and in 1866 he became president of the Chicago YMCA.

After the Chicago fire of 1871, which destroyed the YMCA, his church, and his home, Moody built a new building, the Northside Tabernacle, which he used to feed and clothe thousands of people who had lost their homes. Moody then launched out as an itinerant evangelist. He was received well in Great Britain, and his notoriety across the Atlantic increased his popularity back in North America, where he conducted revival campaigns in Brooklyn, Philadelphia, Manhattan, Boston, and Chicago. One of his more notable campaigns was the one he held in conjunction with the Chicago World's Fair in 1893.

Moody's preaching was simple, homespun, and sentimental. He taught the three Rs: ruin by sin, redemption by Christ, and regeneration by the Holy Spirit. Although he specialized in urban evangelism, Moody's eschatology drifted more and more toward premillennialism and away from social reclamation. "I look upon this world as a wrecked vessel," he once declared. "God has given me a lifeboat and said, 'Moody, save all you can.'"

Perhaps because he had so little formal education himself, Moody sought to provide grounding in evangelicalism for those attracted to his preaching. He established Northfield Seminary for girls in 1879 and Mount Hermon School for boys in 1881; Northfield-Mount Hermon, still located in Moody's hometown, is now an élite preparatory school. Moody also conducted summer conferences at Northfield beginning in 1880, and the 1886 gathering gave rise to the Student Volunteer Movement. He helped to form a Bible institute in Chicago in 1889, a school that became known as Moody Bible Institute after his death.

BIBLIOGRAPHY: William G. McLoughlin, *Modern Revivalism* (1959); John Pollock, *Moody* (1963).

Mott, John Raleigh (1865–1955)
Missionary leader. Born in New York and reared in Iowa, John R. Mott was educated at Upper Iowa University and at Cornell University. Mott was one of the one hundred volunteers for foreign missions at Dwight Moody's Student Conference at Northfield, Massachusetts, in 1886; he soon emerged as chairman of the Student Volunteer Movement for Foreign Missions, an association whose motto was "The world for Christ in this generation." Mott maintained that position for thirty-two years.

At Cornell, Mott's work made the YMCA chapter there the largest in the country, and when he graduated in 1888 Mott became general secretary of the intercollegiate YMCA, with a mandate to integrate that work with that of the Student Volunteer Movement. As an itinerant evangelist, Mott was extraordinarily effective in recruiting students for missionary service. Both an evangelical and an ecumenist, Mott participated in the founding and early work of such organizations as the World Student Christian Federation, the Foreign Missions Conference of North America, and the World Alliance of YMCAs. His most important achievement, however, was his involvement in the formation of the World Council of Churches in 1948, of which he served as president. Because of his relief activities after World War II, Mott was awarded the Nobel Peace Prize in 1946.

BIBLIOGRAPHY: John R. Mott, *Strategic Points in the World's Conquest* (1897); *idem, The Evangelization of the World in This Generation* (1900); *idem, The Decisive Hour of Christian Missions* (1910); *idem, The Present-Day Summons to the World Mission of Christianity* (1931); *idem, Evangelism for the World Today* (1938); C. Howard Hopkins, *John R. Mott: 1865–1955* (1979); M. Craig Barnes, s.v., "John R. Mott," in Charles H. Lippy, ed., *Twentieth-Century Shapers of American Popular Religion* (1989).

Niebuhr, Karl Paul Reinhold (1892–1971)
Theologian, ethicist, and seminary professor. Born in Wright City, Missouri, and reared in the Evangelical Synod of North America, Reinhold Niebuhr graduated from Elmhurst College and Eden Seminary before continuing his studies at Yale Divinity School and Yale University. He served as pastor of the Bethel Evangelical Church in Detroit before moving to Union Theological Seminary in New York City, where he spent the remainder of his career. He published his influential *Moral Man and Immoral Society* in 1932 and was founder and editor of *Christianity and Crisis*, which sought to apply theology and ethics to critical social issues.

Though influenced early on by the Social Gospel, Niebuhr, in the wake of World War I and the Great Depression, came to advocate what he called "Christian realism," which tempered Protestant liberalism's optimism about human goodness and the capacity for social progress. Although initially a pacifist, by 1939 he recognized the necessity of resisting fascism by military means. Niebuhr became profoundly suspicious of assertions about human progress and programs for social perfection, including Marxism.

He became associated with the theological movement known as Neo-Orthodoxy, with its radical understanding of the transcendence of God. By means of grace individuals could learn goodness and even sacrifice for others. Justice, for Niebuhr, was ultimately elusive, available only beyond the bounds of human history, but individuals can—and should—strive for a proximate justice in this world.

Niebuhr became one of the premier oracles for Protestant theology in the middle decades of the twentieth century. He sought throughout his career to relate the claims of Christianity to the secular world.

BIBLIOGRAPHY: Richard Niebuhr, *Does Civilization Need Religion?* (1927);

idem, Leaves from the Notebook of a Tamed Cynic (1929); *idem, Moral Man and Immoral Society* (1932); *The Nature and Destiny of Man*, 2 vols. (1941–43); Richard Wightman Fox, *Reinhold Niebuhr: A Biography* (1986).

Palmer, Phoebe (née Worrall) (1807–74)
Holiness teacher and preacher. Reared in a Methodist household, Phoebe Worrall married a Methodist physician, Walter Clarke Palmer, in 1827, and they became active in the Allen Street Methodist Church in New York City. A few months after Phoebe Palmer's sister, Sarah Lankford, had an experience of entire sanctification on May 21, 1835, the Palmers and the Lankfords moved into the same house on Rivington Street, near the Allen Street church. There, the sisters began their famous Tuesday Meetings for the Promotion of Holiness, and Phoebe Palmer had her own sanctification experience on July 26, 1837.

In 1839 Palmer became the first woman to be designated a Methodist class leader in New York. She spoke at camp meetings and, together with her sister, helped to organize other Tuesday Meetings in New England and the mid-Atlantic states. Her travels took her throughout North America and Great Britain, where she exerted an enormous influence on William and Catherine Booth, founders of the Salvation Army. In addition to her itinerancy, Palmer wrote a number of books on holiness themes. *The Promise of the Father*, published in 1859, offered carefully reasoned arguments for the right of women to preach in churches. The Palmers went into the publishing business with the purchase of the *Guide to Holiness* in 1864, which Phoebe edited for the remainder of her life. They later acquired the *Beauty of Holiness and Sabbath Miscellany*, which they merged into the *Guide to Holiness*.

Phoebe Palmer's work and writings were important in both the shaping and the propagation of holiness doctrines in the nineteenth century. She set forth what she called an "altar theology," derived from the Old Testament practice of sacrifice. Palmer urged those who wanted to be sanctified, which she regarded as "full salvation," to lay their desire for holiness on the "altar" and trust God to deliver entire sanctification. She issued "holiness altar invitations" and invited those who had received the experience of entire sanctification to testify to it immediately. Palmer's theology was adopted by such holiness groups as the Salvation Army, the Free Methodists, the Wesleyan Methodists, and the Church of the Nazarene.

BIBLIOGRAPHY: Phoebe Palmer, *The Way of Holiness* (1845); *idem, The Promise of the Father* (1859); Charles E. White, *The Beauty of Holiness:*

Phoebe Palmer as Theologian, Revivalist, Feminist, and Humanitarian (1986); Harold Raser, *Phoebe Palmer: Her Life and Thought* (1987).

Rauschenbusch, Walter (1861–1918)

Baptist minister and theologian of the Social Gospel. After graduating from Rochester Seminary in 1886, Walter Rauschenbusch became pastor of the Second German Baptist Church in the slum of New York known as Hell's Kitchen. Although he had accepted the pastorate with the intent of saving souls, the squalor everywhere around him prompted a reconsideration of his mission. Drawing on the ideas of such secular reformers as Henry George, Rauschenbusch formulated what became known as the Social Gospel, which insisted that the Gospel was capable not only of reforming sinful individuals but of redeeming sinful social institutions as well.

In 1897 Rauschenbusch left New York and returned to Rochester Seminary, where he formulated his ideas and published them as *Christianity and the Social Crisis* in 1907. For the remainder of his life, Rauschenbusch was in demand as a lecturer and spokesman for the Social Gospel movement. BIBLIOGRAPHY: Walter Rauschenbusch, *Christianity and the Social Crisis* (1907); *idem, Christianizing the Social Order* (1912); *idem, A Theology for the Social Gospel* (1917).

Robertson, Marion Gordon ("Pat") (1930–)

Televangelist and conservative political activist. Born in Lexington, Virginia, Pat Robertson was the son of A. Willis Robertson, a Democratic congressman and U.S. senator. Pat Robertson enjoyed all the emoluments of a patrician upbringing; he attended a preparatory school in Chattanooga, Tennessee, and graduated from Washington and Lee University in 1950 and, after a brief tour of duty with the Marines, from Yale Law School in 1955. In 1954, while still in law school, he married Adelia "Dede" Elme shortly before she gave birth to their first child. Robertson failed the bar exam and decided to forsake law in favor of a career in business.

When Robertson abruptly announced that he was going to be a minister, his mother arranged a meeting with a Dutch evangelist, Cornelius Vanderbreggen, who was something of a mystic. Robertson had an evangelical conversion to Christianity and promptly returned home and poured all of his liquor down the drain. He soon left his startled wife, then seven months pregnant with the couple's second child, for a month-long conference sponsored by InterVarsity Christian Fellowship. While there, Robertson received a note from Dede: "Please come back. I need you desperately."

Robertson, after prayer and reflection, responded: "I can't leave. God will take care of you." He returned at the conclusion of the conference and devoted himself to prayer and Bible study. At one point, after her husband literally heeded the admonition in Luke 12:23 to sell all and give to the poor, Dede returned to find that Pat had sold all of their furniture and moved them to a friend's house in a Brooklyn slum.

In 1956 Robertson entered the Biblical Seminary of New York (renamed New York Theological Seminary in 1965) and became an associate pastor at the First Reformed Church in Mount Vernon, New York. There, under the influence of the senior minister, Robertson had a pentecostal experience, including speaking in tongues. After graduation from seminary in 1959, Robertson considered several pastorates and applied to be a missionary in Israel. He weighed the idea of a ministry in the Bedford Stuyvesant slums, but nothing seemed to capture his interest until he heard that a defunct television station was for sale in Portsmouth, Virginia, for $37,000. Robertson visited the station, climbing through a broken window and scaring away a large rat on the glass-strewn floors. He agreed to buy the station, grandly dubbed it the Christian Broadcasting Network, and by 1961, the same year he was ordained a Southern Baptist by the Freemason Street Baptist Church in Norfolk, Virginia, Robertson began broadcasting three hours of religious television per night.

Although the local clergy remained wary of the struggling enterprise, the station—and Robertson's smooth pentecostalism—began to catch on with pentecostals and charismatics. In 1965 Robertson hired two young Assemblies of God evangelists, Jim and Tammy Faye Bakker, as additional talent. Fund-raising telethons fueled the growth of the station and, eventually, the network. An early telethon solicited seven hundred donors who would pledge ten dollars a month; in 1966 Robertson named his central program the *700 Club*, with a talk and entertainment format unabashedly based on the *Tonight Show*. It was nationally syndicated in 1972.

Aside from his boilerplate dispensationalism and his attraction to various conspiracy theories, Robertson and his theology have always been difficult to categorize. His embrace of pentecostal gifts while putatively a member of the Southern Baptist Convention, which as a whole frowns upon speaking in tongues, would classify him as a charismatic. In the mid-1970s, however, Robertson spurned that label in favor of "Spirit-filled evangelical" and by the 1990s insisted upon "evangelical."

On September 17, 1986, Robertson capitalized on his media exposure, which had been enhanced by CBN's use of satellite technology, and announced that he would become a candidate for the Republican presidential nomination if he could obtain three million signatures of support. Less than a year later he declared his candidacy on a far-right political platform. He took a hiatus from CBN, resigned his Southern Baptist ordination in September 1987, and studiously billed himself as a broadcasting executive, bristling when the media referred to him as a televangelist. The media, however, produced a 1985 broadcast of the *700 Club* when Robertson ordered Hurricane Gloria to change course. "In the name of Jesus," he prayed, "we command you to stop where you are and head northeast, away from land, and away from harm. In the name of Jesus of Nazareth, we command it." In 1995 he took credit for diverting Hurricane Felix from the Virginia coast.

Despite these revelations and with the concerted efforts of politically conservative evangelicals at the grassroots level, Robertson won a straw poll in Michigan and finished second to Bob Dole and ahead of George Bush, the eventual nominee, in the Iowa precinct caucuses. In the face of increased scrutiny, however, he faltered in New Hampshire and eventually dropped out of the race.

In January 1989 Robertson met a young political operative, Ralph Reed, at an inaugural party for Bush. Robertson solicited ideas for transforming the grassroots organizations he had assembled during his campaign into a political lobby for politically conservative evangelicals. Reed's long memorandum in response provided the blueprint for the Christian Coalition, which was formed later that same year. Robertson, as head of the organization (Reed was tapped as executive director), became a major force in American politics and especially within the Republican Party.

With his embrace of such ideologies as Christian Reconstructionism, Robertson has often been accused of wanting to collapse the First Amendment distinction between church and state. His excoriations of abortion, political liberals, feminists, and homosexuals have earned him the label of intolerant, although such denunciations resonated with many politically conservative evangelicals. Robertson's prime-time address before the Republican National Convention in Houston in 1992 was widely criticized as extremist and as contributing to the defeat of Bush for re-election. On June 8, 1998, Robertson predicted that Orlando, Florida, would be hit with earthquakes, hurricanes, terrorist attacks, "and possibly a meteor" for allowing gay groups to display rainbow flags during "Gay Days" at Walt Disney World. "I don't think I'd be waving those flags in God's face if I were you," he declared on the *700 Club*.

In the 1990s Robertson cashed in on his media empire, which had been built with the tax-deductible contributions of the faithful. In 1997 his sale of International Family Entertainment, which included the Family Channel, to Rupert Murdoch's News Corporation raised some eyebrows—and not merely because Robertson had regularly criticized the sleazy programming on Murdoch's Fox Network. Robertson put some of the proceeds from that sale into missions work and millions into Regent University, but he and his son, Tim, reportedly put more than $200 million into their own pockets.

BIBLIOGRAPHY: Pat Robertson, *Shout It from the Housetops* (1972); idem, with Bob Slosser, *The Secret Kingdom* (1983); idem, *America's Date with Destiny* (1986); idem, *The New Millennium* (1990); idem, *Turning the Tide: The Fall of Liberalism and the Rise of Common Sense* (1993); David Edwin Harrell Jr., *Pat Robertson: A Personal, Religious, and Political Portrait* (1987); Tim Stafford, "Robertson R Us," *Christianity Today*, 12 August 1996, 26–33.

Sunday, William Ashley ("Billy") (1862–1935)
Itinerant evangelist. Born in Ames, Iowa, Billy Sunday spent his early years in orphanages until his athletic prowess earned him a baseball contract with the Chicago White Stockings, with whom he played until 1891. While in Chicago Sunday underwent a conversion experience in 1886 at the Pacific Garden Mission, and soon afterwards he joined the Jefferson Park Presbyterian Church. Under the auspices of the YMCA Sunday began his work as an evangelist, and shortly after a trade to the Pittsburgh Pirates he quit baseball and in 1893 began serving as an advance man for the itinerant revivalist J. Wilbur Chapman. When Chapman accepted a call to the pastorate in 1895, Sunday struck out on his own in what he would call the "kerosene circuit" of small towns in the Midwest.

By the turn of the century Sunday had taken his revival campaigns to the cities. He would often use vaudeville antics to attract attention; he spoke in the folksy, salty parlance of the day and would often taunt his audiences. Especially during World War I, Sunday trotted out patriotic and nativistic rhetoric, arguing that "Patriotism and Christianity are synonymous terms." He routinely condemned alcohol, gambling, and licentiousness but cared little for the niceties of theology. "I don't know any more about theology than a jack rabbit knows about ping-pong," he would say, "but I'm on my way to glory."

BIBLIOGRAPHY: Billy Sunday, *Great Love Stories from the Bible and Their Lesson for Today* (1917); idem, *Wonderful, and Other Sermons* (1940); Lyle

W. Dorsett, *Billy Sunday and the Redemption of Urban America* (1991);
Douglas Frank, *Less Than Conquerors: How Evangelicals Entered the Twentieth Century* (1986); John Pahl, s.v., "Billy Sunday," in Charles H. Lippy,
ed., *Twentieth-Century Shapers of American Popular Religion* (1989).

Wallis, Jim (1948–)

Evangelical social activist. Born into a Plymouth Brethren household outside of Detroit, Jim Wallis was "born again" at age six and for several years reflected the evangelical, patriotic values of his parents. At age thirteen, however, as he recalled in his autobiography, *Revive Us Again: A Sojourner's Story*, "the world I had grown up in went sour on me." His family moved to Southfield, an upper-middle-class suburb, and Wallis became sullen and withdrawn, uncomfortable with the accoutrements of his affluent surroundings.

In 1967, the summer of racial disturbances in Detroit, Wallis began to question his evangelical church and his parents. His search led him into Detroit, where he met African American congregations of Plymouth Brethren. "I was beginning to see," he recalled later, "that to stand with those who suffered I would have to shed myself of the assumptions of privilege and comfort on which I had been raised." Wallis's growing impatience with what he believed was the hypocrisy of evangelicalism, especially on the issue of race, led to a break with the church over the Vietnam War, which Wallis deemed an extension of America's racism and its callousness toward the poor. As a student at Michigan State University, Wallis led protests against American policies in Southeast Asia, but as the antiwar fervor began to dissipate early in the 1970s Wallis returned to the Bible. In the Sermon on the Mount, Wallis found a biblical warrant for his own concerns about justice, and in the twenty-fifth chapter of Matthew, he "was deeply struck by a God who had taken up residence among the poor, the oppressed, the outcasts."

Seeking to deepen his understanding of theology, Wallis enrolled at Trinity Evangelical Divinity School in the fall of 1970, a seminary of the Evangelical Free Church of America located in the affluent Bannockburn section of Deerfield, Illinois. There, amid a climate of theological conservatism, Wallis nevertheless found a handful of kindred spirits interested in "recovering the prophetic biblical tradition, the authentic evangelical message, and applying it to our historical situation." The group organized as the People's Christian Coalition, which in turn would form the core of what would eventually become the Sojourners Fellowship. At the seminary, however, this "radical discipleship" met with resistance from the administration, the faculty, and even fellow students. Wallis and his confrères became known as the Bannockburn Seven; they conducted demonstrations, passed out leaflets on campus, and conducted forums on such issues as racism, the war in Vietnam, militarism, and discrimination against women.

While attempting to survive various attempts by the seminary to expel them, Wallis and others began to explore connections with other radical evangelicals. During the summer of 1971 they edited and published the first issue of the *Post-American*, a sixteen-page tabloid so named, Wallis recounted, because it "tried to put forward a Christian faith that broke free of the prevailing American civil religion." As the *Post-American* began to appear quarterly, those involved in its production gradually lost interest in the seminary and relocated to form a Christian community among the poor in the Rogers Park section of Chicago.

In the fall of 1975 Wallis and the *Post-American* relocated to a poor neighborhood in Washington, D.C. Both the community and the magazine took the name *Sojourners*. Wallis continues to this day as editor of the magazine, and also maintains a demanding schedule of travel and lectures. He further serves as leader of Call to Renewal, an organization that offers an alternative religious activism to the agenda of the Religious Right. Under Wallis's direction, *Sojourners* magazine has reflected an eclectic mix of theology and spirituality, ranging from Dorothy Day and Thomas Merton to Dietrich Bonhoeffer, Jacques Ellul, and John Howard Yoder.

BIBLIOGRAPHY: Jim Wallis, *Agenda for Biblical People* (1976); idem, *The Call to Conversion* (1981); idem, *Revive Us Again: A Sojourner's Story* (1983); idem, *The Soul of Politics: A Practical and Prophetic Vision for Change* (1994); Randall Balmer, s.v., "Jim Wallis," in Charles H. Lippy, ed., *Twentieth-Century Shapers of American Popular Religion*; John Wilson, "Mr. Wallis Goes to Washington," *Christianity Today*, 14 June 1999, 41–43.

Whitefield, George (1714–70)

Anglican cleric and itinerant revivalist. George Whitefield, the "grand itinerant" of the Great Awakening, was born in Gloucester, England, and early in life developed a love for the theater. He entered Pembroke College, Oxford University, in November 1732, where he met and befriended Charles and John Wesley and joined their "Holy Club," a regular Methodist gathering. Whitefield experienced an evangelical conversion in 1735, graduated from Pembroke in July 1736, and was ordained a deacon in the Church of England the same year. Whitefield soon established a reputation as an extraordinary preacher. His sermons were all extemporaneous, and he used his stentorian voice and dramatic training to full effect. A contemporary once declared that Whitefield could bring tears to the eyes simply by saying "Mesopotamia."

Whitefield accompanied the Wesleys to Georgia in 1738, where he established an orphanage called Bethesda. When Whitefield returned to England to raise funds for the orphanage he was ordained a priest at Christ Church, Oxford, on January 14, 1739. He went on a preaching tour of Wales in March, and his irregular, open-air preaching aroused the opposition of some fellow Anglicans.

Whitefield found a warmer reception across the Atlantic, arriving in America on October 30, 1739. The colonists, already in the throes of a nascent revival, were captivated by the Anglican preacher, and in a culture with as yet no dramatic tradition, his theatrical flourishes were all the more effective. Whitefield's peregrinations along the Atlantic seaboard knit together the various disparate revivals to unleash what both contemporaries and historians called the Great Awakening.

As Whitefield fanned the revival fires, his opponents sought to muzzle him. Alexander Garden, the Church of England commissary in Charleston, South Carolina, brought ecclesiastical charges against Whitefield for preaching to dissenting congregations and for neglect of his putative charge in Georgia. Old Lights attacked Whitefield for his enthusiasm, for the revival excesses, and for challenging the social order in New England by preaching outside of the meetinghouses. Even Whitefield's relationship with the Wesleys became strained when he clung to the Calvinist doctrine of election and refused to adopt the Wesleys' Arminian leanings and their emerging notion of Christian perfection; Whitefield became leader of the Calvinist Methodists as against the Wesleyan Methodists.

Whitefield's popularity overwhelmed his critics. In the course of his many preaching tours in England, Wales, Scotland, Ireland, and North America he preached approximately eighteen thousand sermons. He preached his final sermon in Exeter, New Hampshire, on September 29, 1770, and expired the following morning in Newburyport, Massachusetts.

BIBLIOGRAPHY: George Whitefield, *George Whitefield's Journals* (1960); William H. Kenney, "George Whitefield, Dissenter Priest of the Great Awakening," *William and Mary Quarterly*, 3d ser., 26 (1969): 75–93; Harry S. Stout, *The Divine Dramatist: George Whitefield and the Rise of Modern Evangelicalism* (1991).

October 31, 1517	Martin Luther nails his *Ninety-five Theses* to the cathedral door at Wittenberg, thereby triggering the Protestant Reformation.
1611	Authorized (King James) Version of the Bible published in England.
1620	Pilgrims (Separatists) come to America aboard the *Mayflower*.
1628	First Protestant worship held in New Amsterdam (New York) under the direction of Dutch minister Jonas Michaëlius.
1630	English Puritans, led by John Winthrop, sail for Massachusetts Bay.
1662	Halfway Covenant.
1730–45	Great Awakening.
1795–1835	Second Great Awakening.
August 1801	Cane Ridge, Kentucky, camp meeting.
October 22, 1844	William Miller's predicted second coming of Christ fails to materialize.
1859	Charles Darwin's *The Origin of Species* published in America.

Summer 1886	Student Volunteer Movement for Foreign Missions organized at Mount Hermon, Massachusetts.
January 1, 1901	Students at Bethel Bible College in Topeka, Kansas, speak in tongues.
1906–09	Azusa Street Revival in Los Angeles.
1910–15	Publication of *The Fundamentals*.
July 1925	Scopes "monkey trial" in Dayton, Tennessee.
1949	Billy Graham conducts his revival "crusade" in Los Angeles.
November 1949	National Council of Churches formed during a meeting of Protestant leaders in Cleveland.
December 1955	Montgomery, Alabama, bus boycott, led by Martin Luther King Jr.
October 12, 1958	Dwight D. Eisenhower lays the cornerstone for the Interchurch Center in upper Manhattan.
August 1963	March on Washington.
April 4, 1968	Martin Luther King Jr. assassinated.
November 2, 1976	Jimmy Carter, avowed evangelical, elected U.S. president.
1980	Newly organized Religious Right, a loose coalition of politically conservative evangelicals, contributes to the defeat of Carter and the election of Ronald Reagan.
1989	Moral Majority, a Religious Right organization founded a decade earlier, folds; Christian Coalition, another Religious Right group, organized by Pat Robertson and Ralph Reed.
1998	Jimmy Creech, a United Methodist minister in Omaha, Nebraska, performs a "marriage" ceremony for two of his openly gay congregants.
1999	Evangelical Lutheran Church in America agrees to cooperation and intercommunion with the Episcopal Church; the Episcopalians ratify the agreement the following year.

Apocalypticism Apocalypticism refers generally to a set of beliefs concerning the end of time. Many evangelicals, because of their penchant for biblical literalism, believe that the prophetic utterances in the Bible, particularly those found in the books of Daniel and Revelation, indicate that human history will soon screech to a halt and the world will end in some kind of apocalyptic judgment. Apocalypticism takes many forms, in large measure because biblical prophecies admit of so many interpretations, but apocalypticism is especially popular among premillennialists, those who believe that Jesus will return to earth before the millennium predicted in the book of Revelation (20:1–10).

Arminianism Arminianism is the doctrine that salvation is available to anyone who exercises faith; it contrasts with the Calvinistic understanding that God alone determines who is and who is not among the elect. In 1610 the disciples of Dutch theologian Jacobus Arminius produced a manifesto called the *Remonstrance*, which they viewed as a corrective to the Calvinist doctrine of election. The *Remonstrance* held that one's election to salvation is based on God's foreknowledge of faith on the part of the believer; that Christ died for all humanity (although only believers benefited); that grace is resistible; and that the believer's perseverance in the faith is dependent upon his or her actions. The Reformed Synod of Dort, a gathering of Dutch Reformed leaders, firmly repudiated Arminian doctrines in 1618, thereby contributing the mnemonic TULIP to the vocabulary of Reformed theology: total depravity; unconditional election; limited atonement (limited to the elect); irresistible grace; perseverance of the saints.

Despite the conclusions of Dort, Arminianism became enormously popular among American evangelicals, especially after the American Revolution. Whereas Jonathan Edwards, a Calvinist, had insisted that the Great Awak-

ening was "a surprising work of God," Charles Grandison Finney, apologist
for the Second Great Awakening, insisted that revival—and salvation itself—
was "the work of man." "Revival of religion is not a miracle," Finney declared
in his *Lectures on Revival*. "There is nothing on religion beyond the ordinary
powers of nature. It consists entirely in the right exercise of the powers of
nature." Finney's emphasis on human volition in the salvation process stood
in opposition to the Calvinist notion of predestination and election, but his
Arminian theology was exquisitely suited to the American context and to the
temper of the times. Among a people who had only recently taken their *political*
destiny into their own hands, Arminianism assured them that they controlled
their *religious* destiny as well.

The almost wholesale adoption of Arminian theology on the part of antebellum evangelicals was a source of consternation to those who sought to
uphold the Calvinist tradition, especially the theologians at Princeton Theological Seminary. The Princetonians emphasized the importance of an educated
clergy, for example, as a way of dampening the enthusiasm of the revivals,
which were hotbeds of Arminianism. They failed, however, and the Arminian
emphasis on individual volition and self-determination came to dominate
American evangelicalism. Billy Graham, for instance, uses the language of
Arminianism in his crusades when he implores his auditors to make a "decision" for Christ, language that Edwards would find utterly foreign to his
understanding of salvation.

Born Again   Taken from the third chapter of Saint John, in which Jesus tells
Nicodemus that in order to enter the kingdom of heaven he must be "born
again," the term has come to be synonymous with evangelical conversion. An
evangelical will often talk about her conversion—which is often a dramatic
turning away from sin—as a "born-again experience" or describe himself as
a "born-again Christian." The latter designation is generally meant to distinguish the evangelical believer from a "liberal" or "nominal" Christian. Evangelicals believe that liberal Christians claim the designation "Christian" falsely,
because they cannot point to a datable experience of grace when they were
born again.

Calvinism   A system of theology dating to John Calvin, Calvinism refers to several formative doctrines that lie at the bedrock of Protestant theology in the
Reformed tradition, which, in turn, is virtually synonymous with Calvinism.
This system is sometimes abbreviated as the "Five Points of Calvinism":
1) unconditional election (God chooses some for salvation according to God's
inscrutable will); 2) definite atonement (Christ died to redeem only the elect);
3) total depravity of all humanity (all have inherited Adam's sin and are therefore unworthy of salvation; 4) efficacious grace (God saves those he elects);
5) preservation (perseverance) of the saints (once saved, always saved). These
doctrines are sometimes referred to by the acronym TULIP: total depravity;

unconditional election; limited atonement; irresistible grace; perseverance of the saints.

These doctrines were hashed out at the Synod of Dort by the Reformed Churches of the Netherlands in response to the Remonstrant Party, which placed more emphasis on human volition in the salvation process. The Remonstrants were led by Jakob Hermanszoon (Jacobus Arminius), Simon Episcopius, Johann Oudenbarneveldt, and Hugh De Groote (Hugo Grotius, the jurist). Anti-Remonstrant Reformed stalwarts included Francis Gomarus, Pieter Platevoet (Petrus Plancius), and others.

These doctrines were also adopted, with varying degrees of rigor, by those who identified with the Reformed tradition elsewhere, including Scotland, the Reformed cantons of Switzerland, the Puritans in England, and the Reformed evangelicals in America.

BIBLIOGRAPHY: John T. McNeill, *The History of Character of Calvinism* (1954); John H. Leith, *An Introduction to the Reformed Tradition: A Way of Being in the Christian Community*, rev. ed. (1977).

Charismatic Movement Whereas classical pentecostalism traces its origins to Agnes Ozman's speaking in tongues on the first day of the twentieth century, the Charismatic Movement brought pentecostal fervor—including divine healing and speaking in tongues—into mainline denominations beginning in the 1960s. The groundwork for such an incursion, however, was laid in the previous decade through the efforts of such pentecostal ecumenists as David Du Plessis, Oral Roberts, and Demos Shakarian, a California layman and founder of the Full Gospel Businessman's Fellowship International, a pentecostal organization.

The Charismatic Movement, also known as the Charismatic Renewal or Neo-Pentecostalism, erupted in 1960 among mainline Protestants with the news that Dennis J. Bennett, rector of Saint Mark's Episcopal Church in Van Nuys, California, had received the baptism of the Holy Spirit and had spoken in tongues. About a hundred parishioners followed suit, much to the dismay of other parishioners, members of the vestry, and the Episcopal bishop of Los Angeles. Although Bennett left Van Nuys for Seattle, Washington, he remained with the Episcopal Church, taking over a struggling parish, Saint Luke's, and transforming it into an outpost of the Charismatic Movement. Bennett's decision to remain an Episcopalian illustrates the distinction between charismatics and pentecostals, even though both believe in the baptism of the Holy Spirit. Whereas "pentecostal" refers to someone affiliated with one of the pentecostal denominations, such as the Assemblies of God or the Church of God in Christ, a "charismatic" remains identified with a tradition that, on the whole, looks askance at pentecostal enthusiasm.

The movement spread to other mainline Protestant denominations in the 1960s: the American Lutheran Church, the Lutheran Church in America (united in 1988 under the name Evangelical Lutheran Church in America), the United Presbyterian Church (U.S.A.), the American Baptist Church, and the United Methodist Church. Charismatic influences also took root in such unlikely settings as the Mennonites, the Churches of Christ, and the United Church of Christ. The Lutheran Church–Missouri Synod, however, vigorously resisted charismatic incursions, as did the Southern Baptist Convention, although Pat Robertson—a self-identified charismatic—retained his ordination as a Southern Baptist until his campaign for the presidency in 1988.

Charismatic impulses made their way into the Roman Catholic Church beginning in February 1967, when a group of students from Duquesne University in Pittsburgh attended a spiritual retreat and received the baptism of the Holy Spirit. The Duquesne Weekend, as it came to be known, led to other gatherings of Roman Catholics looking for spiritual renewal, notably in South Bend, Indiana, and Ann Arbor, Michigan. Both venues became majors centers of the Catholic Charismatic Renewal.

The Charismatic Movement also finds expression in independent congregations and in a number of larger churches that have begun to form their own network of affiliated congregations, similar to denominations. Notable examples include Calvary Chapel in Santa Ana, California; Cathedral of Praise in South Bend, Indiana; Victory Christian Center in Tulsa, Oklahoma; Rock Church in Virginia Beach, Virginia; and Vineyard Christian Fellowship in Anaheim, California.

Ecumenism   Ecumenism or the ecumenical movement takes its cue from John 17, where Jesus expresses the hope that his followers "may all be one." In many ways ecumenism seeks to reverse the fraying effects of the Protestant Reformation, in the wake of which Protestants took seriously Martin Luther's injunction to read and interpret the Bible for themselves. Protestant ecumenism in the twentieth century produced such institutions as the National Council of Churches (formed in 1949) and the Interchurch Center (dedicated in 1958). Ecumenism also produced cooperation on various missionary and social-service activities and led to an attenuation of doctrinal differences between mainline Protestant denominations.

Fundamentalism   The term "fundamentalism" derives from a series of pamphlets that appeared between 1910 and 1915 called *The Fundamentals; or, Testimony to the Truth*. *The Fundamentals* contained conservative statements on doctrinal issues and were meant to counteract the perceived drift toward liberal theology or "modernism" within Protestantism. Those who subscribed to these doctrines became known as "fundamentalists," and "fundamentalism" came to refer to the entire movement.

Fundamentalism has also been described as a militant antimodernism, but that characterization must be qualified. Fundamentalists are not opposed to modernism in the sense of being suspicious of innovation or technology; indeed, fundamentalists (and evangelicals generally) have often been at the fore-front of uses of technology, especially communications technology. Funda-mentalists have an aversion to modernity only when it is invested with a moral valence, when it represents a departure from orthodoxy or "traditional values," however they might be defined.

Finally, fundamentalism can be characterized as confrontational, at least as it has developed in the United States; Jerry Falwell, for instance, insists that he is a "fundamentalist," not an "evangelical." This militancy—on matters of doctrine, ecclesiology, dress, personal behavior, or politics—has prompted George M. Marsden, the preeminent historian of fundamentalism, to remark that the difference between an evangelical and a fundamentalist is that a fun-damentalist is "an evangelical who is mad about something."

BIBLIOGRAPHY: George M. Marsden, *Fundamentalism and American Culture: The Shaping of Twentieth-Century Evangelicalism* (1980); Joel A. Carpenter, *Revive Us Again: The Reawakening of American Fundamentalism* (1997); Robert D. Woodberry and Christian S. Smith, "Fundamentalism et al.: Conservative Protestants in America," *Annual Review of Sociology*, 24 (1998): 25–56.

Mainline Protestantism   Sometimes referred to as "mainstream Protestantism" or, more recently, as "old-line Protestantism," mainline Protestantism generally denotes those Protestant groups or denominations that aspired to cultural as-cendancy in the middle decades of the twentieth century. Mainline Protestants, who espoused a liberal theology on such matters as the divinity of Jesus, the authenticity of miracles, and biblical inspiration, laid claim to the legacy of Protestantism after having defeated conservatives during the fundamentalist-modernist controversies of the 1920s. Mainline Protestantism also invested heavily in the ecumenical movement of the 1950s, 1960s, and beyond, which produced such institutions as the National Council of Churches and the In-terchurch Center as well as greater cooperation among Protestant groups. The drift toward ecumenism, however, gradually contributed to a disaffection among constituents of mainline Protestant denominations, which registered steady declines in membership, attendance, and giving after 1965.

Millennium   The millennium refers to a thousand-year period expected near the end of the world by many evangelicals, based on their understanding of the biblical prophecies in the book of Revelation, especially Revelation 20:1–7. This millennial age is one in which the righteous will rule either before or after the coming of Jesus Christ at the end of time. For evangelicals, the millennium is one of the events on the apocalyptic calendar leading to the end of the world.

For centuries, millennial ideas have been hotly debated in evangelical circles. Some evangelicals, following the lead of Martin Luther, see the book of Revelation as unfit for inclusion in the biblical canon. They prefer to in-terpret Revelation itself as a restatement of pre-Christian Jewish apocalyptic thought or as an allegorical source of comfort to the early, persecuted Christians, an assurance that God would eventually avenge their sufferings.

Evangelicals who insist on a literal interpretation of the millennium generally fall into two camps: postmillennialists and premillennialists. Postmillennialists believe that Jesus will return *after* the millennium, this thousand-year period of righteousness. Implicit in postmillennialist belief is the conviction that it is incumbent upon believers to work toward the establishment of the millennial kingdom. Much of the impulse for social reform among evangelicals in the nineteenth century, for example, came from postmillennial sentiments.

Premillennialism, on the other hand, is a theology of despair, at least insofar as it relates to the impetus for reforming society according to the norms of godliness. It holds that Jesus will return *before* the millennium; Jesus may return, therefore, at any moment. Although there are notable exceptions, premillennialists, by and large, have abandoned hopes of widespread social amelioration. They look instead for divine intervention: the rapture of true believers, the tribulation, and the millennium.

Pentecostalism   Pentecostalism coalesced as a movement in the early years of the twentieth century. On the first day of the new century, January 1, 1901, a student at Bethel Bible College in Topeka, Kansas, Agnes Ozman, began speaking in tongues. This experience, also known as "glossolalia," was explicitly linked to the first Pentecost, recorded in Acts 2, when the early Christians were filled with the Holy Spirit. The movement, with its teachings about the baptism of the Holy Spirit, spread to Texas and then to Los Angeles, where it burst into broader consciousness during the Azusa Street Revival.

The roots of pentecostalism, however, reached back into the nineteenth century and the holiness movement, which sought to promote personal holiness (and John Wesley's doctrine of Christian perfection) within Methodism and other American denominations. By the end of the century, however, holiness advocates were feeling increasingly marginalized, and many left Methodism to form their own denominations. The pentecostal movement, with its distinctive emphasis on the second blessing or baptism of the Holy Spirit, as evidenced by glossolalia, spread quickly after the Azusa Street Revival. Pentecostalism took various denominational forms, including the Pentecostal Holiness Church, the Church of God in Christ, the Church of God (Cleveland, Tennessee), and the Assemblies of God, which was organized in 1914 and is the largest pentecostal denomination in North America.

Pentecostal worship today is characterized by ecstasy and the familiar posture of upraised arms, a gesture of openness to the Holy Spirit. Pentecostals generally believe in the gifts of the Holy Spirit, including divine healing, in addition to speaking in tongues.

BIBLIOGRAPHY: Edith L. Blumhofer, *Restoring the Faith: The Assemblies of God, Pentecostalism, and American Culture* (1993); H. Newton Malony and A.

Adams Lovekin, *Glossolalia: Behavioral Science Perspectives on Speaking in Tongues* (1985); Harvey Cox, *Fire from Heaven: The Rise of Pentecostal Spirituality and the Reshaping of Religion in the Twenty-first Century* (1995).

Pietism   Evangelicalism in America emerged from the eighteenth-century fusion of Puritanism and Pietism. While the strand of Puritanism in New England is well known, Pietism remains more obscure to most historians, in part because it was borne to North America by people of faith who spoke and worshiped in languages other than English.

The *Oxford English Dictionary* defines Pietism as a movement begun by Philipp Jakob Spener at Frankfurt-am-Main "for the revival and advancement of piety in the Lutheran church" and characterized by a "devotion to religious feeling, or to strictness of religious practice." Pietism covers the spectrum from conservative, orthodox, liturgical members of state-church traditions to separatist groups who reviled the "four dumb idols" of the state churches—baptismal font, altar, pulpit, and (in Lutheran lands) confessional—to radical prophetic groups alienated from both social and institutional church life. All Pietists, however, emphasized the importance of experiential (or, in the argot of the day, "experimental") religion, a warm-hearted piety that was more important than mere intellectual assent to prescribed dogmas. Indeed, Pietism in Europe very often arose as a protest against a cold orthodoxy, which bordered on scholasticism, a highly intellectualized or ratiocinated theology.

In North America, Pietists often disrupted ecclesiastical conventions and challenged ecclesiastical hierarchies. The best example of this was Theodorus Jacobus Frelinghuysen's all-out assault on the Dutch Reformed clergy in the Middle Colonies, but there are other examples as well, including Peter Henry Dorsius and Heinrich Melchior Mühlenberg. Pietistic impulses triggered—and were eventually absorbed by—the Great Awakening, and the evangelical tradition in America was born.

BIBLIOGRAPHY: F. Ernest Stoeffler, *The Rise of Evangelical Pietism* (1971); Randall Balmer, *Blessed Assurance: A History of Evangelicalism in America* (1999).

Polity   Polity is the form of church government used by a particular denomination. Essentially, there are three varieties of polity: episcopal, presbyterian, and congregational (all of them should be understood in the generic sense and therefore rendered in lowercase, not to be identified solely with the Episcopal, Presbyterian, and Congregational denominations). Episcopal polity (as, for example, in the Roman Catholic Church, the Episcopal Church, and various forms of Lutheranism) is church government by bishops, who ultimately decide denominational doctrines and policies and may also control the movement of clergy. The presbyterian polity (the Presbyterian church and many denominations in the Reformed tradition) is a more representational form of church government where members of the congregation choose elders, who in turn choose other representatives (sometimes known as "presbyters") to the highest body, usually known as the "general assembly."

The final form of polity is congregational, where all power rests with the individual congregation—the power to make and approve budgets, to hire and fire clergy, to authorize repairs to the church steeple. The aggregate power of local churches that are congregational in polity—such as in the Southern Baptist Convention—is, in theory at least, no more than the sum of its parts.

Religious Right   Sometimes called the Christian Right or the New Christian Right, the Religious Right is a name applied to a loose coalition of personalities and organizations that arose in the late 1970s to articulate a politically conservative agenda. Although evangelicals have long been active in politics, many shied away from political engagement in the political arena in the middle decades of the twentieth century. The immediate catalyst for their return was the presidential campaign of Jimmy Carter, a Southern Baptist Sunday school teacher who openly declared that he was a "born-again Christian." While Carter lured many evangelicals out of their apolitical stupor (southerners especially), many evangelicals turned against him when his administration's Justice Department sought to enforce antidiscrimination laws at Bob Jones University, a fundamentalist school in Greenville, South Carolina. This action represented an incursion into the evangelical subculture, which had been carefully constructed in the decades following the Scopes trial.

After evangelical leaders rallied together to resist the Justice Department's move, they sought to assemble a larger agenda, which in time would include opposition to abortion. Ironically, politically conservative evangelicals turned against Carter in favor of Ronald Reagan in 1980, when the Religious Right established itself as an electoral force. Jerry Falwell's formation of Moral Majority in 1979 was perhaps the most visible eruption of Religious Right impulses, but other organizations that fit beneath that umbrella might include the Religious Roundtable, Traditional Values Coalition, Focus on the Family, Concerned Women for America, and Christian Coalition, among many others. The highly conservative agenda articulated by Falwell, Pat Robertson, Ralph Reed, and others, however, represents a departure from the legacy of nineteenth-century evangelicalism, with its abiding concern for social amelioration and for those less fortunate.

Since 1980 the Religious Right has made steady inroads within the Republican Party, often to the chagrin of long-term party members. In 1988 Pat Robertson made a credible showing in the early Republican presidential primaries, and in 1992 Robertson and Pat Buchanan addressed the Republican National Convention in Houston, where they rehearsed themes dear to the hearts of religious conservatives. The success of the Religious Right in the 1980s and 1990s, however, provoked a backlash not only among the electorate (who elected Bill Clinton in 1992 and re-elected him four years later) but also among evangelicals whose political sympathies leaned to the left on the ideological spectrum. In 1996 Senator Mark O. Hatfield, Republican of Oregon, announced his decision not to seek re-election, complaining that "converted Confederates" had taken over his party. That same year Jim Wallis, Tony Campolo and other politically liberal evangelicals formed an organization called Call to Renewal in order to counteract the impression that leaders of the Religious Right spoke for all evangelicals.

BIBLIOGRAPHY: William Martin, *With God on Our Side: The Rise of the Religious Right in America* (1996); Clyde Wilcox, *Onward Christian Soldiers?: The Religious Right in American Politics* (1996).

NOTES

Preface

1. See, for example, Robert Baird, *Religion in the United States of America* (Glasgow, 1844); Winthrop S. Hudson, *Religion in America* (New York: Charles Scribner's Sons, 1965); Edwin Scott Gaustad, *A Religious History of America* (New York: Harper & Row, 1966); Sydney E. Ahlstrom, *A Religious History of the American People* (New Haven, Conn.: Yale University Press, 1972); Robert T. Handy, *A History of the Churches in the United States and Canada* (New York: Oxford University Press, 1977); and Martin E. Marty, *Pilgrims in Their Own Land: 500 Years of Religion in America* (Boston: Little, Brown, 1984).

2. George M. Marsden, *Fundamentalism and American Culture: The Shaping of Twentieth Century Evangelicalism: 1870–1925* (New York: Oxford University Press, 1980). Marsden followed this volume with *Reforming Fundamentalism: Fuller Seminary and the New Evangelicalism* (Grand Rapids, Mich.: Wm. B. Eerdmans, 1987).

3. Mark Noll, *American Evangelical Christianity: An Introduction* (London: Blackwell, 2001).

1. Protestantism in America

1. There are several excellent biographies of the life of Martin Luther, including Roland H. Bainton, *Here I Stand: A Life of Martin Luther* (Nashville: Abingdon-Cokesbury Press, 1950); and Heiko Oberman, *Luther: Man Between God and the Devil* (New Haven, Conn.: Yale University Press, 1989).

2. On the Second Great Awakening, see David W. Kling, *A Field of Divine Wonders: The New Divinity and Village Revivals in Northwestern Connecticut, 1792–1822* (University Park: Pennsylvania State University Press, 1993); John B. Boles, *The Great Revival, 1787–1805: The Origins of the Southern Evangelical Mind* (Lexington: University Press of Kentucky, 1972); Christine Leigh Heyrman, *Southern*

Cross: The Beginnings of the Bible Belt (New York: Knopf, 1997); and Paul E. Johnson, *A Shopkeeper's Millennium: Society and Revivals in Rochester, New York, 1815–1837* (New York: Hill and Wang, 1978).

3. The best account of the Scopes trial and its reverberations throughout the the twentieth century is Edward J. Larson, *Summer for the Gods: The Scopes Trial and America's Continuing Debate over Science and Religion* (New York: Basic Books, 1997).

4. For a discussion of evangelicals and communication, see Randall Balmer, chap. 4 in *Blessed Assurance: A History of Evangelicalism in America* (Boston: Beacon Press, 1999).

5. John 3:3 New International Version (NIV).

6. H. Richard Niebuhr's useful taxonomy appears in his *Christ and Culture* (New York: Harper & Brothers, 1951).

7. Harvey Cox, *The Secular City: Secularization and Urbanization in Theological Perspective* (New York: Macmillan, 1965).

8. Harvey Cox, *Religion in the Secular City: Toward a Postmodern Theology* (New York: Simon & Schuster, 1984).

9. George Gallup Jr., with D. Michael Lindsay, *Surveying the Religious Landscape: Trends in U.S. Beliefs* (Harrisburg, Pa.: Morehouse Publishing, 1999), 63.

10. Ibid., 64, 65.

11. Ibid., 64.

12. Lyman A.Kellstedt and John C. Green, "The Mismeasure of Evangelicals," *Books & Culture* (January/February 1996): 14.

13. Ibid.

14. Ibid., 14–15.

15. Christian Smith, Michael Emerson, Sally Gallagher, and Paul Kennedy, "Findings from the Evangelical Identity and Influence Project" (paper presented at the ISAE Summer Consultation, June 25–27, 1998).

16. Quoted in Alfred Kazin, *On Native Grounds* (Garden City, N.Y.: Doubleday, 1956), 150.

17. For an example of this phenomenon, see Randall Balmer, chap. 3 in *Grant Us Courage: Travels Along the Mainline of American Protestantism* (New York: Oxford University Press, 1996).

2. A Brief History of Protestantism in America

1. On Puritan spirituality, see Charles E. Hambrick-Stowe, *The Practice of Piety: Puritan Devotional Disciplines in Seventeenth-Century New England* (Chapel Hill: University of North Carolina Press, 1982).

2. Regarding Roger Williams, see Perry Miller, *Roger Williams: His Contribution to the American Tradition* (Indianapolis, Ind.: Bobbs-Merrill, 1953); and Edwin S.

Gaustad, *Liberty of Conscience: Roger Williams in America* (Grand Rapids, Mich.: Wm. B. Eerdmans, 1991).

3. Randall Balmer, chap. 1 in *Blessed Assurance: A History of Evangelicalism in America* (Boston: Beacon Press, 1999).

4. See Milton J. Coalter Jr., *Gilbert Tennent, Son of Thunder: A Case Study of Continental Pietism's Impact on the First Great Awakening in the Middle Colonies* (Westport, Conn.: Greenwood, 1986); James Tanis, *Dutch Calvinistic Pietism in the Middle Colonies: A Study in the Life and Theology of Theodorus Jacobus Frelinghuysen* (The Hague: Martinus Nijhoff, 1967); and Randall Balmer, *A Perfect Babel of Confusion: Dutch Religion and English Culture in the Middle Colonies* (New York: Oxford University Press, 1989).

5. Jon Butler has articulated this view most originally and most forcefully. See Butler, chap. 6 in *Awash in a Sea of Faith: Christianizing the American People* (Cambridge, Mass.: Harvard University Press, 1990).

6. Regarding Whitefield's dramatic artistry and its effect on colonists, see Harry S. Stout, *The Divine Dramatist: George Whitefield and the Rise of Modern Evangelicalism* (Grand Rapids, Mich.: Wm. B. Eerdmans, 1991).

7. Darrett B. Rutman, ed., *The Great Awakening: Event and Exegesis* (Huntington, N.Y.: Robert E. Kreiger Publishing, 1977), 37.

8. For an argument on the close connections between evangelical Christianity and democratic ideals in the early republic, see Nathan O. Hatch, *The Democratization of American Christianity* (New Haven, Conn.: Yale University Press, 1989).

9. Christine Leigh Heyrman, chap. 3 in *Southern Cross: The Beginnings of the Bible Belt* (New York: Knopf, 1997).

10. Richard Allen, *The Life Experience and Gospel Labors of the Rt. Rev. Richard Allen* (1783; reprint, Nashville: Abingdon Press, 1960); and Carol V. R. George, *Segregated Sabbaths: Richard Allen and the Rise of Independent Black Churches, 1760–1840* (New York: Oxford University Press, 1973).

11. Randy J. Sparks, *On Jordan's Stormy Banks: Evangelicalism in Mississippi, 1773–1876* (Athens: University of Georgia Press, 1994), 2.

12. C. C. Goen, *Broken Churches, Broken Nation: Denominational Schisms and the Coming of the Civil War* (Macon, Ga.: Mercer University Press, 1985).

13. Galatians 3:28 NIV.

14. Ernest R. Sandeen, chap. 5 in *The Roots of Fundamentalism: British and American Millennarianism, 1800–1930* (Chicago: University of Chicago Press, 1970).

15. The best secondary account of the Scopes trial is Edward J. Larson, *Summer for the Gods: The Scopes Trial and America's Continuing Debate over Science and Religion* (New York: Basic Books, 1997).

16. Will Herberg, *Protestant-Catholic-Jew: An Essay in American Religious Sociology* (Garden City, N.Y.: Doubleday, 1955), 136.

17. Ibid., 136–37.

3. The Varieties of Protestantism in America

1. For a biography of Chauncy, see Charles H. Lippy, *Seasonable Revolutionary: The Mind of Charles Chauncy* (Chicago: Nelson-Hall, 1981). There are many biographies of Edwards, including Perry Miller, *Jonathan Edwards* (New York: William Sloane, 1949); and Patricia J. Tracy, *Jonathan Edwards, Pastor: Religion and Society in Eighteenth-Century Northampton* (New York: Hill and Wang, 1979).

2. See George M. Marsden, *Fundamentalism and American Culture: The Shaping of Twentieth-Century Evangelicalism: 1870–1935* (New York: Oxford University Press, 1980); and Joel A. Carpenter, *Revive Us Again: The Reawakening of American Fundamentalism* (New York: Oxford University Press, 1997).

3. See Grant Wacker, *Heaven Below: Early Pentecostals and American Culture* (Cambridge, Mass.: Harvard University Press, 2001); Edith L. Blumhofer, *Restoring the Faith: The Assemblies of God, Pentecostalism, and American Culture* (Urbana and Chicago: University of Illinois Press, 1993).

4. George M. Marsden, *Reforming Fundamentalism: Fuller Seminary and the New Evangelicalism* (Grand Rapids, Mich.: Wm. B. Eerdmans, 1987).

4. Williston Federated Church

1. One general, albeit fallible, rule for determining whether or not a person or congregation is evangelical or liberal is pronunciation. Evangelicals generally describe themselves using a short "e," so that the first two syllables of "evangelical" or "evangelicalism" rhyme with "heaven," whereas nonevangelicals use a long "e." With "Amen," however, the pattern, curiously, is reversed. Liberal or mainline Protestants tend to pronounce it "ah-MEN," while evangelicals use a long "a." Again, this is a highly fallible generalization, one that admits of many exceptions, including regional variations.

5. Abyssinian Baptist Church

1. For a fuller treatment of this phenomenon, see Charles V. Hamilton, *The Black Preacher in America* (New York: William Morrow, 1972).

6. New Life Family Fellowship

1. For a fuller treatment of this phenomenon, see Donald E. Miller, *Reinventing American Protestantism: Christianity in the New Millennium* (Berkeley and Los Angeles: University of California Press, 1999).

2. The use of grape juice rather than wine on the part of many evangelical congregations dates to the temperance movement of the nineteenth century. For reasons of hygiene, evangelicals also abandoned the common cup for more sanitary individual servings, while liturgical Protestants use wine and the common cup, or chalice. See Leonard I. Sweet, chap. 6 in *Health and Medicine in the Evangelical Tradition: "Not by Might nor Power"* (Valley Forge, Penn.: Trinity Press International, 1994).

3. On the relation between evangelicalism and democracy, see Nathan O. Hatch, *The Democratization of American Christianity* (New Haven, Conn.: Yale University Press, 1989).

7. Protestants and Feminism

1. Ada María Isasi-Díaz, *Mujerista Theology: A Theology for the Twenty-First Century* (Maryknoll, N.Y.: Orbis Books, 1996), 61.

2. Lynn Japinga, *Feminism and Christianity: An Essential Guide* (Nashville: Abingdon Press, 1999), 13.

3. Elisabeth Schussler Fiorenza, *The Power of Naming: A Concilium Reader in Feminist Liberation Theology* (Maryknoll, N.Y.: Orbis Books, 1996), n. 4.

4. Pamela Dickey Young, *Feminist Theology/Christian Theology: In Search of Method* (Minneapolis: Fortress Press, 1990), 13.

5. Rosemary Radford Ruether, *Sexism and God-Talk: Toward a Feminist Theology* (Boston: Beacon Press, 1993), 116, 134–38; and *Feminist Theology/Christian Theology*, 96–102.

6. Daphne Hampson, *Theology and Feminism* (Oxford: Basil Blackwell, 1990), 59–66.

7. *Feminism and Christianity*, 119–23.

8. *Mujerista Theology*, 148–49; and Mark L. Strauss, *Distorting Scripture?: The Challenge of Bible Translation and Gender Accuracy* (Downer's Grove, Ill.: InterVarsity Press, 1998), 176.

9. *Feminism and Christianity*, 131–32.

10. June Steffensen Hagen, "The Little Pronoun 'She,'" *Daughters of Sarah* 15 (November/December 1989): 23.

11. Nancy A. Hardesty, *Inclusive Language in the Church* (Atlanta: John Knox Press, 1987), 2.

12. *Sexism and God-Talk*, 68; and Elizabeth A. Johnson, *She Who Is: The Mystery of God in Feminist Theological Discourse* (New York: Crossroad, 1992), 39.

13. *She Who Is*, 42; Mary Stewart Van Leeuwen, ed., *After Eden: Facing the Challenge of Gender Reconciliation* (Grand Rapids, Mich.: Wm. B. Eerdmans, 1993), 154; and Thomas Finger, "Holy Wisdom, Love So Bright: Sophia in Scripture and Worship," *Daughters of Sarah* 20 (Fall 1994).

14. Edward C. Lehman, *Women Clergy: Breaking Through Gender Barriers* (New Brunswick, N.J.: Transaction Books, 1985), 228.

15. Mark Chaves, *Ordaining Women: Culture and Conflict in Religious Organizations* (Cambridge, Mass.: Harvard University Press, 1997), 27–30; and *Women Clergy*, 239–40.

16. *Feminism and Christianity*, 19.

17. R. Marie Griffith, *God's Daughters: Evangelical Women and the Power of Submission* (Berkeley and Los Angeles: University of California Press, 1997); the phrase quoted in the text is taken from Griffith's subtitle. Cf. Brenda E. Brasher,

Godly Women: Fundamentalism and Female Power (New Brunswick, N.J.: Rutgers University Press, 1998).

18. Lauren F. Winner, "The Man Behind the Megachurch," *Christianity Today*, 6 November 2000, 56ff.

19. *After Eden*, 7.

20. Virginia Ramey Mollenkott, "Interpreting Difficult Scriptures," *Daughters of Sarah* 7 (September/October 1981): 13.

21. Wayne Grudem, "The Meaning 'Source' Does Not Exist," *CBMW News* 2 (December 1997): 1, 7; *idem*, "The Myth of 'Mutual Submission,'" *CBMW News* 1 (October 1996): 1.

22. D. A. Carson, *The Inclusive Language Debate: A Plea for Realism* (Grand Rapids, Mich.: Baker Book House, 1998), 19.

23. Quoted in *Inclusive Language in the Church*, 73–74.

24. *Inclusive Language in the Church*, 77–78.

25. *Inclusive Language Debate*, 21.

26. Wayne Grudem, *The Gender-Neutral Bible Controversy: Muting the Masculinity of God's Words* (Nashville: Broadman and Holman, 2000), 117.

27. *Inclusive Language Debate*, 150.

28. Ibid., 21–38.

29. For the fullest discussion of the SBC takeover, see Nancy Tatom Ammerman, *Baptist Battles: Social Change and Religious Conflict in the Southern Baptist Convention* (New Brunswick, N.J.: Rutgers University Press, 1990).

30. Mark Wingfield, "SBC Approves Family Statement, Declining to Add Amendments," *Associated Baptist Press*, 10 June 1998, vol. 98–143.

31. Becky Thomas, letter to the editor, *The Biblical Recorder*, 25 September 1998.

32. Tim Ellsworth, "Couple Attends, Joins SBC Church After Convention Takes Family Stance," *Baptist Press*, 10 September 1998.

33. H. Wayne House, *The Role of Women in Ministry Today* (Nashville: Thomas Nelson, 1990), 155.

34. Tammi Reed Ledbetter, "Southern Baptist Leaders Respond to Author's Arguments for Women Pastors," *Baptist Press*, 7 June 2001.

35. Russell D. Moore, "CBF Affiliated Group Urges Women to Leave the SBC," *Baptist Press*, 30 June 2000.

36. Michael Foust, "Fred Luter: Reach Men for Christ, Families, Churches Will Benefit," *Baptist Press*, 24 April 2001.

37. Wingfield, "Promise Keepers Was About Revivalism More Than Gender Issues," *Associated Baptist Press*, 30 November 2000; Jeanne Parrott, "Dale Came Home a Different Husband and Father," in *Standing on the Promises: The Promise Keepers and the Revival of Manhood*, ed. Dane S. Claussen (Cleveland: Pilgrim Press, 1999), 162; and Valerie Bridgeman Davis, "A Womanist/Feminist Lives with a Promise Keeper and Likes It," in *Standing on the Promises*, 154–55.

8. Protestants and Homosexuality

1. Saul M. Olyan, "'And with a Male You Shall Not Lie Like the Lying Down of a Woman': On the Meaning and Significance of Leviticus 18:22 and 20:13," in *Que(e)rying Religion: A Critical Anthology*, ed. Gary David Comstock and Susan E. Henking (New York: Continuum, 1997), 398.

2. Letha Scanzoni and Virginia Ramey Mollenkott, *Is the Homosexual My Neighbor?: A Positive Christian Response*, rev. ed. (San Francisco: HarperSanFrancisco, 1994), 61.

3. Walter Wink, "Homosexuality and the Bible." http://www.melwhite.org/biblesays.html

4. Lewis Smedes, "Like the Wideness of the Sea?," *Soulforce, Inc.* http://www.soulforce.org/lewissmedes.html

5. Victor Paul Furnish, "What Does Scripture Say? How Shall We Listen?: The Bible and Homosexuality," *Open Hands* 9 (Summer 1993): 4–6.

6. Mary Jo Osterman, "Biblical Interpretation: Beyond Judgment to Love," *Open Hands* 9 (Summer 1993): 3.

7. Richard B. Hays, *The Moral Vision of the New Testament: Community, Cross, New Creation: A Contemporary Introduction to New Testament Ethics* (San Francisco: HarperSanFrancisco, 1996), 389–90.

8. John Gallagher and Chris Bull, *Perfect Enemies: The Religious Right, the Gay Movement, and the Politics of the 1990s* (New York: Crown, 1996); and Anita Bryant, *The Anita Bryant Story: The Survival of Our Nation's Families and the Threat of Militant Homosexuality* (Old Tappan: Fleming H. Revell, 1977).

9. *Anita Bryant Story*, 53–58.

10. Ibid., 53, 114.

11. Ibid., 13; and Neil Miller, *Out of the Past: Gay and Lesbian History from 1869 to the Present* (New York: Vintage Books, 1995), 402–409.

12. Didi Herman, *The Antigay Agenda: Orthodox Vision and the Christian Right* (Chicago: University of Chicago Press, 1997), 51–70.

13. *Anita Bryant Story*, 21.

14. Matt Daniels, "United We Fall," *World*, 17 June 2000.

15. Nancy L. Wilson, *Our Tribe: Queer Folks, God, Jesus and the Bible* (San Francisco: HarperSanFrancisco, 1995), 23.

16. *Out of the Past*, 402–403.

17. *Perfect Enemies*, 40.

18. Ibid., 100–124; and *Antigay Agenda*, 137ff.

19. Daniels, "United We Fall."

20. Mary Adelia R. McLeod, "God's Great Gift of Love," *beliefnet*, 24 January 2000. http://129.33.230.60/story/11/story_1120_1.html; and William Sloane Coffin, "Let Us Be Impatient with Prejudice," *Rutland Daily Herald*, 20 January 2000, excerpted at *beliefnet*. http://129.33.230.60/story/11/story_1118_1.html

21. Richard Mouw et al., "Just Saying 'No' Is Not Enough: A *CT* Forum on Homosexuality and Public Policy," *Christianity Today*, 4 October 1999, 50ff.

22. Ibid.

23. John Shelby Spong, *Here I Stand: My Struggle for a Christianity of Integrity, Love, and Equality* (San Francisco: HarperSanFrancisco, 2000), 403.

24. Walter C. Righter, *A Pilgrim's Way* (New York: Knopf, 1998), 59.

25. *James M. Stanton, Bishop of Dallas, et al., Presenters v. Walter C. Righter, Respondent* (1996).

26. This and the following five paragraphs are based on Keith Hartman, *Congregations in Conflict: The Battle over Homosexuality* (New Brunswick, N.J.: Rutgers University Press, 1996), 2–24.

27. Lisa Kennedy, "Creech's Crusade," *Out Magazine*, November 1999, excerpted at *beliefnet*. http://www.beliefnet.com/frameset.asp?pageLoc = /story/ 11/story_1106_1.html&boardID = 1547

28. Barbara Nissen, "Covenanting Ceremony for Same Sex Partners to Be Held at First United Methodist Church in Omaha," United Methodist News Service, 12 September 1997. http://www.umaffirm.org/cornews/creech1.html

29. "Statement by Rev. Jimmy Creech," *Interfaith Working Group Online*, 9 November 1999. http://www.iwgonline.org/docs/jcontrial.html

30. "Creech Trial: Questions & Answers," United Methodist News Service http://umns.umc.org/99/nov/creech.html

31. Leanne McCall Tigert, *Coming Out While Staying In: Struggles and Celebrations of Lesbians, Gays, and Bisexuals in the Church* (Cleveland: United Church Press, 1996), 38–43.

32. Timothy Morgan, "Anglicans Deem Homosexuality 'Incompatible with Scripture,'" *Christianity Today*, 7 September 1998, 32.

33. Art Moore, "One Church, Two Faiths: Will the Episcopal Church Survive the Fight over Homosexuality?" *Christianity Today*, 12 July 1999, 42ff.

34. Troy D. Perry, *The Lord Is My Shepherd and He Knows I'm Gay: The Autobiography of the Rev. Troy D. Perry* (Los Angeles: Nash Publishing, 1972), 150.

35. Mel White, "Open Letter from Mel White to Jerry Falwell," *Soulforce, Inc.*, 5 June 1999. http://www.soulforce.org/falwell.html

36. Jerry Falwell, "My Open Letter to Mel White," *National Liberty Journal Online*, July 1999. http://www.liberty.edu/chancellor/nlj/July1999/Coverstory 3.htm

37. "Book of Uncommon Prayer," *Open Hands* 3 (Winter 1988), 13; and Gregory R. Dell, "The Work of the People," *Open Hands* 9 (Winter 1994), 4–5.

38. Quoted in Gross, 130.

39. Chris Glaser, *Coming Out as Sacrament* (Louisville, Ky.: Westminster John Knox Press, 1998), 11–12.

40. Gross, 133.

41. See "Litany of a Supportive Community," *Open Hands* 4 (Winter 1989): 14; and "Liturgy of Affirmation," *Open Hands* 9 (Winter 1994): 20–21.

42. "A Celebration of a Great Feast," *Open Hands* 7 (Spring 1992): 20–21; and Elizabeth Stuart, "The Dangerous Song of the Wild Geese: Sexuality and Liturgy," *Open Hands* 8 (Summer 1992): 20–21.

9. Protestants and Social Justice

1. Joyce Hollyday, "Sisters of Dignity and Courage," *Sojourners* 21, no. 4 (1992): 25. Joyce Hollyday, "At Home in Joseph's House," *Sojourners* 17, no. 1 (1988): 15–20. The Wardlaw material is based on interviews with the author, conducted in 1999, and John Robert Smith, *The Church That Stayed* (Atlanta: The Atlanta Historical Society, 1979); Nile Harper, *Urban Churches, Vital Signs: Beyond Charity Toward Justice* (Grand Rapids, Mich.: Wm. B. Eerdmans Publishing Company, 1999).

2. Walter Bruggeman, "A World Available for Peace," *Sojourners* 17, no. 1 (1988): 22–26.

3. Patricia J. Rumer, "No More Widows from War," *Sojourners* 20, no. 2 (1991): 15.

4. Daniel Sack, *Whitebread Protestants: Food and Religion in American Culture* (New York: St. Martin's Press, 2000), 166–83.

5. John Perkins, "Culture of Despair," *Prism* 1, no. 1 (1993): 9–13.

6. *Urban Churches*, 11–17, 110–17.

7. Mary Lou Kownacki, "Behold the Nonviolent One," *Sojourners* 18, no. 9 (1989): 22–24.

8. Jim Wallis, *Faith Works: Lessons from the Life of an Activist Preacher* (New York: Random House, 2000); and "Evangelicals and the Poor," *Prism* 6, no. 6 (1999): 6–9.

9. Michael O. Emerson and Christian Smith, *Divided by Faith: Evangelical Religion and the Problem of Race in America* (New York: Oxford University Press, 2000), 65–66, 122–23.

10. David Anderson and Brent Zuercher, *Letters Across the Divide: Two Friends Explore Racism, Friendship, and Faith* (Grand Rapids, Mich.: Baker Books, 2001), 7–29.

11. Spencer Perkins and Chris Rice, *More Than Equals: Racial Healing for the Sake of the Gospel*, rev. ed. (Downers Grove, Ill.: InterVarsity Press, 2000), 19, 82.

12. Michael Verchot, "Taking Steps Toward Racial Justice," *Sojourners* 17, no. 2 (1988): 30–31.

13. *Divided by Faith*, 115–72.

14. David P. Gushee, "Racial Reconciliation or Racial Justice?" *Moral Leadership* 2, no. 4 (2001).

15. "Religious Leaders Skeptical About the Christian Coalition's Outreach to African Americans," Interfaith Alliance News Release, 9 May 1997.

16. Amy Sherman, "Getting to Work," *Prism* 6, no. 1 (1999): 12–16.

17. "Evangelicals and the Poor," *Prism* 6, no. 6 (1999): 6–9.

18. Richard Land, "Constitutionally Safe, Religiously Dangerous?" *beliefnet.* http://www.beliefnet.com/story/70/story_7029_1.html

19. Marvin Olasky, "On the Front Lines," *World*, 23 June 2001.

20. Tim Graham, "O Ye of Too Much Faith," *World*, 24 March 2001.

21. Adelle M. Banks, "Bush's Faith-Based Initiative Divides Black Community," (RNS), 2001.

22. Ibid.

23. Eugene Rivers, "The Race Card," interview by *beliefnet*; Franklin Foer, "Right Reverend?" *The New Republic*, 7 May 2001; and Rebecca Carr, "DiIulio Ends 'Mission' Blessed, Frustrated," *The Atlanta Journal–Constitution*, 19 August 2001.

Conclusion

1. Harry S. Stout, *The New England Soul: Preaching and Religious Culture in Colonial New England* (New York: Oxford University Press, 1986), 15 n. 4.

2. See Michael Warner, ed., *American Sermons: The Pilgrims to Martin Luther King Jr.*, 2 vols. (New York: The Library of America, 1999).

3. Eugene Lowry, "Preaching from Oops to Yeah," in *Patterns of Preaching: A Sermon Sampler*, ed. Ronald J. Allen (St. Louis: Chalice Press, 1998), 93–97.

4. Kathy Black, "Preaching on a Personal Issue," in *Patterns of Preaching*, 90–98.

5. Serene Jones, "Preaching from the Perspective of Postliberal Theology," in *Patterns of Preaching*, 231–36.

6. Michael G. Maudlin, "Help for Doubting Thomases," review of *Help My Unbelief* by Fleming Rutledge, *beliefnet.* http://www.beliefnet.com/frameset. asp?pageLoc = /story/46/story_4643_1.html&boardID = 6223

7. Barbara Brown Taylor, *Home By Another Way* (Cambridge, Mass.: Cowley Publications, 1999), 69–72.

8. See, for example, Marsha G. Whitten, *All Is Forgiven: The Secular Message in American Protestantism* (Princeton, N.J.: Princeton University Press, 1993).

9. Taylor, *Speaking of Sin: The Lost Language of Salvation* (Cambridge, Mass.: Cowley Publications, 2000), 5.

10. Quoted in Rob Marcus and Marshall Allen, "Once and Future Worship," *faithWORKS.* http://www.faithworks.com/archives/once_futureworship.htm

11. Quoted in "Once and Future Worship."

12. Quoted in "Once and Future Worship."

13. Arlene Sanchez Walsh, "Slipping into Darkness: Popular Culture and the Creation of a Latino Evangelical Youth Culture," in *Gen X Religion*, ed. Richard W. Flory and Donald E. Miller (New York: Routledge, 2000), 75.

14. Tom Beaudoin, *Virtual Faith: The Irreverent Spiritual Quest of Generation X* (San Francisco: Jossey-Bass, 1998).

CONCLUSION 269

16. Lauren F. Winner, "Gen X Revisited," *The Christian Century*, 8 November 2000.

17. Dieter and Valerie Zander, "The Evolution of Gen X Ministry," *Regeneration Quarterly* 5, no. 3.

18. Andy Crouch, "For People Like Me," *Regeneration Quarterly* 5, no. 3.

19. Quoted in Lori Jensen, "When Two Worlds Collide: Generation X and Conservative Evangelicalism," in *Gen X Religion*, 139.

20. Dale Neal, "Art Forum: Professing the Passion of Christianity in Paint," review of G. Carol Bomer's paintings, *Asheville Citizen Times*, April 1994, quoted at Soli Deo Gloria Studio. http://www.carolbomer.com/reviews.html

21. Rodney Clapp, *Border Crossings: Christian Trespasses on Popular Culture and Public Affairs* (Grand Rapids, Mich.: Brazos Press, 2000).

22. See, for example, Mark I. Pinsky, *The Gospel According to the Simpsons* (Louisville, Ky.: Westminster John Knox Press, 2001).

23. Willard Thorp, "The Religious Novel as Bestseller in America," in *Religious Perspectives in American Culture*, ed. James Ward Smith and A. Leland Jamison (Princeton, N.J.: Princeton University Press, 1961), 195.

24. Susan Wise Bauer, "Christian Fiction Gets Real," *Christianity Today*, 24 April 2000, 106.

25. Scott La Counte, letter to the editor, *Christianity Today*, 11 June 2001.

26. Lauren F. Winner, "The Wright Stuff," *Christianity Today*, 23 April 2001.

27. Susan Ketchin, *The Christ-Haunted Landscape: Faith and Doubt in Southern Fiction* (Oxford: University Press of Mississippi, 1994), 362.

28. Ibid., 320–25.

29. George M. Marsden, *The Outrageous Idea of Christian Scholarship* (New York: Oxford University Press, 1997), 7.

30. Carl F. H. Henry, *Conversations with Carl Henry: Christianity for Today* (Lewiston, Me.: Edwin Mellen Press, 1986), 49–52, 73–80, 159–64.

31. Mark A. Noll, *The Scandal of the Evangelical Mind* (Grand Rapids, Mich.: Wm. B. Eerdmans, 1994), 238.

32. Thomas Morris, ed., *God and the Philosophers: The Reconciliation of Faith and Reason* (New York: Oxford University Press, 1994), 4–5.

33. Alvin Plantinga, "A Christian Party Lived," in *Philosophers Who Believe: The Spiritual Journeys of 11 Leading Thinkers*, ed. Kelly James Clark (Downer's Grove, Ill.: InterVarsity Press, 1993), 81–82.

34. Arthur F. Holmes, "Confessions of a College Teacher," in *Philosophers Who Believe*, 182–88.

35. Marsden has equivocated on this point. At the November 2000 meeting of the American Academy of Religion in Nashville, Tennessee, Marsden denied ever saying that scholars with religious convictions had to, in his memorable phrase, "check their faith at the door."

36. Plantinga, "Christian Party Lived," in *Philosophers Who Believe*, 79.

INDEX

Abels, Paul, 163
Abernathy, Ralph David, 183
abolitionism, x, 16, 18, 55, 57, 59, 84
abortion, 5, 178, 180, 186, 192, 241,
    256
Abyssinian Baptist Church (Harlem,
    New York), ix, 101–9
Adams, John Hurst, 193
Addams, Jane, 30, 217–18
affluence, 60, 65, 67, 184
Africa, 46, 52, 103, 107; Anglican
    bishops in, 171, 172, 173
African Americans: Baptist, 52,
    101–5; and Biblical basis for slav-
    ery, 56–57; and egalitarianism of
    evangelicalism, 50–54; emancipa-
    tion of, 61–62; evangelicalism
    among, 27; and evangelicals, 175,
    243; and faith-based programs,
    191, 192–93; female, 51, 122, 125;
    and feminism, 122, 125; and poli-
    tics, 103, 105, 106; and racial rec-
    onciliation, 187–89; religions of,
    viii, ix, 42, 52, 82, 101–9; revival-
    ism among, 46–48; separate
    churches of, 61–62; and social ac-

tivism, ix, 103, 105, 184–85. *See
    also* Civil Rights movement; seg-
    regation; slavery
African Methodist Episcopal (AME)
    Church, 52, 53, 128
African Methodist Episcopal Zion
    Church, 128, 130
Ahlstrom, Sidney E., vii
Alabama, 50, 230, 248
Albino, Judith, 160
Allen, Richard, 52, 53, 61
Allen, Ronald, 198
Allen Street Methodist Church (New
    York), 238
Alliance for Marriage, 158, 160
American Baptist Church, 71, 78, 164,
    170, 252. *See also* Baptists;
    Southern Baptist Convention
American Civil Liberties Union, 218
*American Evangelical Christianity: An
    Introduction* (Noll), x
American Lutheran Church, 78, 128,
    251
American Revolution, 16, 44, 48–50
Ames, Williams, 43
Amish, 14

198–99; and translation, 139;
Victorious Life, 60–61; and
Wallis, 243–44; well-defined, 33,
195–96; womanist, 122; works-
oriented, 59–62
Tholuck, F.A.D., 229
Thomas, Becky, 142
Thomas Road Baptist Church
(Lynchburg, Virginia), 76
Thornwell, James Henley, 56
Thorp, Willard, 206
Thurman, Chris, 137
Thurman, Holly, 137
Tibbets, Scott, 112–13, 114
Tickle, Phyllis, 201
Tillich, Paul, 66
Tollstadius, Lars, 43
tongues, speaking in. *See* glossolalia
Topeka (Kansas), 113
Torrey, Reuben A., 227
Transcendentalism, 15
transubstantiation, 6, 25, 26
trinitarianism, 155
Trinity, 113, 124, 126
Trinity Evangelical Divinity School
(Deerfield, Illinois), 243–44
Truman, Harry, 182, 228
Trumbull, Charles, 60
Tudor, Mary (Queen), 13
TULIP (total depravity; uncondi-
tional election; limited atonement;
irresistible grace; perseverance of
the saints), 249, 250–51
Turner, Jamie Langston, 207
Turner, Nat, 18, 56, 105
Tyndale, William, 138

Uncle Tom's Cabin (Stowe), 206
Union Theological Seminary (New
York), 19, 63, 125, 237
Unitarianism, 5, 15, 46, 128, 219
Unitarian Universalist Church, 163

United Church of Christ, ix, 71, 78,
93, 95; and charismatics, 252; and
evangelicalism, 24; and grassroots, 33, 195; on homosexuality,
163, 170; women in, 128
United Methodist Church, ix, 71, 78,
93, 95; and charismatics, 252; and
evangelicalism, 24; on homosexuality, 163–64, 167–70
United Methodist Hymnal, 91, 95
United Nations, 87
United Presbyterian Church (U.S.A.),
78, 252
Universal Fellowship of Metropolitan
Community Churches (MCC),
173–74, 175, 176
Universalism, 15, 94, 128
universities: evangelicalism in,
209–10; secularism in, 214
Updike, John, 206
urbanization: and divisions in Protestantism, 19, 30; and evangelicalism, 15, 49; and mainline Protestantism, 62; and
postmillennialism, 84; and premillennialism, 75; and social activism, 59, 181, 184–85

Valentine, Herbert D., 189
Vanderbreggen, Cornelius, 239
Vanhoozer, Kevin, xi
Van Leeuwen, Mary Stuart, 161
Van Leeuwen, Stewart, 133
Velma Still Cooks in Leeway (Wright),
207
Venite (Benson), 201
Venner, Thomas, 42
Vermont, 158–61
Vesey, Denmark, 105
Victorious Life theology, 60–61
Victory Christian Center (Tulsa,
Oklahoma), 79, 252